An Unauthorized *of* Napoleon Hill's Success Classic

THE NEW
THINK
and
GROW
RICH

TED CIUBA *and*
NAPOLEON HILL

Morgan James Publishing • NEW YORK

THE NEW
THINK ⊷and⊷
GROWRICH

© MMVII ViviaCorp SA, *All rights reserved worldwide*

ISBN: 1-60037-020-9 (Hardcover)
ISBN: 0-9758570-7-X (Paperback)

Published by:

MORGAN · JAMES
THE ENTREPRENEURIAL PUBLISHER ™
www.morganjamespublishing.com

Morgan James Publishing, LLC
1225 Franklin Ave Ste 32
Garden City, NY 11530-1693
Toll Free 800-485-4943
www.MorganJamesPublishing.com

In conjunction with:

Parthenon Marketing Inc
2400 Crestmoor Rd. #36
Nashville, TN 37215
USA

Cover/Interior Design by:

Rachel Campbell
rcampbell77@cox.net

Habitat for Humanity®
Peninsula
Building Partner

VIVIACORP SA
Sandringham House #83 Shirley St
Nassau New Providence 00000
Bahamas
+1-242-326-5205
Fax: +1-242-326-5349
www.HoloMagic.com
info@ehaste.com

ORDERS, ENROLLMENTS:

+1-877- *4 RICHES*
★★★
+1-615-662-3169
Fax: +1-615-662-3108

Ted Ciuba, World's TOP *Think And Grow Rich* **Expert**
Book Ted Ciuba at your event! Speeches, workshops, consulting. Contact publisher.

THESE ARE THE

BEST

OF TIMES!

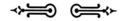

OUR

BEST

IS YET TO COME!

⊶ *acknowledgements* ⊷

As the living author, I express to you, Napoleon Hill, how great it was to work together with you on this project. I was standing on the shoulders of a giant. Imbibers of the same mysteries, businessmen-authors together... It has been, and ever will be, one of the richest experiences of my life.

With profound respect, Infinite Intelligence, I am grateful I was selected to further this project in the Great Work.

Three cheers for the Napoleon Hill Foundation, for continuing to nurture and carry on the Great Work of Hill in so many avenues worldwide.

The living co-author,

Ted Ciuba

Ted Ciuba
2 October 2006

⋯⟹ *dedication* ⟸⋯

To you, reading and studying this book and this work...

To you, preparing yourself for generous contribution, distinction, and reward...

This can be the most important book you ever read – one that *impacts all your days*...

All the things you do, achieve, and contribute to yourself, your family, your community, your society, and the world...

One that sets into motion effects and Fortunes that can endure well beyond your match strike moments on Earth...

To you, I dedicate this book.

Ted Ciuba

Ted Ciuba, living co-author

P.S. Please do let me know how you do!
Email address at **www.HoloMagic.com**

"They *can*, because they *think* they can."

— *Virgil*

⇐ table of contents ⇒

⇒ *author's preface* ⇐

A WORLD OF CAUSE AND EFFECT

Riches Are A Result

The secret to the purposeful creation of wealth can be discovered and applied to your direct benefit.

Here you have the entire philosophy of moneymaking, just as it was organized from the actual achievements of the most successful people known to the world population during the past 100 years. People, who began at scratch with nothing to give in return for riches, except *thoughts, ideas* and *organized plans*.

Here you encounter the famous *Think And Grow Rich* philosophy, *the* philosophy sworn to by millionaires! *The* philosophy that has made *Think And Grow Rich* the greatest selling success book in history! It is a practical philosophy, describing exactly *what* to do and *how* to do it, as well as providing the motivation to get you started or renewed.

It is based on the famous Andrew Carnegie formula of personal achievement by which he accumulated hundreds of millions of dollars for himself and made no fewer than a score of millionaires of men to whom he taught his secret.

> Fortunes gravitate to those whose minds have been prepared to "attract" them, just as surely as water gravitates to the ocean.
>
> In this book, may be found all the stimuli necessary to "attune" any normal mind to the vibrations that will attract the object of your desires.

Perhaps you don't need all that is to be found in the book – not all of the 1,000 men and woman from whose experiences it was written did – but you may need *one idea, plan, insight or suggestion* to start you toward your goal. This could be the very seed that multiplies into your own millions of dollars. Somewhere in the book you will find this needed stimulus.

The book was inspired by Andrew Carnegie, after he had made his millions and retired. It was originally written by Napoleon Hill the man to whom Carnegie disclosed the astounding secret of his riches – the same man to whom over 500 wealthy men revealed the source of their riches. It was updated by Ted Ciuba, the man who carried on the magic work, and brought it into a whole new age 100 years later.

In this volume you find the thirteen principles of money making essential to every person who accumulates sufficient money to guarantee financial independence.

Here's the simple but powerful premise which drives this work…

Success Is A Causable Event

Like *all* things in Nature, knowledge of guiding principles gives you the potential power to *harness* those forces, such as knowledge of aerodynamics allows us to fly hundreds of passengers at a time on intercontinental flights.

In the same manner, the ways to wealth are learnable and applicable by anyone of ordinary intelligence.

Riches are a *result*.

The Most Fully Actualizing Are The Rich

Look around. The people who are living the best lives are the rich and wealthy. Really, it ought to be obvious. It ain't the working stiff trapped into the grind of work, get check, two week's vacation, too broke to go, no time or money to even take care of yourself.

Money gives you resources, reach, opportunities, companions, travel, education, housing, transportation, vacations, ability to have more meaningful relationships, and a thousand and one other gifts.

That's why so many drive mopeds and small motorcycles in many third-world countries… There's no money for no more… And they frequently never leave their neighborhood – borning, living, and dying among their family members.

While there's something to be said about the simplicity of the poor – the simple fact remains:

- Money is power. Power is the ability to do, see, own, experience, and contribute.
- The more money you have, the more advantages you have. And with the more you have, the more you can bestow.

Modest Wealth Can Be Great Prosperity

Speaking of wealth… We throw around a lot of heavyweights in this treatise… I call them *titans* – because they're so exceptional, they're mythic, they're bigger than life. People like Andrew Carnegie, Henry Ford, Thomas Edison, Charles Schwab… People like Bill Gates, Sam Walton, Ray Kroc, Jeff Bezos, Richard Branson, Donald Trump, and Pierre Omidyar.

I wouldn't want you to get the wrong idea... It's not just about joining the ranks of the super rich. A good many of the examples in this book – and especially in the available supplementary materials, feature entrepreneurs who have encountered financial freedom with all the blessings they could ask for on Earth on much less than the *billions* the titans earn.

Besides, this book isn't written for the titans, they already have it... It's written for *you*. And when you cut to the core of it – it's really about achieving the lifestyle you want – doing it consciously and doing it soundly. Being in a state of abundance.

An abundant life always consumes a good sum of money. Therefore, that's the importance of studying the ways and means of acquiring money. According to your own definite chief aims, modest wealth can indeed be great prosperity.

The same rules apply for wealth and actualization at all levels. You get to control the intensity of your vision and your results. The method is the same for any level.

Manifesting Money Manifests Every Other Good Thing

RICHE$ are our target and our end. This book has been confined, exclusively, to instructing the reader how to transmute the *definite purpose of desire for money* into its monetary equivalent.

This treatise is a "manifestation manual for money," and, while it's true, there's more to manifest than money, we unashamedly adopt as our study, our pursuit, and the education we give to worthy students coming up the ranks, the application of the methods of manifestation to *money*.

Besides, earned money brings *actualization*. And actualization fosters a life of contribution.

From everything I've seen, independent wealth gives you the height from which you have the vision to decide how you'd like to contribute to the Earth and the Earth's inhabitants during your brief stay here.

That's a thought of proportions vastly more grand than the daily survival thoughts of the masses of humanity. Need you be reminded?

Fortunately, we're not studying the poor, but the wealthy.

Truly, with the things that wealth gives you, you can live even after your death...

Witness the names before you in this book... Names still resounding in the ears of aware people even 100 years after their crowning achievements played out on the stage of the living moment. Have you heard of the Ford Foundation? How about Carnegie-Mellon University? Vanderbilt University? The Rockefeller Foundation?

This is just a spattering of the worthy Fortunes still working in our generation from the acquisition and investment of wealth.

Of course, we acknowledge *riches* cannot always be measured in money. Money and material things are essential for freedom of body and mind, but there are some who feel the greatest of all riches can be evaluated only in terms of lasting friendships, harmonious family relationships, sympathy and understanding between business associates, and introspective harmony which brings one peace of mind measurable only in spiritual values!

All who read, understand and apply this philosophy will be better prepared to attract and enjoy these higher estates; also, which always have been and always will be denied to all except those who are ready for them.

Actualization. The most highly achieving, contributing people get the most juice out of life.

It's necessary to have an independent income to do that.

Get Ready For Some Changes

Be prepared, when you expose yourself to the influence of this philosophy, to experience a *changed life,* which may help you not only to negotiate your way through life with harmony and understanding, but also to prepare you for the accumulation of material riches in abundance.

Discover The Secret To Countless Fortune

In *every* chapter of this book mention has been made of the money making secret which has made Fortunes for more than a million exceedingly wealthy men and women who have applied these principles since their initial publication. Millions more have followed it to more modest accomplishments.

The secret works as well today as it did in the past, for the simple reason it deals with universal principles. I haven't invented anything, or come up with a new idea or technique, just found and codified for you what works in acquiring wealth.

The secret was brought to my attention by Andrew Carnegie, in a 1908 interview I did of him. The canny, lovable old Scotsman carelessly tossed it into my mind, when I was a big pup. Then he sat back in his chair, with a merry twinkle in his eyes, and watched carefully to see if I had brains enough to understand the full significance of what he had said to me.

When he saw that I had grasped the idea, he asked if I would be willing to spend twenty years or more preparing myself to take it to the world, to men and women who, without the secret, might go through life as failures. I said I would, and with Mr. Carnegie's cooperation, I have kept my promise.

Little did I dream at that time, the actual project would extend over two separate incarnations and more than 100 years. It took me like the quest for the Holy Grail! I worked and wrote with the fever. *And it's still going strong!*

That's the magic in a single powerful impulse of thought – it's a seed that can sprout and grow Fortunes forever.

Think And Grow Rich is *the* book sworn to by nearly every successful person today. Insurance, investment, executive, sales, MLM, and personal achievement organizations of every size and scope have made it *required* reading.

The book has touched millions, still selling a million copies annually… And is called "the book that launched a million millionaires."

There is a secret. This book reveals that secret. It's been put to a practical test by millions of people, in almost every walk of life.

Conventional Schooling Is Of No Value

It was Carnegie's idea that the magic formula, which gave him a stupendous Fortune, ought to be placed within reach of people who do not have time or resources to investigate how people make *BIG* money, and it was his hope that I might test and demonstrate the soundness of the formula through the experience of men and women in every calling.

He believed the formula should be taught in all public schools and colleges, and expressed the opinion that if it were properly taught, it would so revolutionize the entire educational system that the time spent in school could be reduced to less than half.

His experience with Charles M. Schwab, and other young men of Schwab's type, convinced Carnegie that much of that which is taught in the schools is of no value whatsoever in connection with the business of earning a living or accumulating riches.

Indeed, it's true. They just don't teach people how to become outstanding, entrepreneurial contributors to society, how to design and grow your own business… Instead they focus on *norming* the population. Whether you like to admit it or not, you *know* it's true!

When it comes to acquiring financial independence (not *just* a better job – a higher rung on the rat race), study after study has detected no measurable advantage correlated to education.

Carnegie had arrived at this decision because he had taken into his business one young man after another, many of them with little schooling, and by coaching them in the use of this formula, developed in them rare leadership. Moreover, his coaching made Fortunes for everyone of them who followed his instructions.

The Practical Value Of This Philosophy

In the chapter on Faith, you will read the astounding story of the organization of the giant United States Steel Corporation, as it was conceived and carried out, by one of the young men through whom Mr. Carnegie proved that his formula will work for all who are ready for it. This single application of the secret, by that young man – Charles M. Schwab – yielded him a huge Fortune in both money and *opportunity*. Roughly speaking, this particular application of the formula was worth $600 Million. And that at a time when a million dollars was still a staggering sum!

Today, in the New Millennium – the much-heralded twenty-first century, in the upper middle class neighborhoods of cities around the world, a million dollar income is a common thing. Not so at the turn of the Twentieth Century, 100 years ago, when I first began setting the philosophy of success to paper.

Put your ear balls on this one! If you were to take the $600 Million *created from that single idea in* 1903 and adjust it for inflation to today, that's approximately *$12 Billion Dollars!!*

Clearly the realm of Bill Gates thinking – another practical visionary who turned an idea into *billions* of dollars!

These facts – and they are facts well known to almost everyone who knew Mr. Carnegie – give you a fair idea of what the reading of this book may bring to you, provided you *know what it is you want.*

That HoloMagic "c²" Factor

> If you were to take the $600 Million *created from a single idea* in 1903 and adjust it for inflation to today, that's approximately *$12 Billion Dollars!!*
>
> These facts – and they are facts well known to almost everyone who knew Mr. Carnegie – give you a fair idea of what the reading of this book may bring to you, provided you *know what it is you want.*

This is *transmuting desire into money.* Who knows what it will do for you? *Start with an idea!... Make very real money.* Truly, an illustration of the convertibility of an idea into money; as Einstein's formula reveals: $E = mc^2$.

That formula says *Energy* equals *matter* times the *speed of light* squared. Energy is *thought.* Matter is *money.* We're studying in this book that holomagic "c^2" factor.

Hidden In A Hundred Places

The secret to which I refer has been mentioned no fewer than a hundred times throughout this book. It has not been directly named, for it seems to work more successfully when it is merely uncovered and left in sight, where *those who are ready,* and *searching for it,* may pick it up. That is why Mr. Carnegie tossed it to me so quietly, without giving me its specific name.

If you are ready to put it to use, you will recognize this secret at least once in every chapter. I wish I might feel privileged to tell you how you will know if you are ready, but that would deprive you of much of the benefit you will receive when you make the discovery in your own way.

While this book was being written, my own son, who was then finishing the last year of his college work, picked up the manuscript of chapter two, read it, and discovered the secret for himself. He used the information so effectively that he went directly into a responsible position at a beginning salary greater than the average man ever earns.

A peculiar thing about this secret is that those who once acquire and use it, find themselves literally swept on to success with little effort, and they never again submit to failure! If you doubt this, study the names of those who have used it, check their records for yourself, and be convinced.

The Secret Cannot Be Had Without A Price

There is no such thing as *something for nothing!*

The secret to which I refer cannot be had without a price, although the price is far less than its value. It cannot be had at any price by those who are not intentionally searching for it. It cannot be given away; it cannot be purchased for money, for the reason that it comes in two parts. One part is already in possession of those who are ready for it.

The secret serves equally well all who are ready for it. Education has nothing to do with it. Nor does specifically getting your hands on *Think And Grow Rich.* Long before I was born, the secret had found its way into the possession of Thomas A. Edison. He used it so intelligently that he became the world's leading inventor even though he had only three months of schooling. Not to mention that, obviously, Andrew Carnegie had it.

The secret was passed on to a business associate of Mr. Edison. He used it so effectively that, although he was then making only $12,000 a year, he accumulated a great Fortune, and retired from active business while still a young man. You will find his story at the beginning of the first chapter. It should convince...

You Can Enjoy The Money, Fame, Recognition And Happiness You Desire

Riches are not beyond your reach. You can still be what you wish to be. Money, fame, recognition and happiness can be had by all who are ready, and determined to have these blessings.

How do I know these things?

You should have the answer before you finish this book.

You may find it in the very first chapter, or on the last page.

While I was performing the initial twenty year task of research, which I had undertaken at Carnegie's request, I analyzed hundreds of well-known people, many of whom admitted that they had accumulated their vast Fortunes through the aid of the Carnegie secret; among these people:

Henry Ford	Theodore Roosevelt
William Wrigley Jr.	John W. Davis
John Wanamaker	Elbert Hubbard
James J. Hill	Wilbur Wright
George S. Parker	William Jennings Bryan
E. M. Statler	Dr. David Starr Jordan
Henry L. Doherty	J. Odgen Armour
Cyrus H. K. Curtis	Arthur Brisbane
George Eastman	Woodrow Wilson
Charles M. Schwab	Wm. Howard Taft
Harris F. Williams	Luther Burbank
Dr. Frank Gunsaulus	Edward W. Bok
Daniel Willard	Frank A. Munsey
King Gillette	Elbert H. Gary
Ralph A. Weeks	Dr. Alexander Graham Bell
Judge Daniel T. Wright	John H. Patterson
John D. Rockefeller	Julius Rosenwald
Thomas A. Edison	Stuart Austin Wier

Frank A. Vanderlip	Dr. Frank Crane
F. W. Woolworth	George M. Alexander
Col. Robert A. Dollar	J.G. Chapline
Edward A. Filene	Hon. Jennings Randolph
Edwin C. Barnes	Arthur Nash
Clarence Darrow	

Today, 100 years later, you could fill a book with nothing but the *names* of people who attribute their wealth to the secret revealed in *Think And Grow Rich*.

These names represent a small fraction of the countless thousands of well-known people whose achievements, financially and otherwise, prove that those who understand and apply the Carnegie secret reach high stations in life.

I have never known anyone inspired to use the secret who did not achieve noteworthy success in his or her chosen calling. I have never known anyone to distinguish themselves, or to accumulate riches of any consequence, without possession of the secret.

Possession Of The Secret Gives You The "Power"

From these two facts, I draw the conclusion *that the secret is more important* as a part of the knowledge essential for self- determination, *than anything one receives through what is popularly known as "education."*

What is *education*, anyway? This has been answered in full detail.

As far as schooling is concerned, many of these men had very little. John Wanamaker once told me that what little schooling he had, he acquired in very much the same manner as an old-time locomotive takes on water, by "scooping it up as it runs." Henry Ford never reached high school, let alone college.

I am not attempting to minimize the value of schooling, but I am trying to express my earnest belief that those who master and apply the secret will reach high stations, accumulate riches, and bargain with life on their own terms, even if their schooling has been meager.

Celebrate And Give Thanks When You Discover The Secret

If you are ready for it, somewhere, as you read, the secret to which I refer will jump from the page and stand boldly before you. Don't fret... When it appears, you will recognize it.

Whether you receive the sign in the first or the final chapter, stop for a moment when it presents itself, and turn down a glass, for that occasion will mark the most important turning point of your life.

Affirmation
The world works identically as well for me as it does for the rest of humanity...   *With the secret in this book I can achieve anything I put my heart and mind to.*

We pass now, to the Introduction of the book, and to the story of my very dear friend, who has generously acknowledged having seen the mystic sign, and whose business achievements are evidence enough that he turned down a glass.

As you read his story, and the others, remember that they deal with the important problems of life that all people experience. The problems arising from one's endeavor to earn a living, to find hope, courage, contentment and peace of mind, to accumulate riches and to enjoy freedom of body and spirit.

Remember, too, as you go through the book that it deals with facts, and not with fiction. Its purpose is to convey a great universal truth about wealth.

Anyone can do it.

In *The NEW Think And Grow Rich* all who are *ready* may discover, not only *what to do, but also how to do it!* And receive, as well, *the needed stimulus to make a start.*

Choose, Plant, Nurture Life-Affirming Seeds

Therefore, choose, plant, nurture life affirming seeds, the good seed you would realize. Become a conscious co-creator with the Law of Nature. Proactively *cause* the future you desire.

The secret is coded in the very title of this book,

Think! ...and Grow RICH!

A World Of Cause And Effect

The biggest key is recognizing that even with the adventures of daily life, **it is not a haphazard world, but a world that follows the strict regimen of cause and effect**.

When you truly understand that, all mystery is removed from how you can *think* and grow *rich* — because you know that in your thoughts you are planting the seeds that you will harvest in due time. Riches are a *result*.

You then can then place your efforts wholly on energizing your desires, planning your success, setting it into motion, and measuring and adjusting as you climb Mount Money.

Get A Clue

As a final word of preparation, before you begin reading the contents of the book, may I offer one brief suggestion, which may provide a clue by which the Carnegie secret may be recognized?

It is this...

All achievement, all earned riches,
have their beginning in an idea!

If you are ready for the secret, you already possess half of it; therefore, you will readily recognize the other half the moment it penetrates your mind.

The Authors,

Ted Ciuba & Napoleon Hill

introduction

NATURAL LAW

"Plant the seed, eat the fruit"

The Approach Toward Riches

Case Study Reveals Stunning Proof *Think And Grow Rich* Success System Works!

How A Homeless Person Thought His Way To Wealth

Truly, "thoughts are things" when they are mixed with *definiteness of purpose*, *persistence*, and a **burning desire** for their translation into riches.

One day Edwin C. Barnes discovered how true it is that people really do *think and grow rich*. His discovery did not come about at one sitting. It came little by little, beginning with a *burning desire* to become a business associate of the great Edison.

One of the chief characteristics of Barnes' desire was that it was *definite*. He wanted to work *with* Edison, not "for" him.

Observe carefully, the description of how he went about translating his *desire* into reality, and you will have a better understanding of the thirteen principles that lead to riches.

Most People Find It Easier To Whine About Why They Can't Do Something

When this *desire*, or impulse of thought, first flashed into his mind, he was in no position to act upon it. Two difficulties stood in his way. He did not know Mr. Edison, and he did not have enough money to pay his railroad fare to Orange, New Jersey.

These difficulties were sufficient to have discouraged the majority of men from making any attempt to carry out their desire. But his was no ordinary desire! He was so determined to find a way to carry out his desire that he finally decided to travel by "blind baggage," rather than be defeated. (To the uninitiated, this means that he went to East Orange on a freight train).

The disheveled, unbathed Barnes presented himself at Mr. Edison's laboratory, and announced he had come to go into business with the inventor. Check that one out! A bum throws himself before a multimillionaire businessman! How seldom does the bum get a word in that works? However...

Broadcast Louder Than Words

In speaking of the first meeting between Barnes and Edison, years later, Mr. Edison said, "He stood there before me, looking like an ordinary tramp, but there was something in the expression of his face which conveyed the impression that he was *determined* to get what he had come after. I had learned from years of experience with men, that... When person really *desires* a thing so deeply that he or she is willing to stake their entire future on a single turn of the wheel in order to get it, they are sure to win. I gave him the opportunity he asked for, because I saw he had made up his mind to stand by until he succeeded. Subsequent events proved that no mistake was made."

Just what young Barnes said to Mr. Edison on that occasion was far less important than that which he thought. Edison, himself, said so! It could not have been the young man's appearance that got him his start in the Edison office, for that was definitely against him. **It was what he *thought* that counted**.

If the significance of this statement could be conveyed to every person who reads it, there would be no need for the remainder of this book.

Barnes did not get his partnership with Edison on his first interview. He did get a chance to work in the Edison offices, at a very nominal wage, doing work that was unimportant to Edison, but most important to Barnes, because it gave him an opportunity to display his "merchandise" where his intended "partner" could see it.

A Seed, Unseen, Is Growing In The Ground

Months went by. Apparently nothing happened to bring the coveted goal that Barnes had set up in his mind as his *definite major purpose*. But something important was happening in Barnes' mind. He was constantly intensifying his *desire* to become the business associate of Edison.

Mystics for millennia, and psychologists in recent days, have correctly said: "When one is truly ready for a thing, it puts in its appearance." Barnes was ready for a business association with Edison; moreover, he was *determined to remain ready until he got what he was seeking*.

He did not say to himself, "Ah well, what's the use? I guess I'll change my mind and try for a salesman's job." But, he did say, "I came here to go into business with Edison, and I'll accomplish this end if it takes the remainder of my life." He meant it!

What a different story men would have to tell if only they would adopt a *definite purpose*, and stand by that purpose until it had time to become an all consuming obsession!

> What a different story men would have to
> tell if only they would adopt a *definite purpose,*
> and stand by that purpose until it had time
> to become an all consuming obsession!

Maybe young Barnes did not know it at the time, but his bulldog determination, his persistence in standing back of a single *desire,* was destined to mow down all opposition, and bring him the opportunity he was seeking.

"Take Opportunity When It Comes"

When the opportunity came, it appeared in a different form, and from a different direction than Barnes had expected. That is one of the tricks of opportunity. It has a sly habit of slipping in by the backdoor, and often it comes disguised in the form of misfortune, temporary defeat, or work. Perhaps this is why so many fail to recognize opportunity.

Mr. Edison had just perfected a new office device, known at that time, as the Edison Dictating Machine (now the Ediphone). His salesmen were not enthusiastic over the machine. They did not believe it could be sold without great effort. Barnes saw his opportunity. It had crawled in quietly, hidden in a queer looking machine that interested no one, but Barnes and the inventor.

Barnes knew he could sell the Edison Dictating Machine. He suggested this to Edison, and promptly got his chance. He did sell the machine. In fact, he sold it so successfully, that Edison gave him a contract to distribute and market it all over the nation. Out of that business association grew the slogan, "Made by Edison and installed by Barnes."

That business alliance operated for more than thirty years. Out of it Barnes made himself rich in money, but he also did something infinitely greater. He has proven one really may *think* and *grow rich.*

First, An Intangible Impulse Of Thought

How much actual cash that original *desire* of Barnes' has been worth to him, I have no way of knowing. Perhaps it has brought him two or three million dollars (an amount that would be worth over $50 Million in today's money), but the amount, whatever it is, becomes insignificant when compared with the greater asset he acquired in the form of definite knowledge that…

An intangible impulse of thought can be transmuted into its physical counterpart by the application of known principles.

Barnes literally thought himself into a partnership with the great Edison! He thought himself into a Fortune. As the mystics count it, he *projected* himself into good Fortune and riches by an act of will. *This* is what we're talking about in *The NEW Think And Grow Rich*!

Start Exactly Where You Are Right Now

He had nothing to start with, except the capacity to *know what he wanted, and the determination to stand by that desire until he realized it.*

He had no money to begin with. He had little education. He had no influence. But he did have initiative, faith, and the will to win. With these intangible forces he made himself number one man with the greatest inventor who ever lived.

It's really *not* surprising or a secret. Anyone who pursues a single objective, with the same focused passion, is sure to get it. And what critical event elevated Barnes from a clerk to a partner of this pre-eminent businessman? What changed his destiny from a "get by" paycheck to massive wealth, opulence, and privilege?

Listen to these next words with all the fiber of your soul – they hold the key to your advancement with *any* person in the world you wish to partner with!…

A "secret?" Well... It is... But it should be common sense. What he did that got him in to see Edison – and it's the same strategy you can use with *anybody* today... He *solved a problem.* He solved Edison's currently greatest problem.

Edison knew the potential of his invention, but he needed a sales force to carry it out. Up steps Barnes. That's all there is to it...

This is a perfect illustration of why you hear me say so often – entrepreneurs *embrace* problems! Entrepreneurs *search* out problems. Because *problems provide opportunities.*

Entrepreneurs and achievers know this. Ordinary people – like the ordinary competitors Barnes had *who had first dibs* – just see the problem.

Three Feet From Gold

Now, let us look at a different situation, and study a man who had plenty of tangible evidence of riches, but lost it, because he stopped three feet short of the goal he was seeking.

One of the most common causes of failure is the habit of quitting when one is overtaken by temporary defeat. Every person is guilty of this mistake at one time or another.

An uncle of R.U. Darby was caught by the "gold fever" in the gold-rush days, and went out West to *dig and grow rich.* He had never heard that more gold has been mined from the brains of men than has ever been taken from the Earth. He staked a claim and went to work with pick and shovel. The going was hard, but his lust for gold was definite. After weeks of labor, he was rewarded by the discovery of the shining ore. He needed machinery to bring the ore to the surface. Quietly, he covered up the mine, retraced his footsteps to his home in Williamsburg, Maryland, and then told his relatives and a few neighbors of the "strike." They got together money for the needed machinery, and had it shipped to location. The uncle and Darby went back to work the mine.

The first car of ore was mined, and shipped to a smelter. The returns proved they had one of the richest mines in Colorado! A few more cars of that ore would clear the debts. Then would come the big killing in profits.

Down went the drills! Up went the hopes of Darby and Uncle! Then something happened! The vein of gold ore disappeared! They had come to the end of the rainbow, and the pot of gold was no longer there! They drilled on, desperately trying to pick up the vein again — all to no avail. Finally, they decided to *quit*.

A Little Cheap Specialized Knowledge Yields Windfall Profits

They sold the machinery to a junk man for a few hundred dollars, and took the train back home. Some "junk" men are dumb, but not this one! He called in a mining engineer to look at the mine and do a little calculating. The engineer advised that the project had failed, because the owners were not familiar with "fault lines." His calculations showed that the vein would be found *just three feet from where the Darbys had stopped drilling!* That is exactly where it was found!

The "junk" man took millions of dollars in ore from the mine, because he knew enough to seek expert counsel before giving up.

Most of the money, which went into the machinery, was procured through the efforts of R.U. Darby, who was then a very young man. The money came from his relatives and neighbors, because of their faith in him. He paid back every dollar of it, although he was years in doing so.

Long afterward, Mr. Darby recouped his loss many times over, when he made the discovery that *desire* can be transmuted into gold. The discovery came after he went into the business of selling life insurance.

Remembering that he lost a huge Fortune because he *stopped* three feet from gold, Darby profited by the experience in his chosen work, by the simple method of saying to himself, "I stopped three feet from gold, but I will never stop because men say 'no' when I ask them to buy insurance."

Darby is one of a small group of fewer than fifty men who sell more than a million dollars in life insurance annually. He owes his "stickability" to the lesson he learned from his "quitability" in the gold mining business.

Success *Will* Test You

Before success comes in any man's life, he is sure to meet with much temporary defeat, and, perhaps, some failure. When defeat overtakes a man, the easiest and most logical thing to do is to *quit*. That is exactly what the majority of men do.

More than five hundred of the most successful people the world has ever known told the author their greatest success came just one step beyond the point at which defeat had overtaken them. Failure is a trickster with a keen sense of irony and cunning. It takes great delight in tripping one when success is almost within reach.

Apology In Advance

This upcoming story, I must admit, we originally cut from the first manuscript of *The NEW Think And Grow Rich*, for the obvious reason it could excite a racism nerve. We actively embrace *all* races, and the only thing we're intolerant of is intolerance.

However, my MasterMind partners threw a royal fit, and rallied against me. Respecting the good advice of trusted advisors, I put it back in. Why?

Most certainly, this story, here and now, is *not* about or promoting or accepting racism. Don't bloke yourself out imagining racism overtones. This is all of an antique era. But its portrayal of inequality and status position is evergreen.

The story portrays a small Black *child* with no power, no rights, facing off with a powerful businessman who had the right and power to do anything he wanted, including killing her with no real consequence. As readers, we're set with a colossal disparity of power. Overwhelming inequality.

Yet, in one encounter, because of what this young girl possesses, and this is what Napoleon's saying in this episode, she accomplishes her one definite chief aim! Even under the threat of death! When the critical moment of truth comes, *she steps forward!*

No wonder this story couldn't be omitted. This girl is a demonstration of the power of thinking, and to steal that from her would be a travesty. Especially, when we are pro-active in racial sensitivity.

Willing To Accept No Other Outcome

Shortly after Darby paid for his "street seminar," and decided to profit by his experience in the gold mining business, he had the good fortune to be present on an occasion that proved to him that "No" does not necessarily mean no.

One afternoon he was helping his uncle grind wheat in an old fashioned mill. The uncle operated a large farm on which a number of colored sharecroppers lived. Quietly, the door opened, and a small colored child, the daughter of a tenant, walked in and took her place near the door.

The uncle looked up, saw the child, and barked at her roughly, "What d'ya want?"

Meekly, the child replied, "My mammy say send her fifty cents."

"I'll not do it," the uncle retorted, "Now you run on home."

"Yas sah," the child replied. But she did not move.

The uncle went ahead with his work, so busily engaged that he did not pay enough attention to the child to observe that she did not leave. When he looked up and saw her still standing there, he yelled at her, "I told you to go on home! Now go, or I'll take a switch to you."

The little girl said, "Yas sah," but she did not budge an inch.

The uncle dropped a sack of grain he was about to pour into the mill hopper, picked up a barrel stave, and started toward the child with an expression on his face that indicated trouble.

Darby held his breath. He was certain he was about to witness a murder. He knew his uncle had a fierce temper. He knew that colored children were not supposed to defy white people in that part of the country.

When the uncle reached the spot where the child was standing, she quickly stepped forward one step, looked up into his eyes, and screamed at the top of her shrill voice, "*My mammy's gotta have that fifty cents!*"

The uncle stopped, looked at her for a minute, then slowly laid the barrel stave on the floor, put his hand in his pocket, took out half a dollar, and gave it to her.

The child took the money and slowly backed toward the door, never taking her eyes off the man whom she had just conquered. After she had gone, the uncle sat down on a box and looked out the window into space for more than ten minutes. He was pondering, with awe, over the whipping he had just taken.

That Strange Power

Mr. Darby, too, was doing some thinking. That was the first time in all his experience that he had seen a colored child deliberately master an adult white person. How did she do it?

What happened to his uncle that caused him to lose his fierceness and become as docile as a lamb? What strange power did this child use that made her master over her superior? These and other similar questions flashed into Darby's mind, but he did not find the answer until years later, when he told me the story.

Strangely, the story of this unusual experience was told to the author in the old mill, on the very spot where the uncle took his whipping.

Strangely, too, I had devoted nearly a quarter of a century to the study of the power that enabled an ignorant, illiterate colored child to conquer an intelligent man.

As we stood there in that musty old mill, Mr. Darby repeated the story of the unusual conquest, and finished by asking, "What can you make of it? What strange power did that child use, that so completely whipped my uncle?"

Appropriate This Same Power For The Same Results

The answer to his question will be found in the principles described in this book. The answer is full and complete. It contains details and instructions sufficient to enable anyone to understand, and apply the same force that the little child accidentally stumbled upon.

Keep your mind alert, and you will observe exactly what strange power came to the rescue of the child, you will catch a glimpse of this power in the next chapter.

Not only that, you will receive the key that allows you to harness the same power in your own life and affairs. Let it not be overlooked, the child's conquest concerned money. Learn from her, you wise one.

So what was it that she had? It was a *power* **– she was defiant. She was certain. She was fixed. She was willing to accept no other outcome but the outcome rooted in her mind and heart.**

Do most people approach making money, their jobs, their career, and their contributions in that manner? Do most people?...

Anyone, anywhere, anytime can access this holomagic power – the qualities it takes are not education, age, contacts, experience, power, or money.

Somewhere in the book you will find an idea that will quicken your receptive powers and place at your command, for your own benefit, this same irresistible power.

The awareness of this power may come to you in the first chapter, or it may flash into your mind in some subsequent chapter. It may come in the form of a single idea. Or, it may come in the nature of a plan, or a purpose. Again, it may cause you to go back into your past experiences of failure or defeat, and bring to the surface some lesson by which you can regain all that you lost through defeat.

Thirteen Principles To Riches

But what of the man who has neither the time, nor the inclination to study failure in search of knowledge that may lead to success? Where, and how is he to learn the art of converting defeat into steppingstones to opportunity?

In answer to these questions, this book was written. The answer called for a description of thirteen principles. These are not thirteen isolated, linear principles... They are interactive and interdependent, each feeding off of and feeding the other... Each affecting and affected by the other...

They go to the depth of the Universe, encompassing your subconscious and Infinite Intelligence in their scope.

They are multi-dimensional and Quantum. When you understand and apply them in orchestrated consort, they generate an incredible synergy – developing all the while for the sincere wealth seeker.

Also remember, as you read, **the answer** you may be seeking to the questions which have caused you to ponder over the strangeness of life may be found in your own mind, **through some idea, plan, or purpose which may spring into your mind as you read**.

One sound idea is all that one needs to achieve success. The principles described in this book contain the best and the most practical of all that is known, concerning ways and means of creating useful ideas.

Momentum

Before we go any further in our approach to the description of these principles, we believe you are entitled to receive this important suggestion...

When riches begin to come, they come so quickly in such great abundance, that one wonders where they have been hiding during all those lean years.

This is an astounding statement, and all the more so, when we take into consideration the popular belief, that riches come only to those who work hard and long.

Ask any multi-millionaire – they'll tell you the first million was the hardest. After that, with increased knowledge, contacts, ability, and *momentum*, the other millions come much more rapidly.

The Combination That Unlocks The Vault

When you begin to *think* and *grow rich*, you will observe that riches begin with a state of mind, with definiteness of purpose, with little or no hard work.

> Riches begin with a state of mind, with definiteness of purpose, with little or no hard work.

You can compare the possession of the secret with possession of the combination of a vault. Without the combination, you find it *impossible* to open the bank vault, *no matter how hard you try*. But what effort does it take if you *have* the secret? If you *know* the combination? None, of course. How hard is it to twirl a dial on a safe?

In the same way, using the *Think And Grow Rich* secret requires no effort. In the same way, once you've discovered the secret, you can open the door to great riches in your life with little or no effort and hard work. It's the *secret* – it's what you don't know that's preventing you from acquiring the riches you see others enjoying, nothing more.

You, and every other person, ought to be interested in knowing how to acquire that state of mind that attracts riches. All told, I invested 100 years in research, analyzing more than 100,000 people, because I, too, wanted to know the common thread running between wealthy men and women, from different cultures, in different times, in different ways, in radically different markets.

Without that research, this book could not have been written.

Universal Principles

Here take notice of a very significant truth… The Great American Depression started in 1929, and continued on to an all time record of destruction, until sometime after President Roosevelt entered office. Then the Depression began to fade into nothingness. Just as an electrician in a theater raises the lights so gradually that darkness is transmuted into light before you realize it, so did the spell of fear in the minds of the people gradually fade away and become faith.

It's doubtful you've learned the truth about how this was accomplished in your history books – because they just don't talk of this intangible power. Rest assured – I was working with Roosevelt at the time, with an office in the White House. It was actually during this time I wrote the manuscript for the original *Think And Grow Rich*, though it was not published till a few years later.

The Depression didn't just run its course. Its end was engineered with the conscious application of the principles of the *Think And Grow Rich* philosophy on a national level.

These principles can bring wealth to an individual, an enterprise, or an entire nation. Just ask China.

Everything You Touch Turns Into An Asset

Observe very closely, as soon as you master the principles of this philosophy, and begin to follow the instructions for applying those principles, your financial status will begin to improve, and everything you touch will begin to transmute itself into an asset for your benefit. Impossible? Not at all!

It's called *flow*, when things begin to work for you, with you, in you, for you in an automatic, mystical way. When athletes reach this state, they refer to it as being *in the zone*. It's a timeless place of power. It's one of the greatest rewards you encounter when you "live with the license of a higher order of being."

You may have heard a derivative statement… "The rich get richer, the poor get poorer."

One of the main weaknesses of humankind is the average person's familiarity with the word "impossible." He knows all the rules that will *not* work. He knows all the things that *cannot* be done.

These sheeple…feel smug and self-justified, certain in their belief they must totter under the heavy yoke of poverty, just barely getting by in a world of obvious abundance.

Little do they suspect that they are actually proving that the principles *do* work… Only they're using them to step-down the prosperity in their life, which any poor fool can do. What merit is there in that?

This book was written for those daring enough to jump on proving these principles *do* work, those who seek the rules that have made others successful, and are willing to stake everything on those rules.

Truly, by definition, anyone seeking riches *must* be different than the mass of humanity. Normal people will do anything to avoid thinking, and even thinking about being proactive is something they cannot be moved to do.

Harvest Of Like Kind

You, on the other hand, are *pro-active*. Big difference.

Though it happens on a metaphysical level, the metaphor of growth and harvest is perfect. Thoughts are creative seeds, and if not suffocated, starved, denied water or light, or pulled up, *must* manifest in harvest of like kind. This *is* Natural Law in the physical universe, is it not?

Who are we to deny the obvious? Humanity is not above Natural Law. All things in our little world happen according to law, also.

Your thoughts are your seeds. You will become who you think like, if you're not already.

Along those lines, multi-millionaire marketer, TJ Rohleder observes, "Everyone is self-made, but only the successful will admit it!"

This book guides you to know *what* thoughts to think… And with what character. Thoughts you then plant with consciousness in the garden of your life and affairs to flower under that *same* Natural Law that guides the planets, the galaxies, the atoms and the vibratory essence of all creation to manifest according to its seed.

Expansive Vision Or Contracted Vision

You are endeavoring to discover what those right kinds of thoughts are in this book, the right kinds of seeds to sow, and how to nourish them, so that you can *think* and *grow* rich.

A great many years ago I purchased a fine dictionary. The first thing I did with it was to turn to the word "impossible," and neatly razor it out of the book. It was a symbolic gesture, and, though it didn't change the world at large, it registered an important fact to my subconscious. That would not be an unwise thing for you to do.

Success comes to those who become *success conscious.*

Failure comes to those who indifferently allow themselves to become *failure conscious.*

The object of this book is to help all who seek it, to learn the art of changing their minds from *failure consciousness to success consciousness.*

Another weakness found in too many people, is the habit of measuring everything, and everyone, by their own impressions and beliefs. Some will read this, and will believe that no one can *think and grow rich.* They cannot think in terms of riches, because their thought habits have been steeped in poverty, want, misery, failure, and defeat.

For some time I struggled whether to leave this story in *The NEW Think And Grow Rich* or not, because it also could touch a nerve of *prejudice.* It talks of a time *before* we understood and accepted one another... But after reflection and advice, here she stays, because that's exactly what it illustrates – an irrational disability to see the truth due to *parochial vision.* Only through the hard work of raising your consciousness, such as you are doing in the study and application of this work, can you rise above it.

These unfortunate people who can only think in terms of poverty remind me of a prominent Chinese person, who came to America. He attended the University of Chicago. One day President Harper met this young man on campus, stopped to chat with him for a few minutes, and asked what had impressed him as being the most, noticeable characteristic of the American people.

"Why," the Chinaman exclaimed, "the queer slant of your eyes. Your eyes are off slant!" *What do we say about the Chinese?*

We refuse to believe that which we do not understand. We foolishly believe that our own limitations are the proper measure of limitations. Sure, the other fellow's eyes are "off slant," *because they are not the same as our own.*

You Can Equal The Achievements
Of The Richest Persons

Millions of people look at the achievements of Henry Ford, after he has arrived, and envy him, because of his good fortune, or luck, or genius, or whatever it is that they credit for Ford's Fortune. Perhaps one person in every hundred thousand knows the secret of Ford's success, and those who do know are too modest, or too reluctant, to speak of it, *because of its simplicity.* A single transaction will illustrate the "secret" perfectly.

A few years back, Ford decided to produce his now famous V-8 motor. He chose to build an engine with the entire eight cylinders cast in one block, and instructed his engineers to produce a design for the engine. The design was placed on paper, but the engineers agreed, to a man, that it was simply *impossible* to cast an eight-cylinder gas engine block in one piece.

Ford said, "Produce it anyway."

"But," they replied, "it's impossible!"

"Go ahead," Ford commanded, "and stay on the job until you succeed no matter how much time is required."

The engineers went ahead. There was nothing else for them to do, if they were to remain on the Ford staff. Six months went by, nothing happened. Another six months passed, and still nothing happened. The engineers tried every conceivable plan to carry out the orders, but the thing seemed out of the question – *"impossible!"*

At the end of the year Ford checked with his engineers, and again they informed him they had found no way to carry out his orders.

"Go right ahead," said Ford, "I want it, and I'll have it." They went ahead, and then, as if by a stroke of magic, the secret was discovered.

The Ford *determination* had won once more!

How The Universe Works

This is nothing more and nothing less than how the Universe works.

The HoloCosm works itself through psychokinesis.
The SupraConscious takes form through synchronicity.

These two statements are so powerful that just in reaching the point where you understand them, you acquire a significant portion of the Power we speak of in this book.

Here and now is not the place for an in-depth explanation, as that would cheat you of the value that will swell in you when you discover the meaning on your own.

You should take these statements and use them as a constant affirmation.

Powered By Thought

The Ford story may not be described with minute accuracy, but the sum and substance of it is correct. Deduce from it, you who wish to *think and grow rich*, the secret of the Ford millions, if you can. You'll not have to look very far.

Henry Ford is a success, because he understands, and *applies* the principles of success. One of these is *desire*: knowing what one wants. Another is *refusing* to accept anything else. Remember this Ford story as you read and pick out the lines in which the secret of his stupendous achievements have been described. If you can do this, if you can lay your finger on the particular group of principles that made Henry Ford rich, you can equal his achievements in almost any calling for which you are suited.

The Mastery Of Life

When Henley wrote the prophetic lines, *"I* am the Master of my Fate, I am the Captain of my Soul,"* he should have informed us that we are the

Masters of our Fate, the Captains of our Souls, *because* we have the power to control our thoughts.

He should have told us that the Cosmos – this Universal Spirit – in which this little Earth floats, in which we live and move and have our being, is a form of energy moving at an inconceivably high rate of vibration, and that the Cosmos is filled with a form of universal power which *adapts* itself to the nature of the thoughts we hold in our minds, and *influences* us *and all the Universe*, in natural ways, to transmute our thoughts into their physical equivalent.

If the poet had told us of this great truth, we would know *why it is* that we are the Masters of our Fate, the Captains of our Souls. He should have told us, with great emphasis, that this power makes no attempt to discriminate between destructive thoughts and constructive thoughts, that it will urge us to translate into physical reality thoughts of poverty, just as quickly as it will influence us to act upon thoughts of riches… Or mediocrity.

He should have spoken of the magnetism emitted by every organism and every particle of the Universe, and reminded us that magnetism works without effort to attract that which is on its wavelength.

He should have told us, too, that… Our brains become magnetized with the dominating thoughts we hold in our minds, and, by means with which few people understand, these "magnets" attract to us the forces, the people, and the circumstances of life which harmonize with the nature of our dominating thoughts.

He should have told us, before we can accumulate riches in great abundance, we must switch the current in our system, magnetizing our minds and hearts with an intense desire for riches. He should have told us we must become "money conscious" until the *desire* for money drives us to create definite plans for acquiring it.

He also should have told us how to work it… That the entire Universe is *one single organism* – the *HoloCosm*. That, through the seemingly

I

mysterious connections that exist between each entity or "cell" in the Universe, you attract to you the persons, circumstances, events, conditions and opportunities that facilitate your success. He should have given us the instruction manual to *consciously* use these realities to manifest our positive desires.

But, being a poet, and not a philosopher or educator, Henley contented himself by stating a great truth in poetic form, leaving those who followed him to interpret the philosophical meaning of his lines.

Little by little, the truth has unfolded itself, until it now appears certain that the principles described in this book, hold the secret of mastery over our economic fate. It's been proven by well over 70 years of this popular philosophy's published life.

No Experience Required

We are now ready to examine the first of these principles. Maintain a spirit of open-mindedness, and remember as you read, these principles of acquiring riches are the invention of no one person. The principles were gathered from the life experiences of more than 2,000 men and women over the recent 100 years who actually accumulated riches in huge amounts, as well as countless other historical figures in cultures across the world… People, who began in poverty, had little education and were without influence. The principles worked for these people.

My promise to you is, provided you study this book, do the exercises consciously, and *attempt to prove them right*, they will work for you, too.

You will find it easy, not hard, to do.

DESIRE
THE STARTING POINT OF ALL ACHIEVEMENT

THE FIRST STEP TOWARD RICHES

Great souls have wills;
Feeble souls have only wishes.
– Chinese proverb

chapter *1* ➡ When Edwin C. Barnes hopped off the freight train in Orange, New Jersey, USA, more than 100 years ago, he may have resembled a tramp, but his thoughts were those of a king!

As he made his way from the railroad tracks to Thomas A. Edison's office, his mind was racing. He saw himself standing in Edison's presence. He heard himself asking Mr. Edison for an opportunity to carry out the **one consuming obsession of his life**, a *burning desire* to become the business associate of the great inventor. He felt the feelings flooding over him when the great inventor gave him the chance to prove himself.

Barnes' desire was not a hope! It was not a wish! It was a keen, pulsating, passionate *desire* which transcended everything else. It was *definite*.

The desire was not new when he approached Edison. It had been Barnes' dominating desire for a long time. In the beginning, when the desire first appeared in his mind, it may have been, probably was, only a wish, but it was no mere wish when he appeared before Edison with it.

Fast Forward

A few years later, Edwin C. Barnes again stood before Edison, in the same office where he first met the inventor. This time his *desire* had been translated into reality. He was in business with Edison. The dominating *dream of his life* had become a reality.

Many people who knew Barnes envied him because of the "break" life yielded him. They saw him in the days of his triumph, without taking the trouble to investigate the cause of his success.

Barnes succeeded because he chose a definite goal. He placed all his energy, all his willpower, and all his effort – everything back of that goal. He did not become the partner of Edison the day he arrived. He was content to start in the most menial work, as long as it provided an opportunity to take even one step toward his cherished goal.

Five years passed before the chance he had been seeking made its appearance. During all those years, not one ray of hope, not one promise of attainment of his *desire* had been held out to him. To everyone, except himself, he appeared only another cog in the Edison business wheel, but in his own mind, *he was the partner of Edison every minute of the time*, from the very day that he first went to work there.

Win Or Die

It is a remarkable illustration of the power of a *definite desire*. Barnes won his goal, because he **wanted** to be a business associate of Mr. Edison more than he wanted anything else in the world. He **created a plan** by which to attain that purpose, and ***burned all bridges*** behind him. He stood by his *desire* until it became the dominating obsession of his life – and – finally, a fact.

When he went to Orange, he didn't say to himself, "I will try to get Edison to give me a job of some sort." He said, "I will see Edison, and put him on notice that I have come to go into business with him."

He did not say, "I will work there for a few months, and if I get no encouragement, I will quit and get a job somewhere else."

> Barnes succeeded because he chose a definite goal, placed all his energy, all his willpower, and all his effort – *everything* back of that goal.

He did say, "I will start *anywhere*. I will do *anything* Edison tells me to do, but before I am through, *I will be his associate*."

He did not say, "I will keep my eyes open for another opportunity, in case I fail to get what I want in the Edison organization." He said, "There is **one thing in this world that I am determined to have**, and that is a business association with Thomas A. Edison. I will burn all bridges behind me, and stake my *entire future* on my ability to get what I want."

He left himself no possible way of retreat. He had to win or perish! That is all there is to the Barnes story of success!

A long while ago, a great warrior faced a situation which made it necessary for him to make a decision which insured his success on the battlefield. He was about to send his armies against a powerful foe, whose men outnumbered his own. He loaded his soldiers into boats, sailed to the enemy's country, unloaded soldiers and equipment, then gave the order to burn the ships that had carried them.

Addressing his men before the first battle, he said, "You see the boats going up in smoke. That means that we cannot leave these shores alive unless we win! We now have *two* choices – we win or we perish!" They won.

Every person who wins in any undertaking must be willing to burn his ships and cut all sources of retreat. Only by doing so, can one be sure of maintaining that state of mind known as a *burning desire to win*, essential to success.

That's all that distinguished Edwin C. Barnes from thousands of other young individuals who have worked in the Edison organization – not education, looks, connections, or money. It is the same difference that distinguishes practically all who succeed from those who fail.

Every human being who reaches the age of understanding of the purpose of money wishes for it. Wishing will not bring riches. But desiring riches with a state of mind that becomes an obsession, then planning definite ways and means to acquire riches, and backing those plans with persistence which does not recognize failure does bring riches.

The Single Greatest Determinant Of Outrageous Success

In 1951, Yale University is reputed to have begun a longitudinal study. That "long" time stretched 20 years, at which time they re-interviewed the surviving members of that bright and favored business school graduating class.

This is Ivy League Yale, which receives society's most privileged, and breeds in them an advantaged training – along with the contacts that will last them a lifetime.

If *anybody* has a leg up, it's these storied people…Children from across the world, children of magnates and of politicians.

The astonished researchers found that a mere whisper of 3% of the members controlled more wealth, by themselves, than the other 97% combined!

BONUS! 3 FREE Wealth-Building Gifts Worth $97 at HoloMagic.com

Just to put it in understandable terms, here's a mathematical comparison... That means that for each of the 97 losers, the net worth they had accumulated was a whopping total of $16,600. Kinda hard to live too many years of retirement on that one... Especially since that may be represented in equity in a house, paid for furniture and appliances, jewelry, guns, china, and clothing.

How do you spend the china that you need to eat on?...

However, those three great souls who had *written goals and a plan to achieve them* each were worth $16.6 Million each!

Profound difference! Vast!

Those researchers found the largest single facilitator / factor / indicator / determinant of outrageous success was **written goals and a plan to achieve them**.

"This Is A Test"

Now, having just discovered the *one* predictor / determinant of success – and it's not the things the pop culture tells you it is, like money, looks, connections, youth, family, education, or lucky breaks... My question to you is very simple...

Will you *do* the following exercise? Will *you* – right *now!* – create and write down your *goal,* your definite chief aim in life, plus scratch out a plan to achieve it?

It is not necessary to "get it right" the first time. Actually, it's nearly impossible. But getting it down *does* begin the process of clarification and refinement. Doing it forces you to make certain key decisions – and commit to them in a way they manifest...

It separates you from the drifting crowd and signals the HoloCosm to go to work for you.

Hear me – acting on these next few paragraphs is the most important thing you can possibly do in all your life.

BONUS! 3 FREE Wealth-Building Gifts Worth $97 at HoloMagic.com

How To "Think" And Grow Rich

The method by which *desire* for riches can be transmuted into its financial equivalent, consists of six definite, practical steps, being:

Formula For Riches

1. Fix in your mind the exact amount of money you desire. It is not sufficient merely to say, "I want plenty of money." Be definite as to the amount. (There is a psychological reason for definiteness, which will be described in a subsequent chapter).

2. Determine exactly what you intend to give in return for the money you desire. There is no such reality as "something for nothing." The *only* way you can get massively rich is to *contribute* massively to society. It's the Law.

3. Establish a definite date when you intend to possess the money you desire.

4. Create a definite plan for carrying out your desire, and begin at once, whether you are ready or not, to put this plan into action.

5. Write out a clear, concise statement of the amount of money you intend to acquire, name the time limit for its acquisition, state what you intend to give in return for the money, and describe clearly the plan through which you intend to accumulate it.

6. Read your written statement aloud, twice daily, once just before retiring at night, and once after arising in the morning. As you read — *see, feel and believe yourself already in possession of the money.*

BONUS! *3 FREE Wealth-Building Gifts Worth $97 at HoloMagic.com*

It is important that you follow the instructions described in these six steps. It is especially important that you observe and follow the instructions in the sixth step.

And as you do, enter into the feel of the vision until you are seduced to believe it's real, just like a real dream. Where are you? What do you see? Who are you with? What do you hear? What are people saying? What charities are you helping? What is the weather doing? Where are you? What are you wearing? How do you feel? What are you saying and doing? What do you do to celebrate? Are you at dinner? Where? What is the course?…

So Easy, Such Riches?...

Can it be so easy to get rich?… Merely "thinking?"

That's both the good news and the bad news.

It really *is* that easy… Thinking like this is thinking holographically. It includes the principles of this philosophy, which aren't all easy. After all, how many people do you encounter who have one definite chief purpose in life?…

And that's where it starts! That's principle #1.

How many people do you know with written goals, a plan to achieve them, and so much drive, they are currently in action pursuing their dreams?

It's just "thinking" – but everything flows from that.

If You're Skeptical

You may complain that it is impossible for you to "see yourself in possession of money" before you actually have it.

BONUS! 3 FREE Wealth-Building Gifts Worth $97 at HoloMagic.com

You might be complaining that I'm asking you to do / see / believe something you say is *obviously* not "true." But we do it all the time at the movie theater. Everybody knows a movie is "not true," yet that doesn't stop them from getting angry, happy, or scared. Even terrified.

There have even been people who said that seeing a certain movie changed their lives. Hmmm, that's a lot of power for something that's not *real*.

Second, here is where a *burning desire* will come to your aid. **If you truly** *desire* **money so keenly, that your desire is an** *obsession*, **you will have no difficulty in convincing yourself that you will acquire it**.

The object is to want money, and to become so determined to have it that you *convince* yourself you will have it.

"What Does Breaking Boards Have To Do With Your Success?"

Two volunteers came forward. A young diminutive girl broke the board with one clean stroke. The husky country man, after pounding away at it ten times, skulked away – *shamed*.

What gives? Whether you can break a board or not depends entirely on what you "see." When you "see" the top of the board, that's where you stop – *ouch!* When you see the *space beyond the board*, you pass through the board like it's cobweb.

It's not size, might, or even trying hard, as our burly friend with the throbbing hand learned...

> It's not who you are by the Fortunes of
> birth...money, looks, culture...
>
> The difference lies in your *mental focus*. In
> what you SEE!

I can tell you in my own case, as Ted Ciuba, when I was living in a single-axle camper trailer at the end of a long dirt road on the edge of the county-line, a failure for all the world to see, this is what assured me I could and, indeed, *would* be rich. I couldn't predict the exact time – but you can bet I *was* determined that the only variable that could stop me would be a premature death.

Besides, it was such a welcome contrast to the grinding circumstances I was in that it was *easy* and a *joy* to imagine things rich.

Of course, that's how it played out, too. I became everything I was "seeing." You will, too.

Only those who become "money conscious" ever accumulate great riches. "Money consciousness" means that the mind has become so thoroughly saturated with the *desire* for money that one can *see one's self already in possession of it.*

Ceremony Of Initiation

To the uninitiated, who has not been schooled in the working principles of the human mind, these instructions may appear impractical. It may be helpful, to all who fail to recognize the soundness of the six steps, to know that the information they convey was received from Andrew Carnegie, who began as an ordinary laborer in the steel mills, but managed, despite his humble beginning, to make these principles yield him a Fortune of considerably more than $100 Million dollars.

BONUS! 3 FREE Wealth-Building Gifts Worth $97 at HoloMagic.com

Finally, you should chuck any false perfectionism that's stopping you from *simply getting started* right now. Many people are afraid to write anything down, due to nothing but fear, and the unfortunate consequences of conventional schooling. "Write and get judged on it"... But you're dealing with something vastly more important than a homework assignment here – *it's your* life*!!*

You Are Loaned Certain Gifts – What You *Do* With Them Is Up To You

There's two important points to remember on this one... First, Infinite Intelligence loans you some gifts, but *you* yourself get to decide the method and the content of your contribution.

Second, you can and *will* refine the images, routes, resources, and plans of your success... But you have to get started *first*. When you're getting started, you're looking at things as an outsider. How could you possibly know what it will look like when it's done? How can you improve anything when you don't even know what that "thing" is? Ask yourself seriously on that one... And start today, designing, visualizing, affirming, and getting excited about your own life of riches.

It's always the same... Like with Henry Ford – with nothing but a third grade education and a burning desire... Start with the tools you have at hand, and better ones will be found as you go along.

It may be of further help to know that the six steps here recommended were carefully scrutinized by the late Thomas A. Edison, who placed his stamp of approval upon them as being, not only the steps essential for the accumulation of money, but necessary for the attainment of any definite goal.

No Manual Laborers Wanted

The steps call for no "hard labor." They call for no sacrifice. They do not require one to become ridiculous or incredulous. Applying them calls for no great amount of education. But the successful application of these six steps does call for sufficient imagination to enable one to see, and to understand, that **accumulation of money cannot be left to chance, good fortune, and luck.**

One must realize that all who have accumulated great Fortunes first did a certain amount of wishing, hoping, dreaming, *desiring, planning,* and oathing before they acquired money.

The White Heat Of Desire

You may as well know, right here, that you can never have riches in great quantities, *unless* you can work yourself into a white heat of *desire* for money, and actually *believe* you will possess it.

"To See Things In The Seed"

You may as well know also, that every great leader, from the dawn of civilization down to the present, was a dreamer. Both Christianity and Islam are great powers in the world today, because their founders were intense dreamers who had the vision and the imagination to see realities in their mental and spiritual form before they had been transmuted into physical form.

"To see things in the seed, that is genius."
— Lao-Tzu

If you do not see great riches in your imagination, you will never see them in your bank balance. Never, in the history of the world, has there been so great an opportunity for practical dreamers as now exists.

Novus Ordo

Especially because of the Internet, a new race is in the running. The stakes represent huge Fortunes that will be accumulated within the next several years. The rules of the race have changed, because we now live in a *changed world* that definitely favors the masses, those who had little or no opportunity to win under the conditions existing prior to the opening up of the world on the Internet.

A New MegaTrend

Truly, a megatrend… And here we find ourselves!

We, who are in this race for riches, should be encouraged to know that this changed world in which we live is demanding new ideas, new ways of doing things, new leaders, new inventions, new methods of teaching, new methods of marketing, new books, new literature, new features for the radio, new ideas for moving pictures, new strategies, uses, hardware, software, and content for the Internet.

Dazzling Opportunity

However, this most amazing age makes no promises. It just opens up the potential for you to participate.

Back of all this demand for new and better things, there is one quality which one must possess to win, and that is *definiteness of purpose*, the knowledge of what one wants, and a *burning desire* to possess it.

This changed world requires practical dreamers who can and will put their dreams into action. The practical dreamers have always been, and always will be the pattern makers of civilization.

BONUS! 3 FREE Wealth-Building Gifts Worth $97 at HoloMagic.com

We, who desire to accumulate riches should remember the real leaders of the world always have been men who harnessed, and put into practical use, the intangible, unseen forces of unborn opportunity, and have converted those forces (or impulses of thought) into skyscrapers, cities, factories, airplanes, automobiles, and every form of convenience that makes life more pleasant.

Small Minds Need Not Apply

Tolerance and an open mind are practical necessities of the dreamer of today. Those who are afraid of new ideas are doomed before they start. Never has there been a time more favorable to pioneers than the present. True, there is no wild and woolly American West to be conquered, as in the days of the covered wagon; but there is a vast business, financial, industrial, and computer-driven world to be remolded and redirected along new and better lines.

Dreamers *De Facto*

In planning to acquire your share of riches, let no one influence you to scorn the dreamer. To win the big stakes in this changed world, you must catch the **spirit** of the great pioneers of the past, whose **dreams** have given to civilization all that it has of value, to develop and market your talents.

Let us not forget, Columbus dreamed of an unknown world, staked his life on the existence of such a world, and discovered it!

Copernicus, the great Polish astronomer, dreamed of a multiplicity of worlds, and revealed them! No one denounced him as "impractical" *after* he had triumphed. Instead, the world worshipped at his shrine, proving once more that...

BONUS! 3 FREE Wealth-Building Gifts Worth $97 at HoloMagic.com

> *Success requires no apologies,*
> *Failure permits no alibis.*

If the thing you wish to do is right, and you believe in it, go ahead and do it!

Put your dream across, and never mind what "they" say if you meet with temporary defeat, for "they," perhaps, do not know that *every failure brings with it the seed of an equivalent success.*

In The Arena

Actually, as *every* successful person knows… No great success comes without its share of error and shortcoming… How could it be otherwise when you are entering new and unknown ground?

The buccaneering US president, Theodore Roosevelt, quite frankly "couldn't give a spit" about critics with time and worthless second-guessing on their hands…

This is how this winner eloquently expressed his opinion in immortal words in an address in Paris…

> It is not the critic who counts: not the man who points out how the strong man stumbles or where the doer of deeds could have done better.
>
> The credit belongs to the man who is actually in the arena, whose face is marred by dust and sweat and blood, who strives valiantly… Who errs and comes up short again and again…. Because there is no effort without error or shortcoming.
>
> Who knows the great enthusiasms, the great devotions, who spends himself for a worthy cause; who, at the best, knows, in the end, the triumph of high achievement, and who, at the worst, if he fails, at least he fails while daring greatly, so that his

place shall never be with those cold and timid souls who knew neither victory nor defeat.

He knew what he was doing. And, like a modern Odysseus, taking on all adventures, "come shell or high water," he accomplished it. Take note.

Dreamers, Dreamers, And Accomplishments

Henry Ford, poor and uneducated, dreamed of a horseless carriage in every family, and **went to work with what tools he possessed, without waiting for opportunity to favor him**. Now evidence of his dream belts the entire Earth! Exactly, as he planned. He has put more wheels into operation than any man who ever lived, because he was not afraid to back his dreams.

Thomas Edison dreamed of a lamp that could be operated by electricity, began where he stood to put his dream into action, and despite more than ten thousand failures, stood by that dream until he made it a physical reality. Practical dreamers *do not quit!*

Abraham Lincoln, president of the "Land of the Free," dreamed of freedom for Black slaves, put his dream into action, and barely missed living to see a united North and South translate his dream into reality.

The Wright brothers dreamed of a machine that would fly through the air. Now one may see evidence all over the world that they dreamed soundly. Today, we're sending ships to the stars. Tomorrow humans will colonize other planets in distant solar systems.

Marconi dreamed of a system for harnessing the intangible forces of the Cosmos. Evidence that he did not dream in vain may be found in every radio, TV, cell phone and wireless Internet connection in the world. As well, in every plane that flies the skies, every sub that lurks the seas, and every interstellar mission plying through space. This is just the beginning. Marconi's dream has brought the humblest pueblo and the most-stately manor house side by side; it has made the people of every nation on Earth backdoor neighbors.

Incarcerated… *Go figger!*

(Also, as you accelerate into new circumstances, prepare yourself for a bit of negative resistance - gossip, family and friends, the establishment… Etc, yada-yada-yada. It's meaningless, keep it there.)

It gives any leader of any country a medium by which he or she may talk to all the people of their land at one time, and on short notice, or broadcast their notice to the world.

It may interest you to know that Marconi's "friends" had him taken into custody and examined in a psychopathic hospital when he announced he had discovered a principle through which he could send messages through the air without the aid of wires or other direct physical means of communication. But *after* his success, it's a different story!

Dreamers on the bleeding edge always have, always will get treated such. (As a marketer in today's free world, of course, you can *capitalize* on that!)

However, go one step beyond that… The world willingly rewards the dreamer who gives the world a new idea.

"The greatest achievement was, at first, and for a time, but a dream."

"The oak sleeps in the acorn. The bird waits in the egg, and in the highest vision of the soul, a waking angel stirs. *Dreams are the seedlings of reality.*"

Awake, arise, and assert yourself, you dreamers of the world. Your star is now in the ascendancy.

The world is filled with an abundance of *opportunity* the dreamers of the past never knew.

A Burning Desire To Be, To Do, And To Have

A burning desire to be, to do, and to have is the starting point from which the dreamer must take off. Dreams are not born of indifference, laziness, or lack of ambition.

J.C. Penney, a man with the experience of thousands of employees over decades of time says…

> *Give me a stock clerk with a goal,*
> *and I will give you a person who will make history.*

> *Give me a person without a goal,*
> *and I will give you a stock clerk.*

Take Heart

Remember, all who succeed in life get off to a bad start and pass through many heartbreaking struggles before they "arrive." The turning point in the lives of those who succeed usually comes at the moment of some crisis, through which they are introduced to their "other selves."

John Bunyan wrote the Pilgrim's Progress, which is among the finest of all English literature, after he had been confined in prison and sorely punished, because of his views on the subject of religion.

O. Henry discovered the genius, which slept within his brain, after he had met with great misfortune, and was confined in a prison cell in Columbus, Ohio. Being *forced*, through misfortune, to become acquainted with his "other self," and to use his *imagination*, he discovered himself to be a great author instead of a miserable criminal and outcast.

The sports annals are filled with similar examples of outstanding victory coming one step beyond crushing defeat – of desire and determination overcoming adversity and "temporary" setback.

Strange and varied are the ways of life, and stranger still are the ways of Infinite Intelligence, through which people are sometimes forced to undergo all sorts of punishment before discovering their own brains and their own capacity to create useful ideas through imagination.

Edison, the world's greatest inventor and scientist, was a "tramp" telegraph operator. He failed innumerable times before he was driven, finally, to the discovery of the genius which slept within his brain.

Charles Dickens began by pasting labels on blacking pots. The tragedy of his first love penetrated the depths of his soul and converted him into one of the world's truly great authors. That tragedy produced, first, *David Copperfield*, then a succession of other works that made this a richer and better world for all who read his books. Disappointment over love affairs, generally has the effect of driving men to drink, and women to ruin; and this, because most people never learn the art of transmuting their strongest emotions into dreams of a constructive nature.

Helen Keller became deaf, dumb, and blind shortly after birth. Despite her great misfortune, she has written her name indelibly in the pages of the history of the great. Her entire life has served as evidence that no one ever is defeated until defeat has been accepted as a reality.

This amazing lady, with obstacles you'll never encounter, affirmed...

> *"Life is either a daring adventure,*
> *or it is nothing!"*

We should all learn from her.

Robert Burns was an illiterate country lad. Cursed by poverty, he grew up to be a drunkard in the bargain. The world was made better for his having lived, however, because he clothed beautiful thoughts in poetry, and thereby plucked a thorn and planted a rose in its place.

Booker T. Washington was born in slavery, handicapped by race and color. Because he was tolerant, had an open mind at all times on all subjects, and was a *dreamer*, he left his impression for good on an entire race. Actually, the entire *world*.

> Because they dreamed and translated their
> dreams into organized thought.

Beethoven was deaf, Milton was blind, but their names will last as long as time endures, because they dreamed and translated their dreams into organized thought.

Synchronicity

Before passing to the next chapter, awaken in your mind the fire of desire, hope, faith, courage, and tolerance. Visualize the life and achievements you desire. Affirm them.

> If you have these states of mind, and a work-
> ing knowledge of the principles described,
> **all else that you need, will come to
> you when you are *ready* for it.**

If you have these states of mind, and a working knowledge of the principles described, **all else that you need, will come to you when you are *ready* for it.**

Let Emerson state the thought in these words, *"Every proverb, every book, every byword that belongs to thee for aid and comfort shall surely come home through open or winding passages. Every friend whom not thy fantastic will, but the great and tender soul in thee craveth, shall lock thee in his embrace."*

And it doesn't stop with proverbs, books, and bywords – it extends to people, resources, circumstances, and opportunities, as well.

You Get What You *Expect*

There is a difference between *wishing* for a thing and being *ready* to receive it. No one is ready for a thing, until he or she believes they can and will acquire it. The state of mind must be *belief,* an actual state of *knowing,* not mere hope or wish.

Open-mindedness is essential for belief. Closed minds do not inspire faith, courage, and belief.

> No one is ready for a thing, until he or she believes they can acquire it.

You get *what you actually expect, not what you would wish for,* be it abundance and prosperity or misery and poverty. This is another demonstration of *faith* in action. Faith manifests. A poet has correctly stated this universal truth through these lines:

> *I bargained with Life for a penny,*
> *And Life would pay no more,*
> *However I begged at evening*
> *When I counted my scanty store.*

> *For Life is a just employer,*
> *He gives you what you ask,*
> *But once you have set the wages,*
> *Why, you must bear the task.*

> *I worked for a menial's hire,*
> *Only to learn, dismayed,*

That any wage I had asked of Life,
Life would have willingly paid.

"Success Leaves Clues"

I remember the news of the death of Mme. Schuman-Heink. One short paragraph in the news dispatch gave the clue to this unusual woman's stupendous success as a singer. I quote the paragraph, because the clue it contains is none other than *desire*.

> Early in her career, Mme. Schuman-Heink visited the director of the Vienna Court Opera, to have him test her voice. But, he did not test it. After taking one look at the awkward and poorly dressed girl, he exclaimed, none too gently, "With such a face, and with no personality at all, how can you ever expect to succeed in opera? My good child, give up the idea. Buy a sewing machine, and go to work. *You can never be a singer.*"

Never is a long time! The director of the Vienna Court Opera, as much as he knew about the technique of singing, knew little about the **power of desire, when it assumes the proportion of an obsession.** If he had known more of that power, he would not have made the mistake of condemning genius without giving it an opportunity.

Desire Backed By Faith

I believe in the power of *desire* backed by *faith*, because I have seen this power lift men from lowly beginnings to places of power and wealth. I have seen it rob the grave of its victims. I have seen it serve as the medium by which men staged a comeback after having been defeated in a hundred different ways. I have seen it provide my own son, Blair Hill, with a normal, happy, successful life, despite Nature's having sent him into the world without ears.

Wrapped In The Impulse Of Strong Desire

How can one harness and use the power of *desire*? This has been answered through this and the subsequent chapters of this book. Mark well these words...

ALL achievement, no matter what may be its nature or its purpose, begins with an intense, burning desire for something definite.

Through some strange and powerful principle of "mental chemistry" which she has never divulged, Nature wraps up in the impulse of *strong desire* that *something* which recognizes no such word as impossible, and accepts no such reality as failure.

FAITH

HOLOVISUALIZATION OF, AND BELIEF IN, ATTAINMENT OF DESIRE

THE SECOND STEP TOWARD RICHES

chapter 2 ☞ Faith is the catalytic element of this wealth philosophy. When *faith* is blended with the vibration of thought, the subconscious mind instantly picks up the vibration, translates it into its spiritual equivalent, and transmits it to Infinite Intelligence, as in the case of prayer.

The emotions of *faith, love,* and *sex* are the most powerful of all the major positive emotions. When the three are blended, they have the effect of "coloring" the vibration of thought in such a way that it instantly reaches the subconscious mind, where it is changed into its spiritual equivalent, the only form that induces a response from Infinite Intelligence.

Love and faith are related to the spiritual side of man. Sex is purely biological, and related only to the physical. The mixing, or blending, of these three emotions has the effect of opening a direct line of communication between the finite, thinking mind of man, and Infinite Intelligence.

How To Develop Faith

Here's something which will give you a better understanding of the importance the principle of auto-suggestion assumes in the transmutation of desire into its physical, or monetary equivalent:

> *Faith* is a state of mind that may be induced or created by affirmation or repeated instructions to the subconscious mind, through the principle of auto-suggestion.

As an illustration, consider the purpose for which you are, presumably, reading this book. The object is, naturally, to acquire the ability to transmute the intangible thought impulse of *desire* into its physical counterpart, money.

By following the instructions laid down in the chapters on Auto-Suggestion and the Subconscious Mind, you may *convince your subconscious mind* that *you believe* you will receive that for which you ask, **and it will act upon that belief**, which your subconscious mind passes back to you in the form of *faith*, followed by definite plans for procuring that which you desire.

Faith is a state of mind you may develop at will, after you have mastered the thirteen principles, because it is a state of mind which develops voluntarily, through application and use of these principles.

Use Affirmations To Create Faith

Repetition of *effectively crafted affirmations* to your subconscious mind is the only known method of voluntary development of the emotion of faith. (More on how to create *effectively crafted* affirmation in the chapter on Auto-Suggestion.

Perhaps the meaning may be made clearer through the following explanation as to the way men sometimes become criminals. Stated in the words of a famous criminologist, "When men first come into contact with crime, they abhor it. If they remain in contact with crime for a time, they become accustomed to it, and endure it. If they remain in contact with it long enough, they finally embrace it, and become influenced by it."

This is the equivalent of saying that *any impulse of thought which is repeatedly passed on to the subconscious mind is finally accepted and acted upon by the subconscious mind, which proceeds to translate that impulse into its physical equivalent, by the most practical procedure available.*

Which points to the reason we keep hammering home that you want to commit your affirmations to memory, and repeat them time and time again.

Emotionalized Thoughts Have The Power

In connection with this, consider again the statement:

> *All thoughts which have been emotionalized and mixed with faith* begin immediately to translate themselves into their physical equivalent or counterpart.

The emotions, or the "feeling" portion of thoughts, are the factors that give thoughts vitality, life, and action. The emotions of faith, love, and sex, when mixed with any thought impulse, give it greater action than any of these emotions can do singly.

Not only thought impulses which have been mixed with *faith* but, those which have been mixed with any of the positive emotions, or any of the negative emotions, may reach, and influence the subconscious mind.

Guardian At The Door

From this statement, you will understand that the subconscious mind translates into its physical equivalent, a thought impulse of a negative or destructive nature, just as readily as it acts upon thought impulses of a positive or constructive nature. This accounts for the strange phenomenon so many millions of people experience, referred to as "misfortune," or "bad luck."

There are millions of people who *believe* themselves "doomed" to poverty and failure, because of some strange force over which they *believe* they have no control. Though they can't conceive it from their present level of consciousness, they are the creators of their own "misfortunes," because of this negative *belief*, which is picked up by the subconscious mind, and translated into its physical equivalent.

According to Natural Law.

This is exactly why you must rigorously control your thoughts – promoting, allowing, and encouraging *only positive thoughts* and visualizations.

You cannot hold any belief or emotion in your heart that is not manifested in your face and your conditions. This law works equally as well in reverse – with the emotions of jealously, cupidity, revenge, and hatred, as it does with the positive emotions of cooperation, love, encouragement, and teaching.

No one can "hate" someone without feeling the effects of hatred in their own psyche-corpus. In the same token, a gentle spirit can be detected from the gentle manner of the person.

Your Programming, Your Life

What you "are," you present…

Who you really are – deep inside – you project, like the programming of a radio station, to all that have eyes and ears to see.

You can fool yourself, through ignorance, but you can't fool with the actual results you produce.

When Do You Think You Should Start?

That's why it's so important to consciously and positively program your mind and heart. You are like a computer – *whatever* software program you install is specified by your thoughts, goals, emotions, visualizations, plans, and daring – or lack of thereof.

The way the mind creates circumstances from the thoughts encouraged in the mind is how the computer works… It manifests thought.

Hardwired into the hardware – is *how* it works. *What it manifests* is the software each individual installs.

You cannot not get results.

Therefore, choose wisely and with purpose.

And this choosing wisely and rigorously controlling your thoughts need not be difficult in the least! Get fired with passion. Put your imagination to work with the full faith your intelligent organized planning will yield the results you seek. Get engaged early mornings and late nights.

This is an empowered, focused, accomplishing spot.

> Your *belief*, or *faith*, is the catalytic element which determines the action of your subconscious mind

This is an appropriate place to suggest again that you may benefit, by passing on to your subconscious mind, any *desire* you wish translated into its physical, or monetary equivalent, in a state *of expectancy or belief that the transmutation will actually take place.* **Your *belief*, or *faith*, is the catalytic element that determines the action of your subconscious mind.**

Notice the words that have been emphasized in the above paragraph, and you'll understand the razor's edge positioning of your thoughts that is necessary for the conscious creation of the circumstances you desire.

There is nothing to hinder you from "deceiving" your subconscious mind when giving it instructions through autosuggestion, as I deceived my son's subconscious mind when I fed him the impression his "affliction" would be overcome and would, in fact, turn into great benefit.

To make this "artifice" more realistic, conduct yourself just as you would, as *"if"* you were already in possession of the material thing which you are *demanding*, when you call upon your subconscious mind.

The *subconscious lives in the present tense*, so those are the most powerful visualizations, dramas, emotions, beliefs you can use to communicate with your subconscious.

The workings of your subconscious mind transmute into its physical equivalent, by the most direct and physical media available, any order which is given to it in a state of *belief* or *faith* that the order will be carried out, no matter how "coincidental" or *logical* it may appear when it appears…

Experiment And Practice To Prove It Works

Surely, enough has been stated to give a starting point from which one may, through experiment and practice, acquire the ability to mix *faith* with any order given to the subconscious mind. Perfection will come through practice. It cannot come by merely reading instructions.

The Great Mover, Eager Responsibility

If it's true that one may become a criminal by association with crime (and this is a known fact), it is equally true that one may develop faith by voluntarily suggesting to the subconscious mind that one has faith.

The mind comes, finally, to take on the nature of the influences, which dominate it, whatever they may be. When *Think And Grow Rich* was originally published in 1937, this was a controversial stance, which many treated with skepticism or suspicion. In the twenty-first century, this is common knowledge.

> A mind dominated by positive emotions, becomes a favorable abode for the state of mind known as faith.
>
> A mind so dominated may, at will, give the subconscious mind instructions, which it will accept and act upon immediately.

Embrace this truth, and you will grasp why it is essential for you to *encourage the positive emotions as dominating forces of your mind, and discourage and eliminate negative emotions.*

A mind dominated by positive emotions, becomes a favorable abode for the state of mind known as faith.

A mind so dominated may, at will, give the subconscious mind instructions, which it will accept and act upon immediately.

Faith Is A State Of Mind Which May Be Induced By Self-Suggestion

All down through the ages, the religionists have admonished the struggling portion of humanity to "have faith" in this, that, and the other dogma or creed, but they have failed to tell people *how* to have faith. They have not stated that "faith is a state of mind, and that it may be induced by self-suggestion."

BONUS! 3 FREE Wealth-Building Gifts Worth $97 at HoloMagic.com

By Faith You Contact Infinite Intelligence

In language which any normal human being can understand, we will describe all that is known about the principle through which *faith* may be developed, where it does not already exist.

Before we begin, you should be reminded again that:

- *Faith* is the "eternal elixir" which gives life, power, and action to the impulse of thought!
- **Faith is the starting point of all accumulation of riches!**
- *Faith* is the basis of all "miracles," and all mysteries, which cannot be analyzed by the rules of classical science!
- *Faith* is the only known preventative or antidote for *failure*!
- *Faith* is the element, the "chemical" which, when mixed with prayer, gives one **direct communication with Infinite Intelligence**.
- **Faith is the charge, which boosts the ordinary vibration of thought, created by the finite mind of man into its spiritual equivalent.**
- **Faith is the only agency through which the Cosmic Force of Infinite Intelligence can be harnessed and used by man.**

Because reading these Faith affirmations with understanding and emotional acceptance actually creates faith in you, I encourage you to read this brief summary aloud frequently.

Discover "Auto-Suggestion"

Every one of the foregoing statements is capable of proof!

The proof is simple and easily demonstrated. It is wrapped up in the principle of *auto-suggestion*. Let us center our attention, therefore, upon the subject of *self-suggestion*, and find out what it is, and what it is capable of achieving.

It is a well-known fact that one comes, finally, to *believe* whatever one repeats to one's self, whether the statement be true or false. If a person repeats a lie over and over, they will eventually accept the lie as truth. Moreover, they will *believe* it to be the truth. Every person is what he or she is because of the *dominating thoughts,* which they permit to occupy their mind.

Thoughts which a person deliberately places in their own mind, and encourages with sympathy, and with which they mix any one or more of the emotions, constitute the motivating forces, which direct and control their every movement, act, and deed!

And now for a very significant statement of truth…

A Magnetic Force

Science confirms we are bioelectromagnetic beings.

Thoughts which are mixed with any of the feelings of emotions, especially faith, *constitute* a "magnetic" force which attracts, from the vibrations of the Cosmos, other similar, or related thoughts, appropriate circumstances, chance meetings, and who knows what else?…

As a model of how this works, consider the electromagnet. It is an ordinary piece of iron in its normal state. As such, it has no attractive powers.

But when you run an electrical current through the metal, its atoms having been "awakened," it develops magnetic properties. At that point, in a cybernetic-synergetic loop, it is attracted to metal, which is likewise attracted to it.

Note, *the bar of metal did not change…* Only the current flowing through the metal. *Yet the bar's entire reality changed,* and it instantly became possessed with powers unknown and inaccessible to it during periods of ordinary mortality.

Also note, a magnetic force attracts and is attracted by *only* the things on its same "wavelength." Everything else is ignored.

Faith is that current running through your thoughts which stimulates *your* bioelectromagnetic powers. You become a charged person possessed of extraordinary powers and abilities. What you attract is in accord with the dominant thoughts, which occupy your mind.

Therefore, you can appreciate the absolute necessity of designing and controlling the content of your mind, or you may end up surrounded in circumstances not to your liking at all. *What you think about, you bring about.*

In the multi-dimensional, mental-spiritual realm, a thought that's "magnetized" with emotion may be compared to a seed which, when planted in fertile soil, germinates, grows, and multiplies itself over and over again, until that which was originally one small seed, becomes countless millions of seeds of the *same brand*! All life works on the ever-expanding law of increase / leverage.

This reality, as you can clearly see, is the metaphor behind the very title of this book… *Think* and *Grow Rich.*

The Cosmos, that great organic medium in which we live, move, and have our being, is a great cosmic mass of eternal forces of vibration. It is made up of both destructive vibrations and constructive vibrations. It carries, at all times, vibrations of fear, poverty, disease, failure, misery, and vibrations of prosperity, health, success, and happiness, just as surely as it carries the sound of countless thousands of voice and music waves, each which maintain their own individuality and means of identification through the medium of radio and electrical current.

Who understands this better than someone from the Internet Age accustomed to sending and receiving electrons?

Tune into what you *want* – never what you *don't* want!

> From the great storehouse of the Cosmos, the human mind is constantly attracting vibrations, which harmonize with that which *dominates* the human mind. Any thought, idea, plan, or purpose which one holds in one's mind attracts, from the vibrations of the Cosmos, a host of its relatives, adds these "relatives" to its own force, and grows until it becomes the dominating, **motivating master** of the individual in whose mind it has been housed.

From the great storehouse of the Cosmos, the human mind is constantly attracting vibrations on the same magnetic wavelength as those that which *dominate* the human mind.

Any thought, idea, plan, or purpose which one holds in one's mind attracts, from the vibrations of the Cosmos, a host of its relatives, adds these "relatives" to its own force, and grows until it becomes the dominating, *motivating master* of the individual in whose mind it has been housed.

That being the case, it obviously becomes very important we become informed as to how the original seed of an idea, plan, or purpose may be planted in the mind. The information is easily conveyed: *any idea, plan, or purpose may be placed in the mind through repetition of thought.*

This is why you are asked to write out a statement of your major purpose, or definite chief aim, commit it to memory, and repeat it, in audible words, day after day, until these vibrations of sound have reached your subconscious mind.

BONUS! 3 FREE Wealth-Building Gifts Worth $97 at HoloMagic.com

Create Circumstances To Order

If you are not *conscious* and guarded, you can and will be affected by the vibrations of thought which you pick up and register through the stimuli of your heredity and family and daily environment.

Resolve to throw off the influences of any unfortunate environment, and to build your own life to *order*. Taking inventory of mental assets and liabilities, you will discover that your greatest weakness is lack of self-confidence.

This handicap can be surmounted, and timidity translated into courage through the aid of the principle of auto-suggestion. The application of this principle may be made through *affirmations* – a simple arrangement of positive thought impulses stated in writing, memorized, and repeated, until they become a part of the working equipment of the subconscious faculty of your mind.

The Vital Science Of *Affirmations*

There's a reason why you want to do affirmations right – *results*.

You shouldn't just dash off a quick read of the "Self-Confidence Formula" following. You should attack it like a religious convert, because it holds the secrets to your future prosperity.

It consists of a carefully crafted set of affirmations, which create integrity, peace, and self-confidence in yourself.

Study it, sign it, write it out on a note card and carry it with you, *recite it often*, that your dreams may come true…

Self-Confidence Formula

First. I know I have the ability to achieve the object of my definite purpose in life, therefore, I *demand* of myself persistent, continuous action toward its attainment, and I here and now promise to render such action.

Second. I realize the dominating thoughts of my mind eventually reproduce themselves in outward, physical action, and gradually transform themselves into physical reality, therefore, I concentrate my thoughts for thirty minutes daily, upon thinking of the person I am becoming, creating in my mind a clear, vibrant, moving, exciting mental video of that person.

Third. I know through the principle of auto-suggestion, any desire I persistently hold in my mind eventually seeks expression through some practical means of attaining the object back of it, therefore, I devote ten minutes daily to developing the *self-confidence* that empowers me to seek my largest dreams!

Fourth. I have clearly written down a description of my *definite chief aim* in life, and I will never stop making it happen, even when I have developed self-confidence and the attainment of these riches.

Fifth. I fully realize that no wealth or position can long endure, unless built upon truth and justice, therefore, I engage in no transaction, which does not benefit all whom it affects.

I succeed by attracting to myself the forces I wish to use, and the cooperation of other people. I induce others to serve me, because of my willingness to serve others. I eliminate hatred, envy, jealousy, selfishness, and cynicism by developing love for all humanity, because I know that a negative attitude toward others can never bring me success. I cause others to believe in me, because I believe in them, and in myself.

I hereby sign my name to this formula, date it, commit it to memory, and repeat it aloud daily, with full FAITH it gradually influences my *thoughts* and *actions* so I am a self-confident, self-reliant, successful person.

_____   _____

Signature   Date

Back of this formula is a Law of Nature which conventional society has been slow to comprehend. Mystics have possessed the wisdom for millennia. The new Quantum Science, which is still way out there for the average man or woman, offers an elegant explanation of the working of the law.

Modern motivational science of the most advanced degrees, such as you find in this present treatise, is built on these same principles.

However, it's less important to understand *how* it works than it is to *use* it!

It's fascinating. It's baffled scientists of all ages. Psychologists have named this law, "auto-suggestion," and let it go at that.

The name by which one calls this law is of little importance. The important fact about it is it *works* for the glory and success of humankind… *If* used constructively.

On the other hand, if used destructively, it destroys just as readily. In this statement may be found a very significant truth, namely; that those who go down in defeat, and end their lives in poverty, misery, and distress, do so because of negative application of the principle of auto-suggestion.

The cause may be found in the fact that *all impulses of thought have a tendency to clothe themselves in their physical equivalent.*

Be Conscious!

The subconscious mind (the electro-chemical laboratory in which all thought impulses are combined and made ready for translation into physical reality) makes no distinction between constructive and destructive thought impulses. It works with the material we feed it, through our thought impulses. The subconscious mind translates into reality a thought driven by *fear* just as readily as it translates into reality a thought driven by *courage, self-confidence*, or *faith*.

The pages of medical history are rich with illustrations of cases of "suggestive suicide." A man may commit suicide through negative suggestion, just as effectively as by any other means. In a midwestern city, a man by the name of Joseph Grant, a bank official, "borrowed" a large sum of the bank's money, without the consent of the directors. He lost the money through gambling.

One afternoon, the bank examiner came and began to check the accounts. Grant left the bank, took a room in a local hotel, and when they found him, three days later, he was lying in bed, wailing and moaning, repeating over and over these words, "My God, this will kill me! I cannot stand the disgrace." In a short time he was dead. The doctors pronounced the case one of "mental suicide."

Just as electricity will turn the wheels of industry, and render useful service if used constructively; or snuff out life if wrongly used, so will the law of auto-suggestion lead you to peace and prosperity, or down into the valley of misery, failure, disgrace, and death, according to your degree of understanding and application of it.

If you fill your mind with *fear*, doubt, and unbelief in your ability to connect with and use the forces of Infinite Intelligence, the law of auto-suggestion will take this spirit of unbelief and use it as a pattern by which your subconscious mind will translate it into its physical equivalent.

As True As "2 + 2 = 4"

Like the wind, which carries one ship East and another West, the law of auto-suggestion will lift you up or pull you down according to the way you set your sails of *thought*.

The law of auto-suggestion through which any person may rise to altitudes of achievement which stagger the imagination, is well described in the following verse:

> *If you think you are beaten, you are,*
> *If you think you dare not, you don't*
> *If you like to win, but you think you can't,*
> *It is almost certain you won't.*
>
> *If you think you'll lose, you're lost*
> *For out of the world we find,*
> *Success begins with a fellow's will —*
> *It's all in the state of mind.*
>
> *If you think you are outclassed, you are,*
> *You've got to think high to rise,*
> *You've got to be sure of yourself before*
> *You can ever win a prize.*
>
> *Life's battles don't always go*
> *To the stronger or faster man,*
> *But soon or late the man who wins*
> *Is the man who thinks he can!*

Catch the deep meaning the poet had in mind!

Awaken The Giant Within

Somewhere in your make-up (perhaps in the cells of your brain) there lies sleeping, the seed of achievement, which if aroused and put into action, would carry you to heights such as you may never have hoped to attain.

Just as a master musician may cause the most beautiful strains of music to pour forth from the strings of a violin, so may you arouse the genius which lies asleep in your brain, and cause it to drive you upward to whatever goal you may wish to achieve.

Abraham Lincoln was a failure at everything he tried, until he was well past the age of forty. He was a Mr. Nobody from Nowhere, until a great experience came into his life, aroused the sleeping genius within his heart and brain, and gave the world one of its really great men. That "experience" was mixed with the emotions of sorrow and *love*. It came to him through Anne Rutledge, the only woman whom he ever truly loved.

Like The Poets And Songsters Sing

It is a known fact that the emotion of *love* is closely akin to the state of mind known as *faith*, and this for the reason, love comes very near to translating one's thought impulses into their spiritual equivalent.

During research, the authors discovered, from the analysis of the life, work and achievements of hundreds of men of outstanding accomplishment, that there was the influence of a woman's love behind *every one of them*.

The emotion of love in the human heart and brain creates a favorable field of magnetic attraction, which causes an influx of the higher and finer vibrations which are afloat in the Cosmos.

An Idea With The Impetus Of 2,000 Years

If you wish evidence of the power of *faith*, study the achievements of men and women who have employed it. At the head of the list comes the Nazarene. Christianity is still one of the greatest forces, which influences the minds of men. The basis of Christianity is *faith*, no matter how many people may have perverted, or misinterpreted the meaning of this great force, and no matter how many dogmas and creeds have been created in its name, which do not reflect its tenets.

The sum and substance of the teachings and the achievements of Christ, which may have been interpreted as "miracles," were nothing, more or less, than *faith*. If there are any such phenomena as "miracles," they are produced only through the state of mind known as *faith*! More than a few teachers of religion neither understand nor practice *faith*.

The Case Of Gandhi

Let us consider the power of *faith*, as it was demonstrated, by a man who is well known to all of civilization, Mahatma Gandhi, of India. In this man the world has seen one of the most astounding examples known to civilization of the possibilities of *faith*.

Gandhi wielded more potential power than any man living at his time, and this, despite the fact that he had none of the orthodox tools of power, such as money, battle ships, soldiers, and materials of warfare. Gandhi had no money, had no home, did not even own a suit of clothes, but *he did have power*. How did he come by that power?

He created it out of his understanding of the principle of faith, and through his ability to transplant that faith into the minds of two hundred million people.

Gandhi accomplished, through the influence of *faith,* that which the strongest military power on earth could not, and never will accomplish through soldiers and military equipment. He accomplished the astounding feat of *influencing* two hundred million minds to *coalesce and move in unison as a single mind.*

What other force on Earth, except *faith*, could do as much?

Proof A Person Can *Think* And Grow Rich

Because of the need for faith and cooperation in operating business and industry, it will be both interesting and profitable to analyze an event which provides an excellent understanding of the method by which industrialists and business people accumulate great Fortunes, by *giving* **before they try to get.**

The event chosen for this illustration dates back to 1900, when the United States Steel Corporation was being formed. As you read the story keep in mind these fundamental facts, and you will understand how *ideas* have been converted into huge Fortunes.

First, the huge United States Steel Corporation was born in the mind of Charles M. Schwab, in the form of an *idea* he created through his *imagination!*

Second, he mixed *faith* with his *idea.*

Third, he formulated a *plan* for the transmutation of his *idea* into physical and financial reality.

Fourth, he put his plan into action with his famous speech at the University Club.

Fifth, he applied, and followed through on his *plan* with *persistence,* and backed it with firm *decision* until it had been fully carried out.

Sixth, he prepared the way for success by a *burning desire* for success.

If you are one of those who have often wondered how great Fortunes are accumulated, this story of the creation of the United States Steel Corporation will be enlightening. If you have any doubt that a person can *think and grow rich,* this story should dispel that doubt, because you can plainly see in the story of United States Steel, the application of a major portion of the thirteen principles described in this book.

This astounding description of the power of an *idea,* was dramatically told by John Lowell, in the New York World-Telegram, with whose courtesy it is here reprinted…

A Pretty After-Dinner Speech
For A Billion Dollars

When, on the evening of 12 December 1900, some eighty of the nation's financial nobility gathered in the banquet hall of the University Club on Fifth Avenue to do honor to a young man from out of the West, not half a dozen of the guests realized they were to witness the most significant episode in American industrial history.

J. Edward Simmons and Charles Stewart Smith, their hearts full of gratitude for the lavish hospitality bestowed on them by Charles M. Schwab during a recent visit to Pittsburgh, had arranged the dinner to introduce the thirty-eight-year-old steel man to eastern banking society. But they didn't expect him to stampede the convention. They warned him, in fact, that the bosoms within New York's stuffed shirts would not be responsive to oratory, and that, if he didn't want to bore the Stillmans and Harrimans and Vanderbilts, he had better limit himself to fifteen or twenty minutes of polite vaporings and let it go at that.

Even John Pierpont Morgan, sitting on the right hand of Schwab, as became his imperial dignity, intended to grace the banquet table with his presence only briefly. And so far as the press and public were concerned, the whole affair was of so little moment that no mention of it found its way into print the next day.

So the two hosts and their distinguished guests ate their way through the usual seven or eight courses. There was little conversation and what there was of it was restrained. Few of the bankers and brokers had met Schwab, whose career had flowered along the banks of the Monongahela, and none knew him well. But before the evening was over, they — and with them money master Morgan — were to be swept off their feet, and a billion dollar baby, the United States Steel Corporation, was to be conceived.

It is perhaps unfortunate for the sake of history that no record of Charlie Schwab's speech at the dinner ever was made. He repeated some parts of it at a later date during a similar meeting of Chicago bankers. And still later, when the government brought suit to dissolve the Steel Trust, he gave his own version, from the witness stand, of the remarks that stimulated Morgan into a frenzy of financial activity.

It is probable, however, that it was a "homely" speech, somewhat ungrammatical (for the niceties of language never bothered Schwab), full of epigram and threaded with wit. But aside from that, it had a galvanic force and effect upon the five billions of estimated capital that was represented by the diners. After it was over and the gathering was still under its spell, although Schwab had talked for ninety minutes, Morgan led the orator to a recessed window where, dangling their legs from the high, uncomfortable seat, they talked for an hour more.

The magic of the Schwab personality had been turned on full force, but what was more important and lasting was the full-fledged, clear-cut program he laid down for the aggrandizement of Steel. Many other men had tried to interest Morgan in slapping together a steel trust after the pattern of the biscuit, wire and hoop, sugar, rubber, whisky, oil or chewing gum combinations. John W. Gates, the gambler, had urged it, but Morgan distrusted him. The Moore boys, Bill and Jim, Chicago stockjobbers, who had glued together a match trust and a cracker corporation, had urged it and failed. Elbert H. Gary, the sanctimonious country lawyer, wanted to foster it, but he wasn't big enough to be impressive. Until Schwab's eloquence took J. P. Morgan to the heights from which he could visualize the solid results of the most daring financial undertaking ever conceived, the project was regarded as a delirious dream of easy-money crackpots.

The financial magnetism that began, a generation ago, to attract thousands of small and sometimes inefficiently managed companies into large and competition crushing combinations, had become operative in the steel world through the devices of that jovial business pirate, John W. Gates. Gates already had formed the American Steel and Wire Company out of a chain of small concerns, and together with Morgan had created the Federal Steel Company. The National Tube and American Bridge companies were two more Morgan concerns, and the Moore Brothers had forsaken the match and cookie business to form the "American" group – Tin Plate, Steel Hoop, Sheet Steel – and the National Steel Company.

But by the side of Andrew Carnegie's gigantic vertical trust, a trust owned and operated by fifty-three partners, those other combinations were picayune. They might combine to their heart's content, but the whole lot of them couldn't make a dent in the Carnegie organization, and Morgan knew it.

The eccentric old Scot knew it, too. From the magnificent heights of Skibo Castle he had viewed, first with amusement and then with resentment, the attempts of Morgan's smaller companies to cut into his business. When the attempts became too bold, Carnegie's temper was translated into anger and retaliation. He decided to duplicate every mill owned by his rivals. Previously, he hadn't been interested in wire, pipe, hoops, or sheet. Instead, he was content to sell such companies the raw steel and let them work it into whatever shape they wanted. Now, with Schwab as his chief and able lieutenant, he planned to drive his enemies to the wall.

So it was that in the speech of Charles M. Schwab, Morgan saw the answer to his problem of combination. A trust without Carnegie – giant of them all – would be no trust at all, a plum pudding, as one writer said, without the plums.

Schwab's speech on the night of December 12, 1900, undoubtedly carried the inference, though not the pledge, that the vast Carnegie enterprise could be brought under the Morgan tent. He talked of the world future for steel, of reorganization for efficiency, of specialization, of the scrapping of unsuccessful mills and concentration of effort on the flourishing properties, of economies in the ore traffic, of economies in overhead and administrative departments, of capturing foreign markets.

More than that, he told the buccaneers among them where the errors lay concerning their customary piracy. Their purposes, he inferred, had been to, create monopolies, raise prices, and pay themselves fat dividends out of privilege. Schwab condemned the system in his heartiest manner. The shortsightedness of such a policy, he told his hearers, lay in the fact that it restricted the market in an era when everything cried for expansion. By cheapening the cost of steel, he argued, an ever-expanding market would be created; more uses for steel would be devised, and a goodly portion of the world trade could be captured. Actually, though he did not know it, Schwab was an apostle of modern mass production.

So the dinner at the University Club came to an end. Morgan went home, to think about Schwab's rosy predictions. Schwab went back to Pittsburgh to run the steel business for "Wee Andra Carnegie," while Gary and the rest went back to their stock tickers, to fiddle around in anticipation of the next move.

It was not long coming. It took Morgan about one week to digest the feast of reason Schwab had placed before him. When he had assured himself that no financial indigestion was to result, he sent for Schwab — and found that young man rather coy. Mr. Carnegie, Schwab indicated, might not like it if he found his trusted company president had been flirting with the Emperor of Wall Street, the street upon which Carnegie was resolved never to tread. Then it was suggested by John W. Gates the go-between, that if Schwab "happened" to be in the Bellevue Hotel in Philadelphia, J. P. Morgan might also "happen" to be there. When Schwab arrived, however, Morgan was inconveniently ill at his New York home, and so, on the elder man's pressing invitation, Schwab went to New York and presented himself at the door of the financier's library.

Now certain economic historians have professed the belief that from the beginning to the end of the drama, the stage was set by Andrew Carnegie that the dinner to Schwab, the famous speech, the Sunday night conference between Schwab and the Money King, were events arranged by the canny Scot. The truth is exactly the opposite. When Schwab was called in to consummate the deal, he didn't even know whether "the little boss," as Andrew was called, would so much as listen to an offer to sell, particularly to a group of men whom Andrew regarded as being endowed with something less than holiness. But Schwab did take into the conference with him, in his own handwriting, six sheets of copper-plate figures, representing to his mind the physical worth and the potential earning capacity of every steel company he regarded as an essential star in the new metal firmament.

Four men pondered over these figures all night. The chief, of course, was Morgan, steadfast in his belief in the Divine Right of Money. With him was his aristocratic partner, Robert Bacon, a scholar and a gentleman. The third was John W. Gates whom Morgan scorned as a gambler and used as a tool. The fourth was Schwab, who knew more about the processes of making and selling steel than any whole group of men then living. Throughout that conference, the Pittsburgher's figures were never questioned. If he said a company was worth so much, then it was worth that much and no more. He was insistent, too, upon including in the combination only those concerns he nominated. He had conceived a corporation in which there would be no duplication, not even to satisfy the greed of friends who wanted to unload their companies upon the broad Morgan shoulders. Thus he left out, by design, a number of the larger concerns upon which the Walruses and Carpenters of Wall Street had cast hungry eyes.

When dawn came, Morgan rose and straightened his back. Only one question remained.

"Do you think you can persuade Andrew Carnegie to sell?" he asked.

"I can try," said Schwab.

"If you can get him to sell, I will undertake the matter," said Morgan.

So far, so good. But would Carnegie sell? How much would he demand? (Schwab thought about $320,000,000). What would he take payment in? Common or preferred stocks? Bonds? Cash? Nobody could raise a third of a billion dollars in cash.

There was a golf game in January on the frost cracking heath of the St. Andrews links in Westchester, with Andrew bundled up in sweaters against the cold, and Charlie talking volubly, as usual, to keep his spirits up. But no word of business was mentioned until the pair sat down in the cozy warmth of the Carnegie cottage nearby. Then, with the same persuasiveness that had hypnotized eighty millionaires at the University Club, Schwab poured out the glittering promises of retirement in comfort, of untold millions to satisfy the old man's social caprices. Carnegie capitulated, wrote a figure on a slip of paper, handed it to Schwab and said, "All right, that's what we'll sell for."

The figure was approximately $400,000,000, and was reached by taking the $320,000,000 mentioned by Schwab as a basic figure, and adding to it $80,000,000 to represent the increased capital value over the previous two years.

Later, on the deck of a trans-Atlantic liner, the Scotsman said ruefully to Morgan, "I wish I had asked you for $100,000,000 more."

"If you had asked for it, you'd have gotten it," Morgan told him cheerfully.

There was an uproar, of course. A British correspondent cabled that the foreign steel world was "appalled" by the gigantic combination. President Hadley, of Yale, declared that unless trusts were regulated the country might expect "an emperor in Washington within the next twenty-five years." But that able stock manipulator, Keene, went at his work of shoving the new stock at the public so vigorously that all the excess water – estimated by some at nearly $600,000,000 – was absorbed in a twinkling. So Carnegie had his millions, and the Morgan syndicate had $82,000,000 for all its "trouble," and all the "boys," from Gates to Gary, had their millions.

The thirty-eight-year-old Schwab had his reward. He was made president of the new corporation and remained in control until 1930.

The dramatic story of "Big Business," which you have just read, was included in this book because it is a perfect illustration of the method by which *desire can be transmuted into its physical equivalent*!

For The Scoffers

Some readers question the statement that a mere, intangible *desire* can be converted into its physical equivalent. Some take great pride in saying, "You cannot convert *nothing* into *something*!"

The proving reply is in the story of United States Steel.

BONUS! 3 FREE Wealth-Building Gifts Worth $97 at HoloMagic.com

That giant organization was created in the mind of one man. A man who, at the time, was a financial mouse.

It doesn't take money to make money!

The *plan* by which the organization was provided with the steel mills that gave it financial stability was created in the mind of the same man. He had moxie. He had *faith*. He had a huge imagination. He was proactive and decisive. **His *desire*, his *imagination*, his *faith*, his *persistence* were the real ingredients that went into United States Steel.**

What You Can Expect From A *Single Idea*

The steel mills and mechanical equipment acquired by the corporation, *after it had been brought into legal existence*, were incidental, but careful analysis will disclose the fact that the appraised value of the properties acquired by the corporation increased in value by an estimated *$600 Million* – equivalent to approximately $12 Billion in today's money – by the mere transaction which consolidated them under one management.

In other words, Charles M. Schwab's *idea*, plus the *faith* with which he conveyed it to the minds of J. P. Morgan and the others, was marketed for a profit of approximately $600 Million. Not an insignificant sum for a single *idea*!

What happened to some of the men, who took their share of the millions of dollars of profit made by this transaction, is a matter with which we are not now concerned. The important feature of the astounding achievement is that it serves as unquestionable evidence of the soundness of the philosophy described in this book, because this philosophy was the warp and the woof of the entire transaction.

Moreover, the practicability of the philosophy has been established by the fact that the United States Steel Corporation prospered and became one of the richest and most powerful corporations in America, employing thousands of people, developing new uses for steel, and opening new markets; proving that the $600 Million in profit which the Schwab *idea* produced was earned.

Riches begin in the form of thought!

The amount is limited only, by the person in whose mind the *thought* is put into motion. *Faith* removes limitations!

Name Your Price

Remember this when you are ready to bargain with Life for whatever it is that you ask as your price for having passed this way.

Remember, also, that the man who created the United States Steel Corporation was practically unknown at the time. He was a transparent individual working for Andrew Carnegie until he gave birth to his famous *idea*. After that he quickly rose to a position of power, fame, and riches.

THERE ARE NO LIMITATIONS
TO THE MIND EXCEPT THOSE
WE ACKNOWLEDGE

BOTH POVERTY AND
RICHES ARE THE
OFFSPRING OF
THOUGHT

AUTO-SUGGESTION
THE MEDIUM FOR INFLUENCING
THE SUBCONSCIOUS MIND

THE THIRD STEP TOWARD RICHES

chapter 3 ☞ Auto-suggestion is a term which applies to all self-administered suggestions and stimuli. Stated in another way, auto-suggestion is self suggestion. It is the agency of communication between that part of the mind where conscious thought takes place and that which serves as the seat of action for the subconscious mind. It works with the language of the five senses.

Auto-Suggestion Is The Technology You Use To Contact And Influence Your Subconscious Mind

Through the dominating thoughts which one permits to remain in the conscious mind (whether these thoughts be negative or positive is immaterial) the mechanism of *auto-suggestion reaches the subconscious mind and influences it with these thoughts.*

This would immediately suggest that if one could find the "right thoughts" to hold, encourage, and excite the *conscious* mind, the *subconscious* mind would "get it." Discover and think the kind of thoughts the

rich think, discover and think them in the same way, with the same qualities, and in a matter of outworking, you end up rich.

It would seem to remove programming the subconscious mind and
soliciting aid from Infinite Intelligence from the arena of chance, accident, and timing and make it a process you can direct to the specific end
of the accumulation of wealth.

It *is* that simple.

It doesn't necessarily mean it's all that easy, because there are constel-
lations of considerations, science, and effort in the process. Therefore, it
takes an entire book to adequately impart everything you need to access,
organize, and benefit from this technology.

No thought, whether negative or positive, *enters the reservoir of the subconscious without the vehicle of auto-suggestion.* (Except, of course, thoughts picked
up from the Cosmos, which is another related science to cultivate.).

Stated differently, all sense impressions which are perceived through the
five senses, are stopped by the *conscious* thinking mind, and may be either
passed on to the subconscious mind, or rejected, at will. The conscious faculty serves, therefore, as an outer guard to the approach of the subconscious.

The *subconscious* controls everything in our life, except for when we
intervene with the conscious. With this power of intervention, best accomplished with affirmations, we can reprogram our reactions, motivations,
thoughts, and deeds.

We can *change* who we are to who we want to be, in the flash of time
it takes to make a committed decision.

Unless you're already rich beyond your dreams, the entire point is
about reprogramming and recharging your own subconscious so the
right things come to you in flow.

The entire point of repeated contact with Infinite Intelligence, whose
wisdom is captured and crafted into your own personalized affirmations,

is so you begin to act automatically, by *habit*, in such a way that creates the natural result of wealth in your life.

Absolute Control Over Your Future

Few people know this… But the awareness of this fact is the actual tool that gives you near absolute control over your future and your destiny in all respects!

Nature has built the human animal so that each individual has *absolute control* over the material that reaches his or her subconscious mind through the five senses; although this is not meant to be construed as a statement that the individual always *exercises* this control. In the great majority of instances, this is distinctly *not* the case, which explains why so many people go through life in poverty.

No matter what happens, you have control over the *meaning* of any event or feeling… If you exercise it.

I know some on-the-ball business people who refer to the majority of people as "sheeple"… People who cannot and will not think for themselves… Nor imagine that *they cause their world*. Ironically, while imagining it cannot be so, they are living the very sheeple lives their sheeplelistic thoughts have created.

Bottom line… Think the sheeple thoughts the "mass of humanity" think, and you find yourself thoroughly immersed in the unfantastic actualization sheeple have, "lives of quiet desperation" (Thoreau).

You, of course, are willing to step outside your comfort zone and try a new experience well attested to by thousands of super-successful people from all times, cultures, sexes, and professions… People who have found the secret.

BONUS! 3 FREE Wealth-Building Gifts Worth $97 at HoloMagic.com

A Fertile Garden Spot

Recall what has been said about the subconscious mind resembling a fertile garden spot, in which weeds will grow in abundance, if the seeds of more desirable crops are not sown.

Auto-suggestion is the agency of control through which an individual may voluntarily feed his subconscious mind on thoughts of a creative nature, with the seeds of prosperity, or, by neglect, permit thoughts of a destructive nature to find their way there.

Auto-Suggestion Pre-Supposed In *Think And Grow Rich* Exercises

You were instructed, in the last of the six steps described in the chapter on Desire, to read *aloud* twice daily the *written* statement of your *desire for money*, and to *see and feel* yourself *already* in possession of the money!

By following these instructions you communicate the object of your *desire* directly to your *subconscious* mind in a spirit of absolute *faith*.

Through repetition of this procedure, **you voluntarily create thought habits favorable** to your efforts to *transmute desire into its monetary equivalent.*

Go back to these six steps described in chapter one, and read them again, very carefully, before you proceed further.

Then (when you come to it), read very carefully the four instructions for the organization of your "MasterMind" group, described in the chapter on Organized Planning.

By comparing these two sets of instructions with what has been stated on auto-suggestion, you, of course, see that the instructions involve the application of the principle of auto-suggestion.

Emotion Required

Remember, when reading aloud the statement of your desire (through which you are endeavoring to develop a "money consciousness") that the mere reading of the words is of *no consequence unless* you mix emotion, or feeling with your words. If you repeat a million times the famous Emil Coué formula, "Day by day, in every way, I am getting better and better," without mixing emotion and *faith* with your words, you will experience no desirable results.

Your subconscious mind recognizes and acts *only* upon thoughts which have been well mixed with emotion or feeling.

If Auto-Suggestion "Doesn't Work" For You

This is a fact of such importance as to warrant repetition in practically every chapter, because the lack of understanding of this is the main reason the majority of people who try to apply the principle of auto-suggestion get no desirable results.

Plain, unemotional words do not influence the subconscious mind. You will get no appreciable results until you learn to reach your subconscious mind with thoughts, or spoken words, which have been well emotionalized with *belief*.

Do not become discouraged, if you cannot control and direct your emotions the first time you try to do so. Remember, there is no such possibility as *something for nothing.* The ability to reach, and influence your subconscious mind has its price, and you *must pay that price.*

You cannot cheat, even if you desire to do so. The price of ability to influence your subconscious mind is everlasting *persistence* in applying the principles described here. You cannot develop the desired ability for a lower price. You, and *you alone*, must decide whether or not the reward for which you are striving (the "money consciousness") is worth the price you must pay for it in effort.

Wisdom and "cleverness" alone will not attract and retain money except in a few very rare instances, where the law of averages favors the attraction of money through these sources. The method of attracting money described in this philosophy does not depend upon the law of averages. Moreover, the method plays no favorites. It will work for one person as effectively as it will for another.

A Simple Dose Of Reality

Where failure is experienced, it is the individual, not the method, which has failed. If you try and fail, make another effort, and still another, until you succeed.

Where failure is experienced, it is the individual, not the method, which has failed. If you try and fail, make another effort, and still another, until you succeed.

The Easiest Task Of Concentration You'll Ever Encounter

Your ability to use the principle of auto-suggestion will depend, very largely, upon your capacity to *concentrate* upon a given *desire* until that desire becomes a **burning obsession**.

When you begin to carry out the instructions in connection with the six steps described in the first chapter, it will be necessary for you to make use of the principle of *concentration*.

Let us here offer suggestions for the effective use of concentration. When you begin to carry out the first of the six steps, which instructs you to "fix in your own mind the *exact* amount of money you desire," hold your thoughts on that amount of money by *concentration*, or fixation of attention, with your eyes closed, until you can *actually see* the physical appearance of the money. Do this at least once each day.

Remember, your affirmations require the high voltage *emotion* breathes into them…

- Think strongly about your goals

- Form a portfolio of full-bodied, active, bright images and clips of achievement

- Relish frequently in the feelings of accomplishment

- Blend into the *end*, the achievement accomplished, *believing* that it's real!

This is the **emotional present-tense** language of the subconscious.

Here are a few more tips about building effective affirmations and positive visualizations.

Employ The Senses

The more sense input you attach to your images and visualizations, the more impact they have. Enter into the positive emotional feeling of each sensory image. To embellish, ask yourself such questions as…

- What do you see? What colors are involved?

- In what?

- Who are you with?

- What's happening?

BONUS! 3 FREE Wealth-Building Gifts Worth $97 at HoloMagic.com

- How can you infuse *movement* in your visualizations?

- What's going on around you?

These questions are merely meant to be suggestive, there's no end to the variety of life you can zip into your imagination.

The point is, sensory input makes sense to your subconscious. Since the subconscious can't tell the difference between what is "real" and what is vividly imagined, you can use high sensory input and emotion to foment the pressure to achieve in your subconscious mind.

I've invented the cumbersome, but effective acronym, *Vakogëm* to help you remember all the sense elements that insert vitality in your affirmations. Each letter represents a portion of the formula, according to the following table:

v	Visual
a	Auditory
k	Kinesthetic
o	Olfactory
g	Gustatory
ë	Emotional!
m	Movement

Here's an emotional trick… To beef up the impact of the *emotion* component, I've even christened the *e* for *emotion* with two dots above it: *ë*. The double dots signify you give the emotional dimension of your affirmations *extra energy*.

So how do you use the formula? Simple, just use the acronym as an integrity check on the affirmation you're developing.

As an example, let's say you're writing an ebook on making affirmations, and you're visualizing 100,000 downloads of your free lead generator ebook generating $1 million sales dollars from it, one year after publishing.

In your imagination you could create a mental clip that possesses these elements…

> It is now _____(date) and I feel jazzed celebrating with my wife and two business partners on this project. We are huddled together watching the monitor in real time, with the champagne already poured… Sandy is so close I smell her exotic perfume. We're watching sales in real time! This is more exciting than the Oscars! We're whooping and hollering, taking bets on the minute that will be the magic minute – the culmination of four months of writing and one year of distribution of *Affirmation Magic*.
>
> Right now we only need *three* more sales to zip across the finish line! We each lift the champagne glass to our nostrils, and sniff the pungent clean smell of the bubbly champagne, which jumps and hits our cheeks and pops on my eyeglasses…
>
> We're poised, it will be any moment…
>
> And *now – cling, cling, cling* – I strike the Chinese money bell at 9:07 pm with the final sale that flies us past the Million Dollar mark! We lift our glasses – *ching, ching* – and swallow hard the acrid taste of celebratory champagne. *We did it!* Sandy breaks into a dance, we are so beside ourselves we are congratulating and hugging each other, swelling with the pride of accomplishment, of helping so many other human beings make their lives better.

Sensory Input Makes It Real

A quick analysis against our touchstone, *Vakogëm*, reveals, among others, we used…

BONUS! 3 FREE Wealth-Building Gifts Worth $97 at HoloMagic.com

Visual – watching the monitor in real time, the persons involved, what they are doing, seeing the sale that breaks the million barrier

Auditory – whooping and hollering, striking of the bell, the ch-ing-ching of the glasses

Kinesthetic – everything in *present tense,* we are huddled together, bub-bly champagne, champagne jumping onto our cheeks, hugging

Olfactory – Sandy's perfume, sniffing the champagne

Gustatory – the acrid taste of the champagne

Ëmotional! – feeling jazzed, more exciting than the Oscars, the suspense of watching sales in real time, *one* sale away from a win-ner, dancing, hugging, pride of accomplishment

Movement – huddling, preparing for the moment, lifting glasses in ching-ching, dancing, hugging

Also note this action visualization incorporates the members of your MasterMind group, who help you accomplish your ends.

Note as well, the use of *pre-supposition.* In visualizing the *end in mind…* It pre-supposes *many other things / hurdles* have been successfully passed; such as, for instance in this case, getting the product created and pro-duced, getting the website up, getting the copy written and tested, getting your lead generator out there, *doing whatever it takes,* etc.

This is the kind of life substance you can and should inject into the images of your definite chief aim in life; and, likewise with all the impor-tant milestones in the various departments of your life – spiritual, finan-cial, career, family, health, and personal development.

BONUS! 3 FREE Wealth-Building Gifts Worth $97 at HoloMagic.com

As you go through the exercises you receive in this book, follow the instructions given in the chapters on *Faith* and Auto-Suggestion, and vakogëm yourself actually *in possession of the money!*

Kick-Start Your Riches With Metaphysics

Here is a most significant fact: *the subconscious mind takes any orders given it in a spirit of absolute faith and acts upon those orders, although the orders often have to be presented over and over again, through repetition, before they are interpreted by the subconscious mind.*

Following the preceding statement, consider the possibility of playing a perfectly legitimate "trick" on your subconscious mind, by making it believe, because you believe it, that you must have the amount of money you are visualizing, that this money is already awaiting your claim, and that the subconscious mind *must* hand over to you practical plans for acquiring the money which is yours.

Hand over the thought suggested in the preceding paragraph to your *imagination*, and see what your imagination can, or will do, to create practical plans for the accumulation of money through transmutation of your desire.

Do not wait **for a definite plan, through which you intend to exchange services or merchandise in return for the money you are visualizing, but begin at once to see yourself in possession of the money,** *demanding* **and** *expecting,* **meanwhile, that your subconscious mind will hand over the plan or plans you need.**

Be on the alert for these plans, and when they appear, put them into *action immediately.* When the plans appear, they will probably "flash" into your mind through the sixth sense, in the form of an "inspiration." This inspiration may be considered a direct "telegram," or **message from Infinite Intelligence.** Treat it with respect, and act upon it as soon as you receive it. Failure to do this will be *fatal* to your *success.*

BONUS! 3 FREE Wealth-Building Gifts Worth $97 at HoloMagic.com

In the fourth of the six steps, you were instructed to "create a definite plan for carrying out your desire, and begin at once to put this plan into action." You should follow this instruction in the manner described in the preceding paragraphs. Do not trust your "reason" alone when creating your plan for accumulating money through the transmutation of desire. Your reason is faulty. Moreover, your reasoning faculty may be lazy, and it certainly isn't omniscient, and, if you depend entirely upon it to serve you, it may disappoint you.

If there was ever a time to close your eyes, meditate, and connect with you Higher Self, Infinite Intelligence, this is the time.

After you receive the impression of what you'll do to acquire the riches you desire, when visualizing the money you intend to accumulate (with closed eyes), see, feel, and move yourself rendering the service, or delivering the merchandise you intend to give in return for this money. This is important!

Make these images exciting… Make these clips larger than life, louder than normal, more colorful and intense than you'd usually find. Fashion images that *turn you on!* Then play them often. Enjoy yourself thoroughly!

And then you receive the ideas and plans for your unique pathway to riches, you begin fashioning them in your imagination, you jump to work, and the people, resources, circumstances and situations to help you finesse it begin to appear.

When these things begin to happen, embrace them and act on them quickly – and you'll keep the flow going.

Remember, as you carry out these instructions, that you are applying the principle of auto-suggestion for the purpose of giving orders to your subconscious mind. Remember, also, that your subconscious mind will act *only* upon instructions, which are emotionalized, and handed over to it with "feeling." *Faith* is the strongest, and most productive of the emotions. Follow the instructions given in the chapter on *Faith*.

The Mastery Of Life

These instructions may, at first, seem abstract. Do not let this disturb you.

Follow the instructions, no matter how abstract or impractical they may, at first, appear to be. The time will soon come, if you do as you have been instructed, in spirit as well as in act, when a whole new universe of power will unfold to you.

Skepticism, in connection with *all* new ideas, is characteristic of human beings. But if you follow the instructions outlined, your skepticism will soon be replaced by belief, and this, in turn, will soon become crystallized into *absolute faith*. Then you will have arrived at the point where you may truly say, "I am the master of my fate, I am the captain of my soul!"

Many philosophers have made the statement, that man is the master of his own earthly destiny, but most of them have failed to say why he is the master. The reason that man may be the master of his own earthly status, and especially his financial status, is thoroughly explained in this chapter.

Any human may become the master of himself or herself, and of their environment, because he or she has the *power to influence their own subconscious mind*, and through it, gain the cooperation of Infinite Intelligence.

The Other Principles Of The *Think And Grow Rich* Philosophy Empower Auto-Suggestion

You are now reading the chapter that represents the keystone to the arch of this philosophy. The instructions contained in this chapter must be understood and *applied with persistence*, if you are to succeed in transmuting desire into money.

BONUS! 3 FREE Wealth-Building Gifts Worth $97 at HoloMagic.com

The actual performance of transmuting *desire* into money involves the use of auto-suggestion as an agency by which one may contact and influence the subconscious mind. *The other principles are simply tools with which to apply auto-suggestion.* Keep these ideas in mind, and you will, at all times, be conscious of the important part the principle of auto-suggestion plays in your efforts to accumulate money through the methods described in this book.

With The Faith Of A Child

Carry out these instructions as though you were a small child. Inject into your efforts something of the *faith* of a child. The authors have been most careful to see that no impractical instructions are included because of their sincere desire to be helpful.

After you have read the entire book, come back to this chapter and follow in spirit, and in action this instruction:

Read the entire chapter aloud once every night, until you become thoroughly convinced that the principle of auto-suggestion is sound, **that it will accomplish for** *you all that has been claimed for it, and that you now know how to employ it.*

As you read, underscore or highlight every sentence that impresses you favorably.

Follow the foregoing instruction to the letter, and it will open the way for a complete understanding of and mastery of the principles of success.

SPECIALIZED KNOWLEDGE
PERSONAL EXPERIENCES
OR OBSERVATIONS

THE FOURTH STEP TOWARD RICHES

chapter 4 ⊂══► There are two kinds of knowledge. One is general; the other is specialized.

General knowledge, no matter how great in quantity or variety it may be, is of little use in the accumulation of money. The faculties of the great universities possess, in the aggregate, practically every form of general knowledge known to civilization.

Most of the professors have little or no money. They specialize in *teaching* knowledge, but they do not specialize in the organization, or the *use* of knowledge.

Knowledge Doesn't Attract Money

Knowledge does not attract money, unless it is *organized* and *intelligently directed*, through practical *plans of action* to the *definite end* of accumulation of money. Lack of understanding of this fact has been the source of confusion to millions of people who falsely believe that "Knowledge is Power." It is nothing of the sort! Knowledge is only *potential power.* It becomes power only when and if it is organized into definite plans of action, geared to a definite end.

This "missing link" in all systems of education known to civilization today, may be found in the failure of educational institutions to teach their students *how to organize and use knowledge after they acquire it.*

The Shocking Chicago Court Case

Many people make the mistake of assuming that, because Henry Ford had little "schooling," he is not a man of "education." Those who make this mistake do not know Henry Ford, nor do they understand the real meaning of the word "educate." That word is derived from the Latin word "educo," meaning to educe, to draw out – to *develop from within.*

An educated man is not, necessarily, one who has an abundance of general or specialized knowledge. An educated man is one who has so developed the faculties of his mind that he may acquire anything he wants, or its equivalent, without violating the rights of others. Henry Ford comes well within the meaning of this definition.

During the Euro-American World War I, a Chicago newspaper published certain editorials in which, among other statements, Henry Ford was called "an ignorant pacifist." Mr. Ford objected to the statements, and brought suit against the paper for libeling him. When the suit was tried in the courts, the attorneys for the paper pleaded justification, and placed Mr. Ford, himself, on the witness stand, for the purpose of proving to the jury that he was ignorant.

The attorneys asked Mr. Ford a great variety of questions, all of them intended to prove, by his own evidence, that, while he might possess considerable specialized knowledge pertaining to the manufacture of automobiles, he was, for the most part, ignorant.

Mr. Ford was plied with such questions as the following:

"Who was Benedict Arnold?" and "How many soldiers did the British send over to America to put down the Rebellion of 1776?" In answer to the last question, Mr. Ford replied, "I do not know the exact number of soldiers the British sent over, but I have heard that it was a considerably larger number than ever went back."

You catch the drift of the minutiae that, indeed, *few* could answer.

Finally, Mr. Ford became tired of this line of questioning, and in reply to a particularly offensive question, leaned over, pointed his finger at the attorney who had asked the question, and said...

> If I should really *want* to answer the foolish question you have just asked, or any of the other questions you have been asking me, let me remind you that I have a row of electric push-buttons on my desk, and by pushing the right button, I can summon to my aid men who can answer *any* question I desire to ask concerning the business to which I am devoting most of my efforts.
>
> Now, will you kindly tell me *why* I should clutter up my mind with general knowledge, for the purpose of being able to answer questions, when I have men around me who can supply any knowledge I require?

There certainly was good logic to that reply. That answer floored the Chicago lawyer. Every person in the courtroom realized it was the answer, not of an ignorant man, but of a man of *education*. **Any man is educated who knows where to get knowledge when he needs it, and how to organize that knowledge into definite plans of action.**

BONUS! 3 FREE Wealth-Building Gifts Worth $97 at HoloMagic.com

Through the assistance of his "MasterMind" group, Henry Ford had at his command all the specialized knowledge he needed to enable him to become one of the wealthiest men in America. It was not essential that he have this knowledge in his own mind. Surely, no person who has sufficient inclination and intelligence to read a book of this nature can possibly miss the significance of this illustration.

It Is Not Essential The Specialized Knowledge You Need Be In Your *Own* Mind

> Henry Ford had at his command all the specialized knowledge he needed to enable him to become one of the wealthiest men in America.
>
> *It was not essential that he have this knowledge in his own mind.*

Before you can be sure of your ability to transmute *desire* into its monetary equivalent, you will require *specialized knowledge* of the service, merchandise, or profession which you intend to offer in return for Fortune. Perhaps you may need much more specialized knowledge than you have the ability or the inclination to acquire, and if this should be true, you may bridge your weakness through the aid of your "MasterMind" group.

Andrew Carnegie stated that he, personally, knew nothing about the technical end of the steel business; moreover, he did not particularly care to know anything about it. The specialized knowledge he required for the manufacture and marketing of steel, he found available through the individual units of his *MasterMind group.*

The accumulation of great Fortunes calls for *power*, and power is acquired through highly organized and intelligently directed specialized knowledge, but that knowledge does not, necessarily, have to be in the possession of the man who accumulates the Fortune.

Knowledge Is Not The Power

The preceding paragraph should give hope and encouragement to the person with ambition to accumulate a Fortune, who has not possessed themselves of the necessary "education," to supply such specialized knowledge as they may require. People sometimes go through life suffering from "inferiority complexes," because they are not persons of "education." The person who can organize and direct a "MasterMind" group, who possess knowledge useful in the accumulation of money, is just as much a person of education as any person in the group. *Remember this*, if you suffer from a feeling of inferiority, because your schooling has been limited.

Thomas A. Edison had only three months of "schooling" during his entire life. He did not lack education neither did he die poor.

Henry Ford had less than a sixth grade "schooling," but he has managed to do pretty well by himself, financially.

Specialized knowledge is among the most plentiful, and the cheapest forms of service that may be had! If you doubt this, consult the payroll of any university.

What's Really Important Is The *Approach*

Now that we're clear on the *place* of knowledge in your quest for riches – that's it's *not* knowledge that's important, but the organization, use, and *gearing* of knowledge that is… And that knowledge does *not* need to be in the possession of the individual employing it…

BONUS! 3 FREE Wealth-Building Gifts Worth $97 at HoloMagic.com

Knowledge Is Readily Available

Let's recognize that all people, at frequent points, encounter the need to acquire some specialized knowledge, so there's much we need to say on this topic.

First of all, decide the sort of specialized knowledge you require, and the purpose for which it is needed.

To a large extent your major purpose in life, the goal toward which you are working, will help determine what knowledge you need.

With this question settled, your next move requires that you have accurate information concerning dependable sources of knowledge. The more important of these are…

a)　One's own experience and education

b)　Experience and education available through cooperation of others – MasterMind and community with other switched-on persons

c)　The Internet – the greatest, easiest, most powerful, method of all

d)　Colleges and Universities, including distance learning programs

e)　Public Libraries

f)　Special Training through night schools, distance learning, specialized courses, seminars, workshops, and coaching programs

When you need specialized knowledge, in our society today, it's easily available.

The Secret To Gearing Knowledge Into *Power*

Just always remember, to have anything other than darling "life-of-the-party" value, as knowledge is acquired, it must be *organized and put into use* for a definite purpose in practical plans. Most people do not *know* this, and therefore, find it difficult to *actualize* this behavior. You, of course, are different.

Knowledge has no value except that which can be gained from its application toward some worthy end.

As you advance, unless you need the sheepskin as a qualifier to pursue your career, like you would in medicine, you'll find you don't study to get degrees and awards, but you study what you need to get the job done.

This is one reason why college degrees are not valued more highly in the upper echelons of achievement, and why college graduates are not automatically successful. Degrees represent nothing but miscellaneous knowledge.

Those who rely on a certificate, rather than their performance, are treading on thin ice, and, sooner or later, will be found out to the tune of a cold dunking in the frigid wash up pond.

If you contemplate taking additional schooling, first determine the purpose for which you want the knowledge you are seeking, then learn where this particular sort of knowledge can be obtained from reliable sources.

Of course, you may not need any additional "schooling" at all. That's only one hoax the established educational systems bred into you, and it takes a fair bit of independent thinking to break away from that and to think on your own.

What you want is *results* – the knowledge that you *need*. Not the useless trappings… You can find anything you want and need through your wireless connection to the Internet.

Further, through hiring a consultant, outsourcing work, taking on a JV partner, a regular partner, or an employee, you may completely avoid the necessity of acquiring knowledge yourself, engage the skills and knowledge you already possess and excel at, and gear straight into productivity.

While it's true general knowledge *can* improve the quality of your life in certain respects… It's true it's not *knowledge* itself, but what aim you organize the knowledge you acquire toward that which *accomplishes* things.

That is, the unemployed whiz at crossword puzzles is only a legend – in their own mind…

Far better to provide for yourself and your loved ones in such a fashion whereby they can actualize the moments of life they have, and enjoy crossword puzzles as a diversion…

But, for the *learning*…

Successful individuals, in all callings, never stop acquiring specialized knowledge related to their major purpose, business, or profession.

Those who are not successful usually make the mistake of believing that the knowledge acquiring period ends when one finishes school. The truth is that schooling does little more than to put one in the way of learning how to acquire practical knowledge.

Overcome The Adventures, And Get The Training You Need

Most adults truly find it challenging to return to a university or even junior college to get more education, once they decide they need it.

Among the exigencies of a job and kids, maybe some travel on the job or late nights, a social, church, or school event always sprinkled in, a little bit of social time, not a lot of money, a lot of stress, and the simple requirements of human and family life like buying groceries, paying bills, eating, bathing, sleeping, and laundry… there's just not much time left.

However, others *do* make it happen…

And if you're making your start on the road to riches as an employee, you will find also that employers know what it says about the individual who does show the initiative and gets additional schooling.

The Internet and readily available homestudy courses and systems have actually made it unnecessary to actually go out, if you don't want to. Correspondence schools, consultants, Internet merchants, and fully accredited universities are all offering specialized training *anywhere in the world*, on all subjects that can be taught by the distance method – which is vastly greater than once imagined, especially as technology has rocketed forward...

On the other hand, a fixed schedule would be impossible for others. One major advantage of home study training is the flexibility of the program, which permits you to study during your spare time, scheduled to your own convenience.

Another stupendous advantage of home study training (if the school / mentor is carefully chosen) is the fact that most courses offered by home study schools carry with them generous privileges of consultation, which can be of priceless value to those needing specialized knowledge. No matter where you live, you can share the benefits.

However, for several other advantages, including the discipline of a fixed schedule and companionship with others, actual programmed courses of study at educational institutions and businesses in every city are not likely to go out of fashion anytime soon.

Don't Always Think It Must Be "Free" – You Get More From It When You Pay For It

Anything acquired without effort, and without cost is generally unappreciated, and often discredited. Perhaps this is why we get so little from our marvelous opportunity in public schools. As it is, the *self-discipline* one receives from a definite program of specialized study makes up to some extent, for the wasted opportunity when knowledge was available without cost.

BONUS! 3 FREE Wealth-Building Gifts Worth $97 at HoloMagic.com

A Price To Pay Pays Off

Because of the Internet, merchants who hawk with money-back guarantees and no obligation enrollments, and clearly defined refund/no-refund policies in the major institutions, it's not the same today as when I was working in the early years of the twentieth century to make my Fortunes.

Correspondence schools were highly organized business institutions. Their tuition fees were so low they were forced to insist upon prompt payments. (Of course, with my *Ruthless Marketing* mindset Being asked to pay, whether the student made good grades or poor, had the effect of causing one to follow through with the course when they would otherwise have dropped it. In many cases, my own included, their collection departments constituted the very finest sort of training on *decision, promptness, action* and *the habit of finishing that which one begins.*

Years ago, I enrolled for a home study course in Advertising. After completing eight or ten lessons I stopped studying, but the school did not stop sending me bills. Moreover, it insisted upon payment, whether I kept up my studies or not. I decided that if I had to pay for the course (which I had legally obligated myself to do), I should complete the lessons and get my money's worth. I felt, at the time, that the collection system of the school was somewhat too well organized, but I learned later in life that it was a valuable part of my training for which no charge had been made.

Being forced to pay, I went ahead and completed the course. It turned out the efficient collection system of that school had been worth much in the form of money earned, because of the training in advertising I had so reluctantly taken.

"Abracadabra!" The Power Of Words

Over two lifetimes, I became a copywriter able to spin out hundreds of thousands of dollars, sometimes millions, on command, just by writing a single ad, salesletter, or webpage.

Not to mention creating more engaging *content* in my writing and speaking activities, as well.

Copywriting… Which I learned because I "forced" myself to do it… It was possibly the single most momentous decision I ever made in my life, in terms of the impact it had on me, my Fortunes, and all the affairs of all my life.

As soon as I harnessed my fluency with words to a commercial end that had a prospect of paying off during my own lifetime, I became instantly independent.

Strange and imponderable are the ways and coincidences of life in the affairs of a **purpose-driven** individual.

If you'd like to discover the inside secrets to weaving this "magic spell" with words, and lining your pockets with gold, it's one of the leveraged wealth approaches we suggest at **www.HoloMagic.com**

Others' Laziness Gives You Competitive Advantages

There is one weakness in people for which there is no remedy. It is the universal weakness of *lack of ambition!* That weakness gives you, the person with ambition, overwhelming advantages. Just the mere fact that you study and improve yourself, and apply yourself to specific pursuits places you far ahead of others in the race for success.

It's like they prefer to "watch" the sport from the grandstand seats (and complain all the while how "lucky" you are), while you prefer to get in the ring and play. Obviously, you show better than the beer-bellies in the grandstands.

BONUS! 3 FREE Wealth-Building Gifts Worth $97 at HoloMagic.com

Teddy Roosevelt's immortal words in his 1910 Paris address speak to this…

It is not the critic who counts: not the man who points out how the strong man stumbles or where the doer of deeds could have done better.

The credit belongs to the man who is actually in the arena, whose face is marred by dust and sweat and blood, who strives valiantly… Who errs and comes up short again and again…. Because there is no effort without error or shortcoming.

Who knows the great enthusiasms, the great devotions, who spends himself for a worthy cause; who, at the best, knows, in the end, the triumph of high achievement, and who, at the worst, if he fails, at least he fails while daring greatly, so that his place shall never be with those cold and timid souls who knew neither victory nor defeat.

Face it. Everyone *on the field* is leagues ahead of the grandstanders.

Persons, especially salaried people, who schedule their spare time to provide for home study, seldom remain at the bottom very long. Their action opens the way for the upward climb, removes many obstacles from their path, trains them for the climb, and gains the friendly interest of those who have the power to put them in the way of *opportunity*.

BRIEF COMMERCIAL MESSAGE

**H I G H   L E V E R A G E
W E A L T H   S Y S T E M S**

We offer select information on what we have identified as high leverage wealth systems in which the "ordinary person"

BONUS! 3 FREE Wealth-Building Gifts Worth $97 at HoloMagic.com

> can start from scratch and truly grow rich
> quickly and soundly.
>
> Specific training on copywriting, Internet
> Marketing, real estate, information marketing,
> mailorder, and stock, currencies and futures
> trading opportunities, among others...
>
> **www.HoloMagic.com**
>
> Check it out, we may have just what
> you need.

Every employer and entrepreneur appreciates the *doer* because they've *demonstrated* their worth, not "talked" about it. Not to mention the fact that, with increased education you are in a position to *do something more powerful*.

Creative Career Re-Location

There's always something in the economy, the political situation, and life that makes it necessary for waves of people to find additional or new sources of income, or to keep up with new ways of earning their income – such as incorporating a computer into their business. For the majority of these, the solution to their problem may be found only by acquiring specialized knowledge. Many will be forced to change their occupations entirely.

This shouldn't present a big problem... Think about it – when a merchant finds that a certain line of merchandise is not selling, he or she usually supplants it with another that is in demand. The person whose business is that of marketing personal services (i.e. selling themselves in a "job") must also be an efficient merchant. If his or her services do not bring adequate returns in one occupation, they must change to another, where broader opportunities are available.

BONUS! 3 FREE Wealth-Building Gifts Worth $97 at HoloMagic.com

As an example, Stuart Wier prepared himself as a construction engineer and followed this line of work until the down business cycle limited his market to where it did not give him the income he required. At least, as long as he remained in his own country, because for those who are willing to shift their view to the International arena, "The sun is always shining somewhere!" But, whatever a person chooses!...

> He took inventory of himself, decided to change his profession to law, went back to school and took special courses by which he prepared himself as a corporate lawyer. Despite the fact the economic correction had not ended, he completed his training, passed the bar exam, and quickly built a lucrative law practice in Dallas, Texas. In fact, he's turning away clients.

Just to keep the record straight, and to anticipate the alibis of those who will say, "I couldn't go to school because I have a family to support," or "I'm too old," I will add the information that Wier was past forty, and married when he went back to school. Moreover, by carefully selecting highly specialized courses, in colleges best prepared to teach the subjects chosen, Wier completed in two years the work for which the majority of students require four years.

You *can* do the same thing by investigating and enrolling in "distance education" programs over the Internet. You truly don't have any excuses.

It's not opportunity that's lacking, it's the will that's slacking. *Winner* or *wiener* – we each make our choice.

It Pays To Know How To Purchase Knowledge!

The person who stops studying merely because he or she has finished school is forever hopelessly doomed to mediocrity, no matter what may be their calling. Wherever it leads, the way of exceptional success is a way of continuous adventure and learning.

Let us consider an instance you find repeated over and over again in variants, because of the Internet.

An inside buyer in a brisk business California grocery store found himself without a position. A new interstate had come through, diverting traffic that the location had enjoyed for over 180 years – literally from the days of covered wagons!

He was only one of the suddenly unemployed in the store's cascading bad fortunes.

Having previously had some bookkeeping experience, he took a few quick courses in accounting, familiarized himself with the latest laptop computers and accounting software, and went into business for himself.

> It's not opportunity that's lacking, it's the will that's slacking.
>
> *Winner* or *wiener* – we each make our choice.

His idea was so practical that he soon found it necessary to employ other people – all done with outsourcing overseas, at very *little* cost, and no employee headaches or grueling tax reporting. And he does everything from *getting* his clients and workers, to interacting with them via email, the Internet, and an occasional phone call.

He's acquired over 2,200 small business clients, keeping their books at what is, to them, a very nominal monthly fee. Now his future is more secure than it has ever been, with monthly residual income, and new customers coming in regularly.

The Yeast That Makes The Loaf Rise

There are lots of people who know accounting very well, who are also reasonably proficient on the Internet. But *two elements* went into the unemployed salesman's success… Specialized knowledge plus imagination. Yes, this adversity, too, proved to be a blessing in disguise.

But here's the point. The beginning of this successful business was an *idea*!

Nothing more. The ex-salesman put drive and action behind the idea, did what was necessary to organize it into physical expression, and reaped the benefits of his timely idea.

Specialized knowledge, though essential in the process of wealth acquisition is not the magic element − *imagination* is. imagination is the yeast that makes the loaf rise.

Imagination On The Internet − A Lethal Weapon

Stories like these are repeated over and over again in the success annals of Internet Marketing… I'm sure you have a few favorites of your own, too. And when you're getting these news broadcasts from government reports, the evening news, CNN, magazines, newspapers, and webpages, there's got to be something to them.

Of course, there is.

One enthusiastic convert shared confidentially with me in San Francisco, recently, "I made more money last year alone, on the Internet, than I made in the previous 15 years *combined!*"

BONUS! 3 FREE Wealth-Building Gifts Worth $97 at HoloMagic.com

Bill Gates Is Not The Only One Who Can Benefit From Specialized Knowledge About The Internet

If you have imagination and specialized knowledge about how the Internet works you can make a Fortune – radically altering your existence and daily life!

As America's foremost Internet Marketing consultant, I have more than a little to share on this theme. Information Marketing on the Internet is so different from "business as usual!"

You can give great benefit and advantage to others, without depleting your own stocks and resources, so that you have them to sell again! Sound incredible? Well, compare selling an ebook, audio or video download to selling the same thing in a "hard" format (though those are indeed the easiest hard products to sell, too).

With a physical product you have to pay to produce it, ship it to a warehouse, and pay for shipping and storage, then, when you get an order, ship it out to the customer. When your inventory has been sold out you must acquire more inventory. (At more expense.)

However, let's turn that ugly equation around. Once you have your website up and operating with a *digital* product – a product your customer downloads from your website – there is **no cost of producing, storing, or shipping the product.** *Absolutely zero!* An ebook is nothing more than a file download. Brilliant!

And what if you did a "viral" marketing campaign, so your advertising cost on those leads was absolutely *zero!*

You could run your entire business with no costs and *only* profits! You could sell that one ebook, audio, or video hundreds, thousands, or millions of times, and still have it to sell again!

BONUS! 3 FREE Wealth-Building Gifts Worth $97 at HoloMagic.com

You've organized your business to eliminate product and advertising cost, meaning… *You keep* everything *that comes in!*

Of course, it's more complex than that quick stroke of paragraphs portrays, however, this basic plan can make you independently wealthy in short order.

This is an area of specific expertise for me, and I have hundreds of testimonials to this account. Further, I've repeatedly accepted the "Internet Challenge," which goes like this…

> Give me a willing person from the crowd,
>
> Loan me a laptop computer with an Internet connection,
>
> And within 72 hours that person will have a product, a website, and money in the bank!

Time after time as *the World Internet Summit* (**www.TheWorldInternetSummit.com**) visited cities across the globe (the Internet has no boundaries), such as Atlanta, Nashville, Los Angeles, London, Sydney, Gold Coast, Shanghai, and Singapore, I've pulled a person selected by a lottery drawing to the stage, and made money for them right before their astonished eyes! Variously, these people have made, in their first 72 hours online, $11,431, $13,431, $18,090, $28,340, $34,866, $32,346, $24,921, $19,953, and $32,250.

For info on how to get it together on the Internet for yourself visit **www.HoloMagic.com**

Fashions change, and I know this book will outlast the glinting fashions of today… But, as I write, everything that has ever meant El Dorado, California, or Australia is right at home on the Internet.

Don't Linger At The Bottom – It's The Loser's Lounge

It pays to start – or to quickly fulfill your position so you can quickly move up – one or two steps above the bottom. By doing so, one forms the *habit* of looking around, of observing how others get ahead, of seeing *opportunity*, and of embracing it without hesitation.

That's right, those confidently pursuing their vision, *see* abundant opportunity, and recognizing its authenticity, *jump* on it! Within the obvious happy borders of honest, ethical, legal, and moral awareness, those climbing the ladder of industry, commerce, and politics do *whatever it takes* (WEIT) to put themselves there.

Dan Halpin is a splendid example of what I mean. During his college days, he was manager of the famous 1930 National Championship Notre Dame football team, when it was under the direction of the late Knute Rockne.

Perhaps he was inspired by the great football coach to aim high, and *not mistake temporary defeat for failure*, just as Andrew Carnegie, the great industrial leader, inspired his young business lieutenants to set high goals for themselves.

At any rate, young Halpin finished college at a mighty unfavorable time, when the Depression had made jobs scarce, so, after a fling at investment banking and motion pictures, he took the first opening with a potential future he could find selling electrical hearing aids on a commission basis.

It Was Enough

Anyone could start in that sort of job, and Halpin knew it, but it was enough to open the door of opportunity to him.

BONUS! 3 FREE Wealth-Building Gifts Worth $97 at HoloMagic.com

For almost two years, he continued in a job not to his liking, and he would never have risen above that job if he had not done something about his dissatisfaction. He aimed, first, at the job of Assistant Sales Manager of his company, and got the job. **That one step upward placed him high enough above the crowd to enable him to see still greater opportunity; also, it placed him where *opportunity could see him*.**

That's why you *always* want to do something *noteworthy* in your niche – it gets you noticed, it opens doors… It *proves* you're a doer. And all the world is looking for a doer.

Perform, Word Gets Around

Halpin made such a fine record selling hearing aids, that A.M. Andrews, Chairman of the Board of the Dictograph Products Company, a business competitor of the company for which Halpin worked, wanted to know something about that man, Dan Halpin, who was taking big sales away from the long established Dictograph Company. He sent for Halpin.

When the interview was over, Halpin was the new Sales Manager, in charge of the Acousticon Division. Then, to test young Halpin's metal, Mr. Andrews went away to Florida for three months, leaving him to sink or swim in his new job. He did not sink!

Most people like to play it safe –usually through lack of self-confidence. They want guarantees.

The true entrepreneur gets excited about 1% odds, being certain that's plenty to leverage to success.

Knute Rockne's spirit of "All the world loves a winner, and has no time for a loser," inspired him to put so much into his job that he was recently elected Vice-President of the company, and General Manager of the Acousticon and Silent Radio Division, a job which most men would be proud to earn through ten years of loyal effort. Halpin turned the trick in little more than six months.

It is difficult to say whether Mr. Andrews or Mr. Halpin is more deserving of eulogy, for the reason that both showed evidence of having an abundance of that very rare quality known as *imagination*. Mr. Andrews deserves credit for seeing in young Halpin a "go-getter" of the highest order.

Following The Black Girl's Formula

Perhaps you remember the story of the Black girl in the introduction?... See the spirit again in Halpin.

Halpin deserves credit for **refusing to compromise with life by accepting and keeping a job he did not want**, and that is one of the major points I am trying to emphasize through this entire philosophy.

That we rise to high positions or remain at the bottom *because of conditions we can control if we desire to control them.*

Business Associations Are Vital Factors

I am also trying to emphasize another point; namely, that both success and failure are largely the results of *habit!* I have not the slightest doubt that Dan Halpin's close association with the greatest football coach America ever knew, planted in his mind the same brand of *desire* to excel which made the Notre Dame football team world famous.

Truly, there is something to the idea that hero worship is helpful, provided one worships a *winner*. Halpin tells me that Rockne was one of the world's greatest leaders of men in all history.

My belief in the theory that business associations are vital factors, both in failure and in success, was recently demonstrated, when my son Blair was negotiating with Dan Halpin for a position. Mr. Halpin offered him a beginning salary of about one half what he could have gotten from a rival company.

I brought parental pressure to bear, and induced him to accept the place with Halpin, because I *believe that close association with one who refuses to compromise with circumstances he does not like, is an asset that can never be measured in terms of money.*

That is after all, the premise of the MasterMind. Surround yourself with superior beings so that you share in their knowledge, insight, character, influence, and willing assistance to help you rise to the top yourself. (Or stay there – as it's a constant process.)

The bottom is a monotonous, dreary, unprofitable place for any person. That is why you must develop a strong, passionate vision that motivates you – so you *do* the things that are necessary to even get started.

This Is Your Time

Perhaps some will find in the *idea* here briefly described the nucleus of the riches they *desire*!

Specialized Knowledge Works For Wages, Ideas Create Fortunes

Imagination is more important than knowledge. If you have *imagination*, and seek a more profitable outlet for your personal services, any of the ideas mentioned in this very chapter could be the stimulus for which you have been searching.

Many a good idea — I see it daily — is capable of yielding an income far greater than that of the "average" doctor, lawyer, or engineer whose education required several years in college.

Good money can be made in certain positions, especially in sales, but, overall, our research bears out what J. Paul Getty says in his book, *How To Be Rich,* that in order to get really rich, you *must* have your own business.

In short, you must be an employer, not an employee — an originator, not a clerk.

Ideas Don't Tip The Merchant's Scales, But They Make The Cash Register Ring!

Ideas cannot be compared and measured in the commodity market, for the very reason they are worth what the value, timing, vision, drive, and sustained effort of the originator or *marketer* of the idea invests it with!

You will experience this played out in the upcoming story of the Coca-Cola enterprise…

This is good… *Very good.* **There is no fixed price for sound *ideas*!**

To bring all *ideas* to fruit requires specialized knowledge. But specialized knowledge is not the secret. Unfortunate for those who swallow the hoax and specialize in specialized knowledge, fortunate for those with the imagination to gear it toward specific ends, specialized knowledge is more abundant and more easily acquired than IDEAS.

"Rise!"

Because of this very truth, **there is a universal demand and an ever-increasing opportunity for the person who understands and applies these principles**. Capability means you've got *imagination,* the one quality needed to combine specialized knowledge with *ideas* in the form of *organized plans* designed to yield you riches.

If you have *imagination* this chapter may present you with an impulse or idea sufficient to serve as the beginning of the riches you desire. Or quantum you up a few levels if you're already in motion.

The Idea is the main thing

Specialized knowledge may be found just around the corner – any corner! At the local Internet café in any country of the world...

IMAGINATION
THE WORKSHOP OF THE MIND

THE FIFTH STEP TOWARD RICHES

chapter 5 ⌐→ Imagination is literally the workshop wherein are fashioned all plans created by the human thinking animal.

The impulse, the *desire*, in addition to being an imaginative impulse itself, is given shape, form, and *action* through the aid of the imaginative faculty of the mind.

Tune In, Turn On

Of all the ages of civilization, this is the most favorable for the development of the imagination, because it is an age of rapid change. We are in the midst of the exploding Information Age – fueled by the Internet… Barriers of ignorance and misunderstanding bred by isolation are falling, like the Berlin Wall. On every hand, at any URL, one may contact stimuli that develop the imagination.

Through the aid of the imaginative faculty, humanity has discovered and harnessed more of Nature's forces during the past 100 years than during the entire history of the human race. It has conquered the air so completely, that the birds are a joke in comparison. Remember Michel-angelo's first bird-shaped flying contraption?

Humanity has harnessed the Cosmos, and made it serve as a means of instantaneous communication with any part of the world, and even inter-stellar space. It has analyzed and weighed the sun at a distance of millions of miles, and entire galaxies millions of *light years* away, and has determined, guided through *imagination*, the elements of which all the cosmic mass we know of consists.

Humans have discovered that their own brain is both a broadcast-ing and a receiving station for the vibration of thought, and is begin-ning now to learn how to make practical use of this discovery. They have connected humanity into a Global Brain – a massive MasterMind – giving anyone with an Internet connection the means to interact with this massive MasterMind and to publish their work and be heard, to help shape society.

With the increased speed of locomotion, it is now possible to travel at a speed faster than the speed of sound. The time has long since arrived when a person may breakfast in London, lunch in New York, and dine in Panamá. The days are not that far off when humanity will be planet hopping the same way we country hop today. Translation *a la Star Trek* is not too distant.

Humanity's only limitation, within reason, *lies in the development and use of imagination.*

Whatever the human mind can conceive and believe, it can achieve.

The human animal has not yet reached the apex of development in the use of its imaginative faculty. It has merely discovered that it has an imagination, and has commenced to use it in a very elementary way.

Two Forms Of Imagination

The imaginative faculty functions in two forms. One is known as the *synthesizing i*magination, and the other as *creative imagination.*

Synthesizing Imagination – Through this faculty one may arrange old concepts, ideas, or plans into new combinations. This faculty is not a creative faculty. It merely works with the material of experience, education, and observation with which it is fed. It is the faculty used most by the inventor, with the exception of the "genius" who draws upon the creative imagination when he can't solve his problem through synthesizing imagination.

The synthesizing imagination is important, and you'll use it every wealth-building day of your life, but there's another imagination that eclipsed when you learned to color within the lines at school. This is the space where your breakthroughs come from…

Creative Imagination – Through the faculty of creative imagination, the finite mind of man has direct intercommunication with Infinite Intelligence. It is the faculty you use to engage your desires in the HoloCosm, Infinite Intelligence. It is the faculty through which Infinite Intelligence communicates to you in hunches, inspirations, and guidance is received. It is by this faculty that all basic, or new ideas are handed over to humanity.

It is through this faculty that thought vibrations from the minds of others are received. It is through this faculty that one individual may "tune in," or communicate with the subconscious minds of other individuals.

It is the channel of synchronicity and serendipity. It is through this faculty chance meetings, events, circumstances, and opportunities present themselves in your life. It is through this faculty Infinite Intelligence communicates to you through a book, magazine, radio, TV spot, spoken

BONUS! 3 FREE Wealth-Building Gifts Worth $97 at HoloMagic.com

words of another, or a thousand different ways… Those tuned into this faculty love to play on the word *coincidence.*

The creative imagination works automatically, in the manner described in subsequent pages. This faculty functions *only* when the conscious mind is vibrating at an exceedingly rapid rate, as for example, when the conscious mind is stimulated through the emotion of a strong desire – creating passion in your quest for wealth.

The creative faculty becomes more alert, able to send sharper images, more receptive to vibrations from the sources mentioned, in proportion to its development through USE. This statement is significant! Ponder over it before moving on.

Discover Meditation

Learn how to meditate, and practice it daily. It is in the silence you connect the profound strength of Infinite Intelligence in your personal affairs, including, of course, creating wealth. You plug into the power.

Keep in mind, as you follow these principles that the entire story of how one may convert *desire* into money cannot be told in a single statement. The story will be complete only when you have *mastered, assimilated,* and *begun to make use* of all the principles.

Follow the several examples you encounter in this book. When you meditate, meditate in a causative, creative, magnetic fashion. Intend to accomplish your definite chief aim. Have *faith* you will. Intend to encounter the answers you seek in your quest for success, and to attract the personalities, funds, and organization necessary for its eventual completion.

As you enter the alpha state repeat the Formula For Riches and the Self-Confidence Formula, *remolding your character and charging what you are contributing to this world.* Set up vibes that attract the same from all dimensions of the Cosmos.

BONUS! 3 FREE Wealth-Building Gifts Worth $97 at HoloMagic.com

Meditate with an attitude of gratitude, because, truly, all things of life are a gift, loaned to us – we should be grateful... And you really enjoy life more, and contribute at a deeper level coming from that space.

Develop Creative Imagination

The great leaders of business, industry, finance, and the great artists, musicians, poets, and writers became great, because they developed the faculty of **creative imagination**.

Both the synthesizing and creative faculties of imagination become more alert with use, just as any muscle or organ of the body develops through use.

Desire is only a thought, an impulse. It is nebulous and ephemeral. It is abstract, and of no value, until it has been transformed into its physical counterpart. While the synthesizing imagination is the faculty used most frequently in the process of transforming the impulse of *desire* into money, you must keep in mind the fact that you will face circumstances and situations which demand use of the creative imagination as well, especially as it relates to the *idea* that will make you rich.

The synthesizing imagination may be relied upon for working out the details, but the voice of Divinity speaks in the still small voice of Creative Intelligence.

Re-Ignite Your Imagination

Your imaginative faculty may have become weak through inaction. It can be revived and made alert through *use*. This faculty does not die, though it may become quiescent through lack of use.

BONUS! 3 FREE Wealth-Building Gifts Worth $97 at HoloMagic.com

Focus First On Developing Your Synthesizing Imagination

Center your attention, for the time being, on the development of the synthesizing imagination, because this is the faculty that you will use more often in the process of converting desire into money.

Transformation of the intangible impulse, *desire*, into the tangible reality of *money* calls for the use of a plan, or plans. These plans must be formed with the aid of the imagination, and mainly, with the synthesizing faculty.

Start there. Start now.

As you continue reading this book, let the wheels turn… Start making notes… Then, when you've finished, come back to this chapter, and begin at once to put your imagination to work on the building of a plan, or plans, for the transformation of your *desire* into money.

Put Your Plan In Writing

Detailed instructions for the building of plans have been given in almost every chapter. Carry out the instructions best suited to your needs. Reduce your plan to writing, if you have not already done so. Putting it on paper forces you to be more exact – to develop your reach and your reasons. It gives your plans clarity and *force*. It can be referred to and built upon.

The moment you commit your plan to writing, you have *definitely* given concrete form to the intangible *desire*.

Read the preceding sentence once more. Read it aloud, very slowly, and as you do so, remember that the moment you reduce the statement of your desire and a plan for its realization to writing, you have actually *taken the first* of a series of steps that converts the thought into its physical counterpart.

> The moment you **reduce the statement of your desire, and a plan for its realization, to writing**, you have actually *taken the first* of a series of steps that converts the thought into its physical counterpart.

Mind Into Matter

The Earth in which you live, you yourself, and every other material thing, are the result of evolutionary change through which microscopic bits of matter have been organized and arranged in an orderly fashion.

Moreover – and this statement is of stupendous importance – this Earth, every one of the billions of individual cells of your body, and every atom of matter, began as an intangible form of energy.

You are not separate from everything else. You are made from the same Cosmic Soup – made of the same interconnecting relationships as all the substance and organisms of the Universe. "As above, so below." "As within, so without." The Laws of the Universe don't change for you – you are an expression of the same laws that rendered every other thing and process in creation… This is the way the Universe works. This is the way you work it. It starts with…

Desire is thought impulse! Thought impulses are forms of energy. When you begin with the thought impulse, *desire*, to accumulate money, you are drafting into your service the same "stuff" that Nature used in creating this Earth and every material form in the Universe, including the body and brain in which the thought impulses function.

E = mc²

As far as science has been able to determine, the entire Universe consists of two elements – matter and energy. And matter is nothing other than "solidified" energy.

All of creation, everything perceptible to humanity, from the largest star which floats in the heavens down to and including the "aware" human animal is created throughout the shifting combinations of energy and matter.

You are now engaged in the task of trying to profit by Nature's method. You are working to adapt yourself to Nature's Laws. Then you will have the power to convert *desire* into its physical or monetary equivalent.

Then, as simply as getting the words to a magic spell – you will possess the power that converts desire into its physical or monetary equivalent. And while its power sounds like some mythical force, it's really quite ordinary.

Possession of the secret gives you the power to open the locks on the vaults of life and choose what you would have, as easily as possession of the secret – the combination – lets you twist a dial on a door a few times, and swing open the door of the vault at the bank.

It's about *getting in on the secret.* That's what the deal is. It's not about how hard you work… It's *getting the secret. That's* how hard it is, access to riches swings on a hinged door, and requires no more work and effort than that.

You can do it! It has been done before!

You Need To Know How

You can build a Fortune through the aid of laws that are immutable. But, first, you must become familiar with these laws, and learn to *use* them.

The Secret Revealed

Through repetition, and by approaching the description of these principles from every conceivable angle, the authors hope to reveal to you the secret through which every great Fortune has been accumulated. Strange and paradoxical as it may seem, however, the "secret" is *not a secret* at all!

Nature herself broadcasts it in the Earth on which we live, the stars, the planets suspended within our view, in the elements above and around us, in every blade of grass, and every form of life within our vision.

Nature advertises this "secret" in the terms of biology, in the conversion of a tiny cell, so small that it may be lost on the point of a pin, into the *human being* now reading this line. The conversion of desire into its physical equivalent is, certainly, no more miraculous!

Development Comes In Layers

Do not become discouraged if you do not fully comprehend all that has been stated. Unless you have long been a student of the mind, it is not to be expected that you will assimilate all that is in this chapter upon a first reading.

But you will, in time, make good progress.

The principles that follow open the way for understanding of imagination. Assimilate that which you understand, as you read this philosophy. Then, every time you reread and study the book, a chapter, or a passage, marvel as you discover new things, get more clarity, experience a deeper understanding, and develop an unwavering faith and conviction – sure signs of your growth.

Above all, *do not stop* or hesitate in your study of these principles until you have read the book at least *three* times, for then, you will *never* want to stop.

BONUS! 3 FREE Wealth-Building Gifts Worth $97 at HoloMagic.com

Once you read the book seven times you can begin to truly feel like you own it. Your eyes will be opened.

How To Make Practical Use Of Imagination

Ideas are the beginning points of all Fortunes. Ideas are products of the imagination. Let us examine a few well-known ideas that have yielded huge Fortunes, with the hope that these illustrations will convey definite information concerning the method by which imagination may be used in accumulating riches.

The Enchanted Kettle

Well over 100 years ago, an old country doctor drove to town, hitched his horse, quietly slipped into a drug store by the backdoor, and began "dickering" with the young drug clerk.

His mission was destined to yield great wealth to many people. It was destined to bring to the South of the United States the most far-flung benefit that has ever arrived. Even today it employs thousands of people in this city, and in *all countries of the world*, and contributes to the welfare of many, many thousands more.

It all began between two men meeting in a drugstore after hours, and turned into a Fortune that now generates **billions** *of dollars annually!*

Remember this the next time you tend to think small. It is, indeed, true that all things, like the mighty oak, or a mighty enterprise, like Coca-Cola, grow from small and humble seeds or beginnings.

For more than an hour behind the prescription counter, the old doctor and the clerk talked in low tones. Then the doctor left. He went out to the buggy and brought back a large, old-fashioned kettle and a big wooden paddle, used for stirring the contents of the kettle, and deposited them in the back of the store.

The clerk inspected the kettle, reached into his inside pocket, took out a roll of bills, and handed it over to the doctor. The roll contained exactly $500 – the clerk's entire savings!

The doctor then handed over a small slip of paper on which was written a secret formula. The words on that small slip of paper were worth a king's ransom!

But not to the doctor!

This should encourage all who feel they are not "gifted" or "creative"… You don't have to be the inspired inventor, author, programmer, or performer to make a Fortune. You can be the one who organizes it to happen!

Magic Words Written On A Slip Of Paper

Those magic words were needed to start the kettle to boiling, but neither the old doctor or the young clerk knew what fabulous Fortunes were destined to flow from that kettle.

It was a good deal, well in tune with our promise to ourselves to "engage in no transaction that does not benefit all whom it affects."

The old doctor was glad to sell the outfit for $500. The money would pay off his debts, and give him freedom of mind.

The clerk, for his part, was taking a big chance by staking his entire life's savings on a mere scrap of paper and an old kettle! He never dreamed his investment would start a kettle to overflowing with gold that would surpass the miraculous performance of Aladdin's lamp.

"The Fault Is Not In The Stars..."

What the clerk really purchased was an *idea*. The old kettle, the wooden paddle, and the secret message on a slip of paper were incidental. The strange performance of that kettle began to take place after the new owner mixed with the secret instructions, an ingredient of which the doctor knew nothing.

This story bears a resemblance that you should note to the story of Edwin Barnes' great opportunity. **It's *not the opportunity* – but from the *person* wherein springs the magic**. Edwin Barnes was the *last* person, not the first choice, to receive the opportunity that brought him Fortune. Asa Chandler only got the kettle opportunity because another was not sufficiently visionary, skilled, or motivated to act on it.

Read this story carefully and give your imagination a test! See if you can discover what it was that the young man added to the secret message, which caused the kettle to carbonate over with gold. Remember as you read, that this is not a story from *Arabian Nights*. Here you have a story of facts, stranger than fiction; facts which began in the form of an *idea* – a sterling illustration of the "c^2" factor, of Quantum energy in force, the generative power of holomagic.

You need to catch it. A model for you today!

Vast Fortunes From A Secret Formula

Let us take a look at the vast Fortunes of gold this idea has produced. It has paid and still pays huge Fortunes to men and women all over the world, who distribute the contents of the kettle to millions of people.

The Old Kettle is now one of the world's largest consumers of sugar providing jobs of a permanent nature to thousands of men and women engaged in growing sugar cane and in refining and marketing sugar.

The Old Kettle annually consumes millions of glass and plastic bottles and aluminum cans, providing jobs to huge numbers of workers.

The Old Kettle gives employment to an army of clerks, accountants, chemists, lawyers, copywriters, programmers, and advertising experts throughout the world. It has brought fame and Fortune to scores of artists who have created magnificent pictures describing the product, and overflowed to the tune of millions to famous entertainers who have sung, danced, or appeared in its praises.

The Old Kettle has converted a small southern city into the business capital of the South, where it now benefits, directly or indirectly, every business, resident, and visitor to the city.

The influence of this idea now benefits every country in the world, pouring out a continuous stream of gold to all who touch it.

Gold from the kettle built and maintains one of the most prominent colleges of the South, where thousands of young people receive the training essential for success.

The Old Kettle has done other marvelous things. All through the downs of various business cycles, with factories, banks, and businesses folding up and dying by the thousands, laying off thousands of employees per wave, the business of this Enchanted Kettle goes marching on, giving continuous employment to an army of men and women all over the world, *meanwhile,* paying outrageous portions of gold to those who long ago had faith in the idea.

Tales Of Romance

If the product of that old brass kettle could talk, it would tell thrilling tales of romance in every language.

The author is sure of at least one such romance, for he was a part of it, and it all began not far from the very spot on which the drug clerk purchased the old kettle. It was here that the author met his wife, and it was she who first told him of the Enchanted Kettle. It was the product of that Kettle they were drinking when he asked her to accept him "for better or worse."

Otra Tarde Romántica	*Another Romantic Afternoon*
Como escribo estas palabras exactas que ves, estoy sentado con mi hermosa compañera al frente del Mar Caribe en El Malecón en Santo Domingo, la República Dominicana.	As I write these very words, I'm sitting with my beautiful companion on the waterfront of the Caribbean Sea on the Malecón in Santo Domingo, the Dominican Republic.
Al lado de nosotros, un joven agil sube a una palma de coco, derriba uno de ellos, se desliza, y porta su ganancia a mamá.	Beside us a lithe young black boy shimmies up a palm tree, knocks down a coconut, slips down, and carries off his take to mama.

"Disfruta Coca-Cola"

The first year sales of all Coca-Cola products in 1886 totaled $50. (Which, by the way, cost $70 to generate.) All out of a single soda fountain in Atlanta, Georgia USA, run by a sole proprietor.

Worldwide sales of Coca-Cola last year surpassed $21 Billion dollars, and the company directly employs 49,000 people worldwide. (That doesn't count the millions of other merchants, institutions, and governments that also make money on the product.)

Is it coincidence that I'm drinking this same cool beverage that provides stimulation of thought without intoxication – just what an author needs in order to do his or her best work – 118 years later?!

Is it coincidence that the red and white beach umbrella cooling us under the intense Caribbean sun says, "*Disfruta Coca-Cola*"? ("Enjoy Coca-Cola.")

BONUS! 3 FREE Wealth-Building Gifts Worth $97 at HoloMagic.com

Or is it a demonstration of how the principles described in this book play out in this HoloGraphic Universe?

The Secret Ingredient

Whoever you are, wherever you may live, whatever occupation you may be engaged in, just remember in the future, every time you see the words "Coca-Cola," that its vast empire of wealth and influence grew out of a single IDEA, and that the mysterious ingredient the drug clerk, Asa Candler, mixed with the secret formula was… *imagination*!

Stop and think on that for a moment. Remember, the country doctor had the same "goods."

However, the clerk was seeing a radically different vision than the doctor. Something else was flashing the neural circuits of his brain…

That imagination, that idea was that he could *sell* this refreshing beverage to his customers.

Then he set about growing his customer base. He began in his own neighborhood with a single soda fountain…Then elsewhere in the city…Then elsewhere in the state…Then over the southeast region of the country…followed by the entire country…Then international markets opened, and expansion continues to this day. No doubt, when we get to the stage when we're making settlements on other planets, casks of Coca Cola will ride the supply cargo of every passage.

Setback And Indignation Brings Secret Chicken Recipe To Light

One of the most famous secret recipe accounts of recent times involves Harlan Sanders.

BONUS! 3 FREE Wealth-Building Gifts Worth $97 at HoloMagic.com

Setback: A victim of progress in the rural town of Corbin, Kentucky when the new interstate took his business away, at 62 years of age, he decided it was time to retire anyway.

Indignation: When he received his first Social Security check for $105, he thought it was some kind of a joke. Once he realized it was for real, he sat down to take stock of his options.

He'd lost his restaurant in the induced downturn… Had zero funds left… And the only thing he knew how to do that people valued was cook – especially chicken.

Taking the only thing he had he went to work. He valued his *chicken recipe* as an asset that could be sold and hit the road.

It wasn't necessarily easy – in fact, success literature touts him as having received a thousand *no*'s before he got his first *yes*.

But he persisted, and the lovable Colonel Sanders of Kentucky Fried Chicken created a string of 600 franchise locations before being approached eight years later by the big investment boys waving countless millions in his face.

The recipe became famous because the Colonel's chicken was "Finger Licking Good" – just a marketing slogan anyone could have thought of. What genius is there in that?

But mixed with *faith* and *imagination* it became the cornerstone of a dynasty. Today the business generates $10 *Billion* annually.

This adversity, too, brought some unsuspected powers out of the man…

The Best Hamburger In The World

Oh, excuse me! *Nobody* (except a kid) has ever said McDonald's has the best hamburger in the world. So that ain't the secret ingredient.

And he *didn't* invent the concept of the fast-food hamburger, either. Like Bill Gates and Asa Chandler, he *bought* the system that would make him fabulously rich.

BONUS! 3 FREE Wealth-Building Gifts Worth $97 at HoloMagic.com

Imagination, daring, faith, and the drive to forge ahead were the secret ingredients Ray Kroc blended with his hamburger meat. There's something in a *McDonald's* experience that attracts so many people, but it's sure not the best hamburger in the world.

That never made any difference to Kroc, however, because he understood something very clearly. Ray Kroc was *not* in the hamburger business. He was in the *money* business, using the hamburger experience as a vehicle.

Starting from a single clone of the McDonald's Brothers' popular restaurant (they were *already* on to something), he built a restaurant chain that now has over 30,000 locations strong, in 117 countries of the world, serving 47 *million* customers per *day!*

Hi-Tech Chicken And Burgers

Oops, again! Here we're talking about chickens and hamburgers… And both of these have been around a *long* time…There's nothing hi-tech or deeply specialized about chicken and burgers. They would seem to be pretty ordinary, wouldn't they?

This should be heartening to anyone who fears they don't have advanced technical or specialized knowledge in some cutting edge field. It doesn't take it. Fortunes can be made from the simplest of propositions… *If* you mix *imagination* with definite plans to get rich – *that's* where the magic is.

The Fire Of Imagination

Winners have the ability to *see* what others cannot see. It's kind of like where others see a bar of glass, they are seeing *through* it – they see the glorious colors of the spectrum dancing around their passion. They get '*taken*' by their own great vision!

Walt Disney went out to what would be Disney World in a swamp boat. It came to pass.

Marketing circles tell the story of a young Bill Gates, fired with the dream of a computer for every person in the world. In a downtown Albuquerque upstairs alley Bill dared form his simple definite chief aim and marketing plan… "A PC on every desk, Microsoft inside it."

These principles of success always move in orchestrated waves… and *imagination* is the *key* element in your plans for success. The heat of your imagination guides you in choosing your definite chief aim… Believing in your imagination, you go to work in earnest. You use and encourage supercharged emotions in the plans and affirmations you create, driving *power* into the seeds you plant, reaping in like kind.

It is your imagination that gives you the magical quality of persistence, and your imagination that makes you as strong as the small Black child facing off Darby's uncle.

It takes imagination…

- To discern the dream
- To *believe* the dream
- To fashion and form the dream
- To project the dream
- To form the positive affirmations
- To *see* it while it is a dream
- To form the plans
- To go to work on those plans in earnest
- To sustain under all circumstances and events

Just ask Disney, *imagination is magic.*

BONUS! 3 FREE Wealth-Building Gifts Worth $97 at HoloMagic.com

A Magic Took In Asa Chandler

A magic took in Asa Chandler and he saw what was not seeable.

A frater gave me this following anonymous quote, which Asa Chandler, Edwin Barnes, Henry Ford, Bill Gates, and others so clearly illustrate...

> History makers have always had overmastering convictions in regard to their life's work. They have believed in their visions, and in the part they had to play. They believed their vision foreshadowed a prophecy, that it was a substance of things expected, and not a mere figment of the imagination.

With that kind of faith Asa Chandler went to work.

It called for risk, and it was something in which Asa Chandler had no direct experience. Certainly he had no money left to fund his proposed plans... But he had *imagination* and the *Faith* to put his plans into action. That's all it takes. Don't look for material advantage, connections, education, age, race, religion or any of the dozens sundry excuses people use to explain their failures as the secret.

Desire. Imagination. Action.

Think Big, Act On Your Opportunity

Also, recognize that the thirteen steps to riches, described in this book, were the media through which the influence of Coca-Cola has been extended to every city, town, village, and cross-roads of the world, and that *any idea* you may create, as sound and meritorious as Coca-Cola, has the possibility of duplicating the stupendous record of this worldwide thirst killer.

Opportunity can be a trickster, showing in different clothes to different people. Sometimes it presents destiny in the simplest of propositions.

If the country doctor hadn't sold his kettle and formula to Asa Chandler, Coca-Cola probably would have been thrown out as an old man's debris after he died.

Asa Chandler didn't *have* to think big, but he did.

And look at the results he achieved! Take Donald Trump's statement to heart… "Since you have to *think* anyway, you might as well think *big*!"

Truly, thoughts are things, and their scope of operation is the world itself.

When you yourself are fully in alignment with your desire, the Universe brings all necessary players together. See it in action with Asa Chandler and Frank W. Gunsaulus.

How One Man Manifested $1 Million Dollars In 36 Hours

This story proves the truth of that old saying, "Where there's a will, there's a way." It was told to me, by that beloved educator and clergyman, the late Frank W. Gunsaulus, who began his preaching career in the stockyards of South Chicago.

While Dr. Gunsaulus was going through college, he observed many defects in our educational system, defects which he believed he could correct if he were the head of a college. His deepest desire was to become the directing head of an educational institution in which young men and women would be taught to "learn by doing."

He made up his mind to organize a new college in which he could carry out his ideas, without being handicapped by orthodox methods of education.

He needed a million dollars to put the project across. Where was he to lay his hands on so large a sum of money?.. That was the question that absorbed most of this ambitious young preacher's thoughts.

We should point out that $1 Million in 1890, when Gunsaulus preached his famous "Million Dollar Sermon," would be equivalent, conservatively, to $22 Million dollars in New Millennium money. It was a l-a-r-g-e figure.

It's Easier To Quit

He thought about the money, but he couldn't seem to make any progress. Every night he took that thought to bed with him. He got up with it in the morning. He took it with him everywhere he went. He turned it over and over in his mind until it became a consuming obsession with him. A million dollars is a lot of money. He recognized that fact, but he also recognized the truth that *the only limitation is that which one sets up in one's own mind.*

Being a philosopher, as well as a preacher, Dr. Gunsaulus recognized as do all who succeed in life, that *definiteness of purpose* **is the starting point from which one must begin. He recognized, too, that definiteness of purpose takes on animation, life, and power when backed by a** *burning desire* **to translate that purpose into its material equivalent.**

> **Definiteness of purpose takes on animation, life, and power when backed by a** *burning desire* **to translate that purpose into its material equivalent.**

He knew all these great truths, yet he did not know where or how to lay his hands on a million dollars. The natural procedure would have been to give up and quit, saying, "Ah well, my idea is a good one, but I can't do anything with it, because I can never procure the million dollars."

That is exactly what the majority of people would have said, but it is not what Gunsaulus said. He *knew* these truths. What he said, and what he did, are so important that I now introduce him, and let him speak for himself.

Answer In Alpha

"One Saturday afternoon I sat in my room thinking of ways and means of raising the money to carry out my plans. For nearly two years, I had been thinking, but I had done nothing but think!

The time had come for *action*!

A *Decision* Moves All The Universe

"I *made up my mind*, then and there, that I would get the necessary million dollars within a week. How? I was not concerned about that. The main thing of importance was the decision to get the money within a specified time, and I want to tell you that the moment I reached a definite decision to get the money within a specified time, a strange feeling of assurance came over me, such as I had never before experienced.

"Something inside me seemed to say, 'Why didn't you reach that decision a long time ago? The money was waiting for you all the time!' Things began to happen in a hurry. I called the newspapers and announced I would preach a sermon the following morning entitled, 'What I Would Do If I Had A Million Dollars.'

"I went to work on the sermon immediately, but I must tell you, frankly, the task was not difficult, because I had been preparing that sermon for almost two years. The spirit back of it was a part of me!

BONUS! 3 FREE Wealth-Building Gifts Worth $97 at HoloMagic.com

Anticipation

"Long before midnight I had finished writing the sermon. I went to bed and slept with a feeling of confidence, for I could see myself already in possession of the million dollars.

"Next morning I arose early, went into the bathroom, read the sermon, then knelt on my knees and asked that my sermon might come to the attention of someone who would supply the needed money.

"While I was praying I again had that feeling of assurance that the money would be forthcoming. In my excitement, I walked out without my sermon, and didn't discover the oversight until I was in my pulpit and about ready to begin delivering it.

Infinite Intelligence Takes The Wheel

"It was too late to go back for my notes, and what a blessing that I couldn't go back! Instead, my own subconscious mind yielded the material I needed. When I arose to begin my sermon, I closed my eyes, and spoke with all my heart and soul of my dreams. I not only talked to my audience, but I fancy I talked also to God.

"I told what I would do with a million dollars if that amount were placed in my hands. I described the plan I had in mind for organizing a great educational institution, where young people would learn to do practical things, and at the same time develop their minds.

"When I had finished and sat down, a man slowly arose from his seat, about three rows from the rear, and made his way towards the pulpit. I wondered what he was going to do. He came into the pulpit, extended his hand, and said, 'Reverend, I liked your sermon. I believe you can do everything you said you would, if you had a million dollars. To prove that I believe in you and your sermon, if you will come to my office tomorrow morning, I will give you the million dollars. My name is Phillip D. Armour.'"

Young Gunsaulus went to Mr. Armour's office and the million dollars was presented to him. With the money, he founded the Armour Institute of Technology.

Infinite Intelligence did it all – arranged every needful detail and all the players… Gunsaulus forgot his notes – don't guess Infinite Intelligence needed them. Infinite Intelligence delivered an inspiring, persuasive message – using the preacher's own unique vision, oratory effort, and subconscious trained mind.

That school, now merged with Illinois Institute of Technology continues to this day, 112 years later, to benefit bright engineering students. And all indications are it has hundreds more years to run.

All from a single flash of thought – that intangible substance that can be harnessed to very real, positive, and tangible results. Of *huge* proportions!

Remarkable Results From Single Application Of Secret

That is *more money than the majority of preachers ever see in an entire lifetime, yet the* **thought impulse** *back of the money was created in the young preacher's mind in a* **fraction of a second**. The necessary million dollars came as a result of an idea. Back of the idea was a *desire* that young Gunsaulus had been nursing in his mind for almost two years.

Observe this quantum fact –

He got the money within thirty-six hours after he…

1. **Reached** *a definite decision* **in his own mind to get it and…**

2. **Decided upon a definite plan for getting it!**

There was nothing new or unique about young Gunsaulus' vague thinking about a million dollars, and weakly hoping for it. Others before him, and many since his time, have had similar thoughts. But there was something very unique and different about the decision he reached on that memorable Saturday afternoon when he put vagueness into the background, and definitely said, "*I will* get that money within a week!"

The uninitiated imagine the Gods throw themselves on the side of the fortunate few.

Initiates know the Gods favor the person, any person, who knows exactly what he or she wants, provided he or she is determined to get *just that!*

Remember our powerful affirmation:

The HoloCosm works itself through psychokinesis.
The SupraConscious takes form through synchronicity.

Absolutely, the principle through which Dr. Gunsaulus got his million dollars is still alive! It is available to you! This universal law is as workable today as it was when the young preacher made use of it so successfully. This book describes, step by step, the thirteen elements of this great law, and suggests how they may be put to use.

It Does *Not* Take Money To Make Money

Observe that Asa Candler and Dr. Frank Gunsaulus had one characteristic in common. Both knew the astounding truth **that *ideas can be transmuted into cash through the power of definite purpose mated with definite plans geared relentlessly into positive action.***

Hard Work Is Not The Answer, Either

If you are one of those who believe that hard work and honesty, alone, will bring riches, perish the thought! It is not true!

BONUS! 3 FREE Wealth-Building Gifts Worth $97 at HoloMagic.com

Riches, when they come in huge quantities, are *never* the result of *hard* work!

As Price Pritchett says in *You²*...

> "Trying harder" isn't necessarily the solution to achieving more. It may not offer any real promise for giving what you want out of life. Sometimes, in fact, it's a big part of the problem.
>
> If you want to make a quantum leap, quit thinking about trying harder. More effort isn't the answer.

But it is necessary to work *smarter*. Riches come in response to definite demands, based upon the application of definite principles, and not by chance or luck.

A Single Idea

Generally speaking, an idea is an impulse of thought that impels action, by an appeal to the imagination. All master salesmen know that ideas can be sold where merchandise cannot. Ordinary salesmen do not know this – that is why they are "ordinary."

> If you are one of those who believe that hard work and honesty, alone, will bring riches, perish the thought! It is not true! Riches, when they come in huge quantities, are *never* the result of *hard* work!
>
> Riches come in response to definite demands, based upon the application of definite principles, and not by chance or luck.

Some years back a publisher of books made a discovery that has made millions for marketers who learned the value of *testing*. He learned that many people buy titles, and not contents of books. By merely changing the name of one book that was not moving, his sales on that book jumped upward more than a million copies. The inside of the book was not changed in any way. He merely ripped off the cover bearing the title that did not sell, and put on a new cover with a title that had "box-office" value.

That, as simple as it may seem, was an *idea*! A single deployment of *imagination*.

By the way, if you want to get the in-depth story on the publisher's genius written in his own words, check out **www.HoloMagic.com**

You'll find the program called *Copywriting Classics*, which contains the full and valuable text of E. Julius Haldeman's, *The First One Hundred Million*. (That's *dollars* by the way! And it's *still* possible to duplicate his Fortunes in this business!)

Name Your Price

Truly… There is no standard price on ideas. The creator of ideas sets their own price, and, if he or she is smart, gets it.

That's the BIG advantage you have over selling your personal services in a job. In the job market, there's a well-established competitive rate. But the idea market is wide open.

The Opportunity Continues

The moving picture industry has created flocks of millionaires, from creative people, actors, producers, to distributors. However, most of them have been folks who couldn't create ideas – *but* possess the imagination to recognize ideas when they see them. This is a phenomenon continuing to this very day, with all prospects of continuing on into the future.

The next flock of millionaires grew out of the radio business. Then along came television. Then along came the phone and the cell phone. These communications industries have made and will continue to make millionaires.

But today it's computing and the Internet that's making the hottest Fortunes for people. Who doesn't know Bill Gates is the richest business-person in the world? And he did it all with computers – in an industry that didn't exist just a few short years ago!

And Jeff Bezos who fashioned the largest bookstore on Earth, with Amazon.com – in *cyberspace*! And the "billionaire nerd with a conscience," founder of eBay, Pierre Omidyar, founding the business in his living room that today conducts over $24 Billion annually!!

I've seen it said that *Forbes*, never a publication given to exaggeration, gushes…

"If we could be alive at any one time, to get rich, it would be here and now – because of the Internet."

USA Today says that the Internet, in its brief period of existence, has already made more millionaires than any other industry in history.

If the foregoing comments on the opportunities on the Internet haven't cranked your idea factory, you'd best forget it. Your opportunity is in some other field. If the comments intrigue you in the slightest degree, then go further into it, and you may find the one *idea* you need to round out your career.

As a start check out…

www.TheWorldInternetSummit.com
www.AutoPilotRiches.com
www.HoloMagic.com

BONUS! 3 FREE Wealth-Building Gifts Worth $97 at HoloMagic.com

Fortune's Waiting For You At The Crossroads

Never let it discourage you if you have no experience on the Internet. The field is so new, no one does.

Further it's not necessary… Andrew Carnegie knew very little about making steel – I have Carnegie's own word for this – but he made practical use of the principles described in this book, and made the steel business yield him a Fortune.

Bill Gates didn't have any experience. He was still wet behind the ears when he got the IBM contract that launched him – in an emerging industry that even the giant IBM didn't have any experience in. Nobody did.

You Just Have To Play A Part – You Don't Have To Do It All

The story of practically every great Fortune starts with the day when a *creator of ideas* and a *seller of ideas* get together and work in harmony. Carnegie surrounded himself with men who could do all that he could not do – men who created ideas, and men who put ideas into operation, and that made him and the others fabulously rich.

> The story of practically every great Fortune starts with the day when a *creator* of ideas and a *seller* of ideas get together and work in harmony.

The *idea's* the thing – if you have a great idea, you can find all the supporting technical and marketing expertise you need. That's *specialized knowledge.*

BONUS! 3 FREE Wealth-Building Gifts Worth $97 at HoloMagic.com

Mystical literature disappearing into the mists of the beginnings of time, have said, "When the student is ready, the teacher appears."

Ted Ciuba and Napoleon Hill, modern businessman mystics, say… "Put yourself on the curb, the vehicle will appear."

Bill Gates did not invent the computer-operating platform. Like Asa Chandler, who bought the idea of Coca-Cola, Bill Gates bought the imperfect DOS operating system from some other nameless entity for a mere $50,000. Ray Kroc didn't come up with the idea of McDonald's. He bought a license to the idea from the McDonald brothers.

All these enterprises have and *are* generating *Billions*.

Most People Hugely Overestimate The "Lucky Break"

Millions of people go through life hoping for favorable "breaks." Perhaps a favorable break can get one an opportunity, but the safest plan is not to depend upon luck. It was a favorable "break" that gave me the biggest opportunity of my life, but twenty-five years of determined effort had to be devoted to that opportunity before it became an asset.

The "break" consisted of my good fortune in meeting and gaining the cooperation of Andrew Carnegie. On that occasion Carnegie planted in my mind the idea of organizing the principles of achievement into a philosophy of success. Thousands of people have profited by the discoveries made in those first twenty-five years of research, and a million Fortunes have been accumulated through the application of the philosophy.

Then, with another lifetime I continued the quest and the task, and now you see before you *The NEW Think And Grow Rich*.

The beginning was simple – it was an *idea* that anyone might have developed.

BONUS! 3 FREE Wealth-Building Gifts Worth $97 at HoloMagic.com

The favorable break came through Carnegie, but I was not the *first* to whom Carnegie offered this identical opportunity. Others had the chance before me.

Nevertheless, the favorable break did come through Carnegie. But what about the *determination, definiteness of purpose, desire to attain the goal,* and *persistent effort of 100 years?* It was no ordinary *desire* that survived disappointment, discouragement, temporary defeat, criticism, and the constant reminding of "waste of time." Not to mention the changing Fortunes of life that affect us all. It was and still is a *burning desire,* an *obsession!*

Let that same passion be yours, and you can't help but succeed!

Ideas Take On A Life Of Their Own

When the idea was first planted in my mind by Carnegie it was coaxed, nursed, and enticed to remain alive.

Then came the turnabout – gradually, at first, then with a passion – **the idea became a giant under its own power, and it coaxed, nursed, and drove me**.

Ideas are like that. First you give life and action and guidance to ideas; then they take on a power of their own and sweep aside all opposition.

Ideas are *forces.* Don't be fooled by their intangible appearance. Ideas are *intangible* forces, but they have more power than the physical brains that give birth to them. They have the power to live on after the brain that creates them has returned to dust.

For example, take the power of Christianity. Regardless of your particular creed of religious beliefs, this applies. It began with a simple idea, born in the brain of an ordinary wage earner. Fast-forward and you find the entire history of the Western world closely entwined with the figure of the Christ even to this day. And through that influence, of course, you find proponents of the philosophy in nearly every country of this shifting globe. And who knows how many more centuries or millennium this phenomenon may continue?

And, just as this philosophy of the Christ was carried across oceans to settle new lands, the next step may be across the vast of space, carried by believers, to settle new planets, within or beyond the solar system which spawned the original *idea*.

All based on an idea, something spun from the mind of an individual with *imagination* and the willingness to work to promote his ideas.

$UCCE$$

REQUIRES NO EXPLANATIONS

FAILURE
PERMITS
NO ALIBIS

ORGANIZED PLANNING
THE CRYSTALLIZATION OF DESIRE INTO ACTION

THE SIXTH STEP TOWARD RICHES

chapter 6 ⇌ You have learned that everything the human animal creates or acquires begins in the form of *desire*, and that desire is taken on the first lap of its journey, from the abstract to the concrete, in the workshop of the *imagination*, where *plans* for its transition are created and organized.

In chapter one, you were instructed to take six definite, practical steps as your first move in translating the desire for money into its monetary equivalent. One of these steps is the formation of a *definite*, practical plan, or plans, through which this transformation may be made.

The Planning Process

Building plans need not be a difficult, time-consuming project. With your definite chief aim burning in your heart, it's just a matter of following some basic planning procedures *on paper*, and then recursively refining them as you move forward, as further thought, results, or opportunities suggest.

In its simplest essence it's just a matter of starting with a clear description of where you want to end up (your goal or definite chief aim), connecting that with where you are now, and filling in the blanks along a time line of the things you must do / achieve to reach your goal.

Of course, there's more detail than that… And thorough planning includes making an inventory of required knowledge and resources, the criteria you establish, as well as an analysis of alternative options, including potential obstacles and solutions, models who have done something similar, likelihood of success, etc.

Entire books have been written on the technical aspects of goal achievement and problem solving, so I'm not going into it here. More information is available at **www.HoloMagic.com**

How To Build Plans Which Are Practical

Here are the instructions on how to build plans which are practical:

1. Ally yourself with a group of as many people as you may need for the creation, and carrying out of your plan, or plans for the accumulation of money – making use of the "MasterMind" principle described in a later chapter. (Compliance with this instruction is absolutely essential. Do not neglect it.)

2. Before forming your "MasterMind" alliance, decide what advantages and benefits you may offer the individual members of your group in return for their cooperation. No one will work indefinitely without some form of compensation. No intelligent person will either request or expect another to work without adequate compensation, although this may not always be in the form of money.

3. Arrange to meet with the members of your "MasterMind" group at least twice a week, and more often if possible, until

you have jointly perfected the necessary plan, or plans for the accumulation of money.

4. Maintain *perfect harmony* between yourself and every member of your "MasterMind" group. If you fail to carry out this instruction to the letter, you may expect to meet with failure. The "MasterMind" principle cannot succeed where *perfect harmony* does not prevail.

Two Axioms Of Success

Keep in mind these facts…

First. You are engaged in an undertaking of major importance to you. To be sure of success, you must develop plans that work.

Second. You must have the advantage of the experience, education, native ability and imagination of other minds. This is in harmony with the methods followed by every person who has accumulated a great Fortune.

No individual has sufficient experience, education, knowledge, native ability, contacts, and/or resources to insure the accumulation of a great Fortune without the cooperation of other people.

Every plan you adopt, in your endeavor to accumulate wealth, should be the joint creation of yourself and every other member of your "MasterMind" group. You may originate your own plans, either in whole or in part, but see that those plans are checked and approved by the members of your MasterMind alliance.

> ### Why MasterMind?
> No individual has sufficient experience, education, knowledge, native ability, contacts'

> and/or resources to insure the accumulation
> of a great Fortune without the cooperation
> of other people.

If the first plan you adopt does not work successfully, replace it with a new plan, if this new plan fails to work, replace it, in turn with still another, and so on, until you find a plan which *does work*. Right here is the point at which the majority of people meet with failure, because of their lack of *persistence* in creating new plans to take the place of those which fail.

The most intelligent human living cannot succeed in accumulating money – or in any other undertaking without plans that are practical and workable.

Temporary Defeat Is *Not* Failure

Just keep this fact in mind, and **remember when your plans fail, that temporary defeat is not permanent failure. It may only mean that your plans have not been sound. Build other plans. Start all over again.**

Thomas A. Edison "failed" ten thousand times before he perfected the incandescent electric light bulb. That is, he met with temporary defeat ten thousand times, before his efforts were crowned with success.

Reframing "Temporary Defeat" To "Counsel"

Temporary defeat should mean only one thing, the certain knowledge that there is something incomplete with your plan. Millions of people go through life in misery and poverty, because they lack a sound plan through which to accumulate a Fortune.

Henry Ford accumulated a Fortune, not because of his superior mind, but because he adopted and followed a *plan* which proved to be sound. A thousand men could be pointed out, each with a better education than Ford's, yet each of whom lives in poverty, because he does not possess **the right plan for the accumulation of money**.

Henry Ford, as do all who reach great heights of success, met with numerous episodes of temporary defeat...

That's just it... A quitter never wins, a winner never quits.

No person is ever whipped, until they quit in their own mind.

This fact will be repeated many times, because it is so easy to "take the count" at the first sign of defeat.

Success Follows Organized Planning Backed By A Persistence That Does Not Recognize Failure

James J. Hill met with temporary defeat when he first endeavored to raise the necessary capital to build a railroad from the East to the West, but he, too, turned defeat into victory through *new plans*.

Henry Ford met with temporary defeat, not only at the beginning of his automobile career, but after he had gone far toward the top. He created new plans, and went marching on to financial victory.

Harlan Sanders suffered a series of temporary defeats – he lost his business, he ended up broke, on social security, and suffered a thousand rejections before he every got a yes to his "Kentucky Fried Chicken" idea.

We see men and women who have accumulated great Fortunes, but we often recognize only their triumph, overlooking the temporary defeats which they had to surmount before "arriving."

I've been coming in and out of Nashville, Tennessee USA, capital of country music, for decades. I'm not a musician, but it is a source of constant amusement to this musician-oriented town about how the world falls to adulate the latest "instant success"... Repeatedly.

Only thing is, we knew they'd arrived twelve years earlier, slept in their car for six months, shared a trailer with a song-writing buddy four years, and got their chops up playing for tips in dirty blue jeans on Broadway for five years. Throw in six years of touring, three albums that took off like wet firecrackers and…

When public recognition comes they explode on the scene. The media machine touts an "overnight success." The audience eats it up! Music Row pushes that concept because it sells more CD's and downloads. What those long-suffering musicians say, like Willie Nelson, one for instance, however, is more like, "Overnight success, my ash!"

All great success requires organized planning backed by a persistence that does not recognize failure.

No Follower Of This Philosophy Can Reasonably Expect To Accumulate A Fortune Without Experiencing "Temporary Defeat"

When defeat comes, accept it as a signal that your plans are not sound, rebuild those plans, and set sail once more toward your coveted goal. Want another reframe?… Taken from the marketing profession, we call it a *test*. A test advises us something needs to be changed. If you give up before your goal has been reached, you are a "quitter."

A Quitter Never Wins, A Winner Never Quits

Highlight this sentence in the book, type it in your word processor in 96 point font, print it out, and staple it somewhere, or scotch tape a copy on the mirror where you shave or put on your **morning** makeup, another on the wall where you work during the **day**, and a final copy by where you turn off your lamp to go to sleep at **night**.

You can spot a winner a mile off, because this concept pulsates with vitality in their aura. You feel it. You see it. You sense it.

You can develop this same character; first by understanding it's true, second by affirming it incessantly until it "takes."

Where And How One May Find Opportunities To Accumulate Riches

Now that we have analyzed the principles by which riches may be accumulated, we naturally ask, "Where may one find favorable opportunities to apply these principles?" Very well, let us take inventory and see what the person seeking riches, great or small, has at their disposal.

First of all, you'd have to put the Internet at the top of the list.

As I write this very line, Bill Gates is the richest man on Earth. He accomplished it with computers and the Internet.

While he certainly is an atypical case, the fact is that citizens of all countries of the Earth can post a global storefront from the privacy of their own homes. And while, in some of the less developed and more tightly controlled countries, not everyone has the luxury of a computer in their home, yes, anyone *can* get on the Internet somehow, someway, and turn it into profit.

As America's Foremost Internet Marketing Consultant, I have friends, customers, clients, and protégées in 57 different countries of the world doing it, including all the major countries and continents, of course, and every nationality that exists under the sun.

Of course, in my profession, with my position, with my multi-cultural sensitivities, I attract them – but that's not the point… The point is, it's a capitalistic society in cyberspace, and anybody of any age, in any country can make money online.

If you want more info on this, follow any link from **HoloMagic.com**

BONUS! 3 FREE Wealth-Building Gifts Worth $97 at HoloMagic.com

Opportunity Has Never Been Better!

Let us remember, all of us, that we live in a time in which (most) every law-abiding world citizen enjoys freedom of thought and freedom of deed unequaled ever before. Most of us have never taken inventory of the advantages of this freedom. We have never compared our unlimited freedom with the curtailed freedom of earlier epochs.

In this New Millennium we enjoy unparalleled freedom of thought, freedom in the choice and enjoyment of education, freedom in religion, freedom in politics, freedom in the choice of a business, profession, or occupation, freedom to accumulate and own without molestation *all the property we can accumulate*, freedom to choose our place of residence, freedom in marriage, freedom through equal opportunity to all races, freedom of travel from one state, province, or country to another, freedom in our choice of foods, and freedom to *aim for any station in life for which we prepare ourselves.*

We have other forms of freedom, of course, but this list gives a bird's eye view of the most important, which constitutes *opportunity* of the highest order.

The Global Village

And while these freedoms are not absolute, and while every sane adult knows there are all too frequent miscarriages of justice, and while these freedoms are not equally enjoyed in all countries of the world – they are more widespread, better distributed, and more accessible than at any time in history. The Internet has helped speed along the Global Village. Things are definitely evolving at light speed.

It's never been a more multi-cultural world, with more people "voting with their feet" than at any other time in the history of the world. If these freedoms are not available in a person's country of origin, they are so widely available in so many different countries of the world, that they can be won by any adult who is willing to pursue them – the evidence is too visible to argue otherwise.

A Riddle On The Three Basics Of Food, Clothing, And Shelter

Next, let us recount some of the blessings this widespread freedom has placed within our hands. Take an average family, for example (meaning the family of average income, which is sure *not* rich), and sum up the benefits available to every member of the family…

NOTE: In the pages of this "Food, Clothing, and Shelter" example, I have not modernized the prices… With the ever-present inflation fueled by unbacked currencies of the modern political world, any updated figures, too, would soon appear hopelessly out of date. The truths revealed in this book are perennial; let this serve as a working "to scale" model…

Food

Next to freedom of thought and deed comes *food*, *clothing*, and *shelter*, the three basic necessities of life.

Because of the universal freedom we enjoy in this global economy, the average family has available at its very door, an incredible selection of food coming from all parts of the world, at prices within its financial range.

A family of two, living in the heart of Times Square district of New York City, far removed from the source of production of foods; took careful inventory of the cost of a simple breakfast, with this astonishing result:

BONUS! 3 FREE Wealth-Building Gifts Worth $97 at HoloMagic.com

Articles Of Food	Cost
Grape Fruit Juice, (From Florida)	$0.020
Wheat cereal (From Kansas Farm)	.020
Tea (From China)	.020
Bananas (From South America)	.025
Toasted Bread (From Kansas Farm)	.010
Fresh Country Eggs (From Utah)	.070
Sugar (From Cuba, or Utah)	.005
Butter and Cream (From New England)	.030
Grand Total	20¢

It's not very difficult to obtain *food* when two people can have breakfast consisting of all they want or need for a dime apiece! Observe that this simple breakfast was gathered, by some strange form of magic from China, South America, Utah, Kansas and the New England States, and delivered on the breakfast table, ready for consumption, in the very heart of the most crowded city in America, at a cost well within the means of the most humble laborer.

Shelter

This family lives in a comfortable apartment, with electric heat and air, with gas for cooking, all for $65.00 a month. In a smaller city, or a more sparsely settled part of New York City, the same apartment could be had for as low as $20.00 a month.

The toast they had for breakfast in the food estimate was toasted on an electric toaster, which cost a few dollars; the apartment is cleaned with a vacuum sweeper that is run by electricity. Hot and cold water is available at all times in the kitchen and the bathroom. The food is kept cool in a refrigerator run by electricity. The wife curls her hair, washes her clothes and irons them with easily operated electrical equipment, by power obtained by sticking a plug in the wall. The husband shaves with an electric shaver, and they receive entertainment from all over the world, twenty four hours a day, if they want it, with little or no cost, by merely turning the dial of their radio, switching on their cable TV, or playing on the Internet with an international group of gamers.

When they're tired of email and chat rooms, they can pick up their cell phones and dial anywhere in their country or the world at very affordable rates.

There are other conveniences in this apartment, but the foregoing list gives a fair idea of some of the concrete evidences of the freedom of the New Millennium we enjoy.

Clothing

Anywhere in the world, the woman of average clothing requirements can dress very comfortably and neatly for less than $200 a year, and the average man can dress for the same, or less.

Only the three basic necessities of food, clothing, and shelter have been mentioned. The average person has other privileges and advantages available in return for modest effort, not exceeding eight hours per day of labor. Among these is the privilege of automobile transportation, with which one can come and go at will, at very small cost.

The "Miracle" That Has Provided These Blessings

We often hear politicians taking credit and making promises when they solicit votes, but seldom do they take the time or devote sufficient effort to the analysis of the source or nature of the unparalleled privileges we enjoy these days. Having no axe to grind, no grudge to express, no ulterior motives to be carried out, I have the privilege of going into a frank analysis of that mysterious, abstract, greatly misunderstood "*something*" which gives to every world citizen opportunities to accumulate wealth and freedom of every nature.

I have the right to analyze the source and nature of this *unseen power*, because I know, and have known for more than a century, many of the men and women who organize and use that power, and many who are now responsible for its maintenance.

The name of this mysterious benefactor of humankind is *capital!*

Capital consists not alone of money, but more particularly of highly organized, intelligent groups of people who plan ways and means of using money efficiently for the good of the public, and profitably to themselves.

> *Capital* consists not alone of money, but more particularly of highly organized, intelligent groups of people who plan ways and means of using money efficiently for the good of the public, and profitably to themselves.

These groups consist of scientists, educators, chemists, inventors, business analysts, publicists, transportation experts, accountants, lawyers, doctors, and both men and women who have highly specialized knowledge in all fields of industry and business. They pioneer, experiment, and blaze trails in new fields of endeavor. They support colleges, hospitals, public schools, build good roads, publish newspapers, pay most of the cost of government, and take care of the multitudinous details essential to human progress.

Stated briefly, the capitalists and entrepreneurs are the brains and heart of civilization, because they supply the entire fabric of which all education, enlightenment, and human progress consists.

We Take Organized Capital For Granted – But Its Powers Are Miraculous!

Money without brains always is dangerous. Properly used, it is the most important essential of civilization. The simple breakfast here described could not have been delivered to the New York family at a dime each, or at any other price, if organized capital had not provided the machinery, the ships, the railroads, and the huge armies of trained men, women, robots, and computers to operate them.

Some slight idea of the importance of *organized capital* **may be had by trying to imagine yourself, burdened with the responsibility of collecting without the aid of capital, and delivering to the New York City family, the simple breakfast described.**

To supply the tea, you would have to make a trip to China or India, both a very long way from America. Unless you are an excellent swimmer, you would become rather tired before making the round trip. Then, too, another problem would confront you. What would you use for money, even if you had the physical endurance to swim the ocean?

To supply the sugar, you would have to take another long swim to Cuba, or a long walk to the sugar beet section of Utah. But even then, you might come back without the sugar, because organized effort and money are necessary to produce sugar, to say nothing of what is required to refine, transport, and deliver it to the breakfast table anywhere in the United States.

The eggs, you could deliver easily enough from the barnyards near New York City, but you would have a very long walk to Florida and back, before you could serve the two glasses of grapefruit juice.

You would have another long walk to Kansas, or one of the other wheat growing states, when you went after the four slices of wheat bread.

Even if you drove it could take a week, and even if you flew, getting there and back could eat up an entire day.

The Rippled Wheat cereal would have to be omitted from the menu, because they would not be available except through the labor of a trained organization of workers and suitable machinery, *all of which call for capital.*

While resting, you could take off for another little swim down to South America where you would pick up a couple of bananas, and on your return, you could take a short walk to the nearest farm having a dairy and pick up some butter and cream. Then your New York City family would be ready to sit down and enjoy breakfast, and you could collect your two dimes for your labor!

Seems absurd, doesn't it? Well, the procedure described would be the only possible way these simple items of food could be delivered to the heart of New York City if we had no capitalistic system.

Put Yourself In The Way Of Great Riches

The sum of money required for the building and maintenance of the caravans of trucks, railroads, and ships used in the delivery of that simple breakfast is so huge that it staggers one's imagination. It runs into hundreds of millions of dollars, not to mention the armies of trained employees required to operate the trucks and ships and trains.

But, transportation is only a part of the requirements of modern civilization in a capitalistic system. Before there can be anything to haul, something must be grown from the ground, or manufactured and prepared for market. This calls for more millions of dollars for equipment, machinery, boxing, marketing, and for the wages of millions of men and women.

> These individuals are known as capitalists. They are motivated by the desire to build, construct, achieve, render useful service, earn profits and accumulate riches. And, because they *render service without which there would be no civilization*, they put themselves in the way of great riches.

Trucks, great ships and railroads do not spring up from the earth and function automatically. They come in response to the call of civilization, through the labor and ingenuity and *organizing ability* of individuals who have *imagination, faith, enthusiasm, decision*, and *persistence*!

These individuals are known as capitalists. They are motivated by the desire to build, construct, achieve, render useful service, earn profits and accumulate riches. And, because they *render service without which there would be no civilization*, they put themselves in the way of great riches.

Be Careful Where You Get Your Training

Just to keep the record simple and understandable, I will add that these capitalists are the selfsame individuals of whom most of us have heard soapbox orators speak. They are the same men and women to whom radicals, racketeers, dishonest politicians and grafting labor leaders refer as "the predatory interests" or "Wall Street" insiders.

I am not attempting to present a brief for or against any group of people or any system of economics. I am not attempting to condemn collective bargaining when I refer to "grafting labor leaders," nor do I aim to give a clean bill of health to all individuals known as capitalists.

Adapt Yourself To The System That Controls All Approaches To Fortune

The purpose of this book, a purpose to which I have faithfully devoted over a century of development to, is to present to all who want the knowledge, the most dependable philosophy through which individuals may accumulate riches in whatever amounts they desire.

I have here analyzed the economic advantages of the capitalistic system for the twofold purpose of showing:

1. That all who seek riches must recognize and adapt themselves to the system that controls all approaches to Fortunes, large or small, and…

2. To present the side of the picture opposite to that being shown by religious leaders, teachers, politicians and demagogues who deliberately becloud the issues they bring up, by referring to organized capital as if it were something poisonous.

It really doesn't matter what the current political persuasion is in your particular country. Riches come from capitalism, and no other way.

All progress has been developed through the organized planning of capital. And we who claim the right to partake of the blessings of freedom and opportunity, we who seek to accumulate riches, may as well know that neither riches nor opportunity would be available to us if *organized capital* had not provided these benefits.

To Kill The Goose That Lays Golden Eggs

For more than 150 years, it has been a somewhat popular and growing pastime for radicals, self-seeking politicians, racketeers, crooked labor leaders, and on occasion religious leaders, to take potshots at "Wall Street, The Money Changers, and Big Business." Entrepreneurs get thrown in the same pot when it's convenient.

The practice became so general that we witnessed during the Great Business Depression of America, the unbelievable sight of high government officials lining up with the cheap politicians and labor leaders with the openly avowed purpose of throttling the system, which had made industrial America the richest country on Earth at that time.

Their stupidity worked, all right. The line-up was so general and so well organized that it prolonged the worst depression America has ever known. It cost *millions* of people their jobs, because those jobs were inseparably a part of the industrial and capitalistic system which formed the very backbone of the nation.

How could it be otherwise? It's like the bowels of your body revolting against the heart, and impeding, fighting, and blood bathing the heart. Ignorant of the cause or not… The bowels die, too, when the heart is defeated.

During this unholy alliance of government officials and self-seeking individuals who were endeavoring to profit by declaring "open season" on the American system of industry, a certain type of labor leader joined forces with the politicians and offered to deliver voters in return for legislation designed to permit men to take riches away from industry by organized force of numbers.

Seems unconscionable in a democracy, but this malfeasance continues to this day.

You'd think any sane human would understand, if you want to trade your hours for the "security" of a job, which by definition severely limits your chances of getting *rich*, you ethically owe it to your employer to keep him or her healthy for your own job security.

About that goose? Kill it, feast on the entrails for a day... And where do you find yourself tomorrow?

This violates every Law of Nature. This policy will always fail.

Thank the Gods all peoples and nations don't share these values, but, unfortunately, many of the currently more developed Western nations do... Millions of men and women throughout the United States and the other socialized nations of the Earth, particularly the United Kingdom, Sweden, Germany, and other countries of Europe, are still engaged in this popular pastime of trying to *get* without *giving*. Some of them are *still* lined up with labor unions, demanding *shorter hours and more pay*, and socialized medicine to boot.

The reckoning is coming.

Others do not take the trouble to work at all. *They demand government relief and are getting it.*

Their idea of their *rights* of freedom was demonstrated in New York City recently, where violent complaint was registered with the Postmaster by an ungrateful group of welfare beneficiaries because the postal person awakened them at 7:30 delivering their government relief checks. They *demanded* that the time of delivery be set up to ten o'clock, presumably so, even though the deadbeats could sleep in, they'd still have time before the day ended to *cash* them. What a waste.

If you are one of those who believe that riches can be accumulated by the mere act of men who organize themselves into groups and demand *more pay* for *less service*, if you are one of those who *demand* government relief without early morning disturbance when the money is delivered to you, if you are one of those who believe in trading their votes to politicians in return for the passing of laws which permit the raiding of the public treasury, you may rest securely on your belief, with certain knowledge that no one will disturb you, because *you may think as you please.*

You Cannot Get Rich By "Taking" – It Just Doesn't Work That Way

However, you should know the full truth concerning this rape of freedom of which so many poor people boast, and so few understand. *You may escape work, but you'll always be poor.*

You may blame others and luxuriate in the warm feelings you get. Most losers do. If that's the path you take or continue – I hope you enjoy it in those brief warm moments you get at the beginning.... Because, like a vampire, it will drain you of your blood, you'll turn white, and you'll die.

As far as it reaches, as many supposed "privileges and rights" as socialism provides, *it does not, and cannot bring riches without effort.* There's a law operating here, unseen though it may be... But then so is gravity.

People can organize with governments against productive business interests, but they will always remain poor.

This is not a law of humanity, or a pet political theory of Ted Ciuba or Napoleon Hill, but a *Law of Nature.*

> There is one dependable method of accumulating and legally holding riches, and that is by *rendering useful service.*

There is one dependable method of accumulating and legally holding riches, and that is by *rendering useful service.*

Mere force of numbers won't do it. Sure, numbers and the force of political systems can "impose" their view on the populace... But the correction always comes...

BONUS! 3 FREE Wealth-Building Gifts Worth $97 at HoloMagic.com

No system has ever been created by which the human animal can acquire riches without giving in return an equivalent or greater value of one form or another.

Awake! Believe! Integrate!

Leverage The Law Of Economics

This is the principle known as the law of *Economics!* This is more than a theory. It is a law no individual can beat.

Mark well the name of the principle and remember it, because it is far more powerful than all the politicians and their machinations. It is above and beyond the control of all labor unions. It cannot be swayed, nor influenced nor bribed by racketeers, lobbyists, or self-appointed leaders in any calling.

Moreover, *it has an all-seeing eye, and a perfect system of bookkeeping*, in which it keeps an accurate account of the transactions of every human being engaged in the business of trying to get without giving. Sooner or later its auditors come around, look over the records of individuals both great and small, and demand an accounting.

You can depend upon this much – capitalism *insures every person in the world the* opportunity *to render useful service and to collect riches in proportion to the value of the service.*

"Wall Street, Big Business, Capital Predatory Interests," or whatever name you choose to give the system which has given the citizens of the world freedom, represents a group of super productive people who understand, respect, and adapt themselves to this powerful *law of Economics!* Their financial continuation depends upon them respecting the law.

You, as an entrepreneur, salesperson, or wealth seeker are one of those same people. "Oh happy day!"

Rise To Victory

Opportunity spreads its wares before you. Step up to the front, select what you want, create your plan, put the plan into action, and follow through with *persistence*. The divine law of "as you give so shall you receive" or "as you sow, so shall you reap" will do the rest.

If you study the ways of providing a service, and invest the time necessary to make organized plans to acquire the means of marketing and delivery of your goods and services, implement your plans with a MasterMind team with passion and determination, and adjust and adapt your plan as you get feedback from your implementation, you will, riding on the back of the law of Economics, rise to victory in your chosen field.

A QUITTER

NEVER **WINS**

A WINNER

NEVER **QUITS**

DECISION

THE MASTERY OF PROCRASTINATION

THE SEVENTH STEP TOWARD RICHES

"Fortune favors the bold."

— Round Table

chapter 7 ☞ Accurate analysis of over 25,000 men and women who had experienced failure disclosed the fact that **lack of decision was near the head of the list of the 30 major causes of failure.** This is no mere statement of a theory – it is a fact.

Procrastination, the opposite of *decision*, **is a common enemy,** which practically every individual must conquer.

You will have an opportunity to test your capacity to reach quick and definite *decisions* when you finish reading this book, and are ready to begin putting into *action* the principles that it describes.

Millionaires Reach Decisions Promptly

Analysis of various thousands of people who had accumulated Fortunes well beyond the million dollar mark disclosed the fact that every one of them had the habit of *reaching decisions promptly*, and of changing these decisions *slowly*, if, and when they were changed. People who fail to accumulate money, without exception, have the habit of reaching decisions, *if at all*, very slowly, and of changing these decisions quickly and often.

One of Henry Ford's most outstanding qualities was his habit of reaching decisions quickly and definitely, and changing them slowly. This quality was so pronounced in Ford, that it earned him the reputation of being obstinate. It was this quality which prompted him to continue manufacturing his famous Model "T"– "the world's ugliest car," when his advisors, and many of the purchasers of the car, were urging him to change it.

Perhaps, Mr. Ford delayed too long in making the change, but the other side of the story is that Ford's firmness of decision yielded a huge Fortune before the change in model became necessary. There is little doubt that Ford's habit of definiteness of decision assumes the proportion of obstinacy, but this quality is preferable to slowness in reaching decisions and quickness in changing them.

The Weak Are Influenced By Opinions

The majority of people who fail to accumulate money sufficient for their needs are generally easily influenced by the "opinions" of others. They permit the newspapers and the "gossiping" neighbors to do their "thinking" for them. "Opinions" are the cheapest commodities on Earth! Everyone has a flock of opinions ready to be wished upon anyone who will accept them. If you are influenced by "opinions" when you reach decisions, you will not succeed in any undertaking much less in that of transmuting *your own desire* into money.

> If you are influenced by "opinions" when you reach *decisions*, you will not succeed in any undertaking.

If you are influenced by the opinions of others, you will *have* no *desire* of your own.

Keep Your Own Counsel

Keep your own counsel, when you begin to put into practice the principles described here, by reaching your own decisions and following them. Take no one into your confidence, *except* the members of your "MasterMind" group, and be very sure in your selection of this group, that you choose *only* those who will be in *complete sympathy and harmony with your purpose.*

Close friends and relatives, while not meaning to do so, often handicap one through "opinions" and sometimes through ridicule, which is meant to be humorous. Millions of men and women carry inferiority complexes with them all through life, because some well-meaning, but ignorant person destroyed their confidence through "opinions" or ridicule.

Only The Courageous Rise To Positions Of Success

You have a brain and mind of your own. *Use it*, and reach your own decisions. Only the courageous rise to positions of success. *All* people get the free opinions of others, welcome or not.

Exercise your nobility! Ignore the criticism. Bless the fools if you must… Follow your own counsel.

Don't Talk Too Much, Fools Do And Other Wisdom You Can Use

If you need facts or information from other people, to enable you to reach decisions, as you probably will in many instances; acquire these facts or secure the information you need quietly, without disclosing your purpose.

BONUS! 3 FREE Wealth-Building Gifts Worth $97 at HoloMagic.com

It is characteristic of people who have a smattering or a veneer of knowledge to try to give the impression that they have much knowledge. Such people generally do *too much* talking, and *too little* listening.

Keep your eyes and ears wide open – and your mouth *closed*, if you wish to acquire the habit of prompt *decision*. Those who talk too much do little else. If you talk more than you listen, you not only deprive yourself of many opportunities to accumulate useful knowledge, but you also disclose your *plans* and *purposes* to people who will take great delight in defeating you, because they envy you.

Remember, also, that every time you open your mouth in the presence of a person who has an abundance of knowledge, you display to that person, your exact stock of knowledge, *or your lack* of it! Genuine wisdom is usually conspicuous through modesty and silence.

Keep in mind the fact that every person with whom you associate is, like yourself, seeking the opportunity to accumulate money. If you talk about your plans too freely, you may be surprised when you learn that some other person has beaten you to your goal by *putting into action ahead of you*, the plans of which you talked unwisely.

Let one of your first decisions be to *keep a closed mouth and open ears and eyes*.

As a reminder to yourself to follow this advice, it will be helpful if you copy the following epigram in large letters and place it where you will see it daily. Any fool can and *does* talk – it requires nothing…

> *Tell the world what you intend to do –*
> *but let your actions speak for you.*

This is the equivalent of saying that "Deeds, and not words, are what count most."

Freedom Or Death On A Decision

The value of decisions depends upon the courage required to render them. The great decisions, which served as the foundation of civilization, were reached by assuming great risks, which often meant the possibility of death.

Lincoln's decision to issue his famous Proclamation of Emancipation, which gave freedom to the Black people of America, was rendered with full understanding that his act would turn thousands of friends and political supporters against him. He knew, too, that the carrying out of that proclamation would mean death to thousands of men on the battlefield. In the end, it cost Lincoln his own life. You can bet he had that one figured in as a possibility. That decision required courage.

Socrates' decision to drink the cup of poison, rather than compromise in his personal belief was a decision of courage. It turned time ahead a thousand years, and gave to people then unborn, the right to freedom of thought and of speech.

The decision of Gen. Robert E. Lee, when he came to the parting of the way with the Union, and took up the cause of the American South, was a decision of courage, for he well knew that it might cost him his own life, and that it would surely cost the lives of others.

The Driving Power Of History

But, the greatest decision of all time, as far as any American citizen is concerned, was reached in Philadelphia, July 4, 1776, when 56 men signed their names to a document which they well knew would bring freedom to all Americans, or leave every one of the 56 hanging from a gallows!

Now, there have surely been other events in other places and times with the same momentousness, and I'm not trying to force American politics, ideology, or history down the throats of my International audience. …And I know this is a *political*, not a *commercial* story. However…

There are two simple facts that persuade me to tell it…

1)　As an American myself, I *know* it – it requires no weeks of midnight research to find and tailor a suitable story to illustrate the intangible power.

2)　It's a story that's complete in itself – like a movie… That is, even if you don't know anything about the society or times, the story itself reveals all the human drama you need to understand and apply its principles to your own quests to grow rich.

On to our illustrative history lesson – making the past meaningful to *you* today!

56 Men Defy The Gallows

You have heard of this famous document these 56 men signed, but you may not have drawn from it the great lesson in **personal achievement** it so plainly teaches.

All Americans remember the date of this momentous decision. Hey, it's a national holiday, the day of barbecues, lakes, and fireworks. But few realize what courage that decision required. They remember a spot or two of their history, as it was duly instructed. They remember a few dates, and the names of some of the men involved might ring a bell. They remember Valley Forge and George Washington, of course, who's on the face of every dollar bill in the land.

But they haven't even dreamed of **the *real forces* back of these names, dates, and places**. They know less of that intangible *power*, which insured freedom long before Washington's armies reached Yorktown.

They read the history of the Revolution, and falsely imagine George

Washington was the Father of our Country, and that it was he who won the fledgling nation's freedom. While the truth is, Washington was only an accessory after the fact, because victory for his armies had been insured long before Lord Cornwallis surrendered. This is not intended to rob Washington of any of the glory he so richly merited. Its purpose, rather, is to give greater attention to the astounding *power* that was the real cause of his victory.

Appropriate This Same Irresistible *Power*

It is nothing short of a tragedy that the writers of history have missed entirely, or even give the slightest reference **to this irresistible *power***.

It is a tragedy, because **it is the selfsame *power* which must be used by every individual who surmounts the difficulties of life, and forces life to pay the price asked!**

You would *think* this is the kind of training children would get… Training that would make them successful, productive, self-determining individuals. However, you do get it here…

Surely, no one will be so coarse as to ask how this political drama applies in getting wealthy in business. It portrays the irresistible *power* in action! Grasp it, and model it in your in your own pursuits.

Let us briefly review the events that gave birth to this *power*.

An Occupying Army

The story begins with an incident in Boston on 5 March 1770. British soldiers were patrolling the streets, by their presence, openly threatening the citizens. The colonists resented armed men marching in their midst. Who wouldn't resent an occupying army? (That's the way they looked at it.) They began to express their resentment openly, hurling stones as well as epithets at the marching soldiers, until the provoked commanding officer gave orders, "Fix bayonets.... Charge!!"

A Decision Gears Into *Huge* Outcomes

The battle was on. It resulted in the death and injury of many. The incident aroused such resentment the Provincial Assembly (made up of prominent colonists) called a meeting for the purpose of taking definite action. Two of the members of that Assembly, John Hancock and Samuel Adams, spoke up courageously, and declared that a move must be made to eject all British soldiers from Boston.

> **This irresistible** *power* is the selfsame *power,* which *must be used by every individual who surmounts* the difficulties of life, and forces life to pay the price asked.

Remember this – a *decision,* in the minds of two men, might properly be called the beginning of the United States. Remember, too, the *decision* of these two men called for *faith* and *courage,* because it was dangerous.

"Mene Mene Tekel Upharsin"

Before the Assembly adjourned, Samuel Adams was appointed to call on the Governor of the Province, Hutchinson, and demand the withdrawal of the British troops.

The request was granted, the troops were removed from Boston, but the incident was not closed. How do you call a bullet back from a gun? It had already triggered a situation destined to change the entire trend of civilization. *Writing on the wall...*

Beginnings In Circumstances Which Seem Unimportant

Strange, is it not, how the great changes, such as the American Revolution and World Wars, often have their beginnings in circumstances which seem unimportant? It is interesting, also, to observe that these important changes usually begin in the form of a *definite decision* in the minds of a relatively small number of people.

Few know the history of the United States well enough to realize that John Hancock, Samuel Adams, and Richard Henry Lee (of the Province of Virginia) were the real 'Fathers of the Country' destined to become the United States of America.

Richard Henry Lee became an important factor in this story by reason of the fact that he and Samuel Adams communicated frequently (by correspondence), sharing freely their fears and their hopes concerning the welfare of the people of their Provinces.

By any definition of the word, these heroes were terrorists. They were seeking to undermine the established government under which they were supposed to remain peaceable subjects. They were planning the overthrow of their government, planning, and ultimately using, the use of force to accomplish their ends. At any moment they risked rout and arrest in the middle of the night, loss of their property, and execution without a trial.

They were at grave risk.

Two Years' Incubation

From this practice of maintaining interchange through correspondence, Adams conceived the idea that a mutual exchange of letters between the thirteen Colonies might help to bring about the coordination of effort so badly needed in connection with the solution of their problems. Two years after the clash with the soldiers in Boston (March 1772), Adams presented this idea to the Assembly, in the form of a motion that a Correspondence Committee be established among the Colonies, with definitely appointed correspondents in each Colony, "for the purpose of friendly cooperation for the betterment of the Colonies of British America."

The Die Is Cast

Mark well this incident! It was the beginning of the *organization* of the far-flung *power* destined to give freedom to many. (And, of course, enslavement to others, but that's another story.) The MasterMind had already been organized. It consisted of Adams, Lee, and Hancock.

The Committee of Correspondence was organized. Observe that this move provided the way for increasing the power of the MasterMind by adding to it men from all the Colonies. Take notice that this procedure constituted the first *organized planning* of the disgruntled Colonists.

Organization Generates Power

In union there is strength! The citizens of the Colonies had been waging disorganized warfare against the British soldiers, through incidents similar to the Boston riot, but nothing of benefit had been accomplished. Their individual grievances had not been consolidated under one MasterMind. No group of individuals had put their hearts, minds, souls, and bodies together in one definite *decision* to settle their difficulty with the British once and for all, until Adams, Hancock, and Lee got together.

When Man Doesn't Fear The Government

Meanwhile, the British were not idle. They, too, were doing some *planning* and "MasterMinding" on their own account, with the advantage of having back of them money and organized soldiery.

The Crown appointed Gage to supplant Hutchinson as the Governor of Massachusetts. One of the new Governor's first acts was to send a messenger to call on Samuel Adams, for the purpose of endeavoring to stop his opposition – by *fear*.

We can best understand the spirit of what happened by quoting the conversation between Col. Fenton (the messenger sent by Gage) and Adams.

Col. Fenton: "I have been authorized by Governor Gage, to assure you, Mr. Adams, that the Governor has been empowered to confer upon you such benefits as would be satisfactory [an endeavor to win Adams by promise of bribes] upon the condition that you engage to cease in your opposition to the measures of the government. It is the Governor's advice to you, Sir, not to incur the further displeasure of his majesty. Your conduct has been such as makes you liable to penalties of an Act of Henry VIII, by which persons can be sent to England for trial for treason, at the discretion of a governor of a province. But, *by changing your political course,* you will not only receive great personal advantages, you will also make your peace with the King."

Samuel Adams had the choice of two *decisions*. He could cease his opposition, and receive personal bribes, or he could *continue, and run the risk of being hanged!*

Adams encountered his fate that night, when he was forced into a showdown between the easy way out and his own conscience. The majority of men would have found it difficult to reach such a decision. The majority would have sent back an evasive reply, but not Adams! He insisted upon Col. Fenton's word of honor, that the Colonel would deliver to the Governor the answer exactly as Adams would give it to him.

Adams' answer, "Then you may tell Governor Gage that I trust I have long since made my peace with the King of Kings. No personal consideration shall induce me to abandon the righteous cause of my Country. And, *tell Governor Gage it is the advice of Samuel Adams to him*, no longer to insult the feelings of an exasperated people."

Comment as to the character of this man seems unnecessary. It must be obvious to all who read this astounding message that its sender possessed loyalty of the highest order. This is important. (Racketeers, dishonest politicians, and paranoid and warlording presidents have prostituted the honor for which such men as Adams died).

Violent Opposition Besets Your Way

When Governor Gage received Adams' caustic reply, he flew into a rage, and issued a proclamation which read, "I do, hereby, in his majesty's name, offer and promise his most gracious pardon to all persons who shall forthwith lay down their arms, and return to the duties of peaceable subjects, excepting only from the benefit of such pardon, *Samuel Adams* and *John Hancock*, whose offences are of too flagitious a nature to admit of any other consideration but that of condign punishment."

When You Take The Position *"This, And Only This!"*

As one might say, in modern slang, Adams and Hancock were "on the spot!" The threat of the irate Governor forced the two men to reach another *decision*, equally as dangerous. They hurriedly called a secret meeting of their staunchest followers. (Here the MasterMind began to take on momentum.)

After the meeting had been called to order, Adams locked the door, placed the key in his pocket, and informed all present that it was imperative that a Congress of the Colonists be organized, and that *no man should leave the room until the decision for such a congress had been reached.*

Great excitement followed. Some weighed the possible consequences of such radicalism. (Old Man Fear.) Some expressed grave doubt as to the wisdom of so definite a decision in defiance of the Crown. However, also locked in that room were *two* **men immune to Fear, blind to the possibility of Failure**. Hancock and Adams. Through the influence of their minds, the others were induced to agree that, through the Correspondence Committee, arrangements should be made for a meeting of the First Continental Congress, to be held in Philadelphia, 5 September 1774. *Ticky-tock.*

Remember this date. It is more important than 4 July 1776. *Ticky-tock.* If there had been no *decision* to hold a Continental Congress, there could have been no signing of the Declaration of Independence.

You'll Encounter Others With Your Vision

Before the first meeting of the new Congress, another leader, in a different section of the country, was deep in the throes of publishing a "Summary View of the Rights of British America." He was Thomas Jefferson, of the Province of Virginia, whose relationship to Lord Dunmore (representative of the Crown in Virginia) was as strained as that of Hancock and Adams with their Governor.

Shortly after his famous Summary of Rights was published, Jefferson was informed that he was subject to prosecution for high treason against his majesty's government. Inspired by the threat, one of Jefferson's colleagues, Patrick Henry, boldly spoke his mind, concluding his remarks with a sentence, which shall remain forever a classic, "If this be treason, then make the most of it."

The Seeds: Determination

It was such men as these who, without power, without authority, without military strength, without money, sat in solemn consideration of the destiny of the colonies, beginning at the opening of the First Continental Congress, and continuing at intervals for two years – until on 7 June 1776, Richard Henry Lee arose, addressed the Chair, and to the startled Assembly made this motion: "Gentlemen, I make the motion that these United Colonies are, and of right ought to be free and independent states, that they be absolved from all allegiance to the British Crown, and that all political connection between them and the state of Great Britain is, and ought to be totally dissolved."

Lee's astounding motion was discussed fervently, and at such length that he began to lose patience. Finally, after days of argument, he again took the floor, and declared, in a clear, firm voice, "Mr. President, we have discussed this issue for days. It is the only course for us to follow. Why, then Sir, do we longer delay? Why still deliberate? Let this happy clay give birth to an American Republic. Let her arise, not to devastate and to conquer, but to reestablish the reign of peace and of law. The eyes of Europe are fixed upon us. She demands of us a living example of freedom, that may exhibit a contrast, in the felicity of the citizen, to the ever increasing tyranny."

Before his motion was finally voted upon, Lee was called back to Virginia because of serious family illness, but before leaving, he placed his cause in the hands of his friend, Thomas Jefferson, who promised to fight until favorable action was taken. Shortly thereafter, the President of the

Congress (Hancock), appointed Jefferson as Chairman of a Committee to draw up a Declaration of Independence.

Grace Under Pressure

Long and hard the Committee labored, on a document which would mean, when accepted by the Congress, that *every person who signed it would be signing their own death warrant* should the Colonies lose in the fight with Great Britain which was sure to follow.

The document was drawn, and on 28 June the original draft was read before the Congress. For several days it was discussed, altered, and made ready.

To Commit To Dying On The Strength Of Your Signature

On 4 July 1776 Thomas Jefferson stood before the Assembly and fearlessly read one of the most momentous decisions ever placed upon paper.

"When in the course of human events it is necessary for one people to dissolve the political bands which have connected them with another, and to assume, among the powers of the Earth, the separate and equal station to which the Laws of Nature, and of Nature's God entitle them, a decent respect to the opinions of mankind requires that they should declare the causes which impel them to the separation..."

When Jefferson finished, the document was voted upon, accepted, and signed by the 56 men, **every one staking his own life upon his *decision* to write his name**.

By decisions made in a similar spirit of Faith, and only by such decisions, can men solve their personal problems, and win for themselves high estates of material and spiritual wealth.

Let us not forget this!

BONUS! 3 FREE Wealth-Building Gifts Worth $97 at HoloMagic.com

> When Jefferson finished, the document was voted upon, accepted, and signed by the 56 men, **every one staking his own life upon his** *decision* **to write his name.**
>
> **By decisions made in a similar spirit of Faith, and only by such decisions, can men solve their personal problems, and win for themselves high estates of material and spiritual wealth.**

Destiny Flows From Decision

Analyze the events, which led to the Declaration of Independence, and be convinced that this nation, which yet holds a position of commanding respect and power among the nations of the world, was born of a *decision* created by a MasterMind consisting of 56 men.

Note well, the fact that it was their *decision,* which insured the success of Washington's armies, **because the spirit of that decision** was in the heart of every soldier who fought with him, and served as a **spiritual power** which recognized no such thing as *failure.*

Note, also (with great personal benefit), that the *power,* which gave the USA its freedom, is the selfsame power that must be used by every individual who becomes self-determining.

This *power* is made up of the principles described in this book. It will not be difficult to detect, in the story of the Declaration of Independence, every one of the thirteen pillars of the *Think And Grow Rich* philosophy… Desire, Imagination, Passion, Decision, Faith, Auto-Suggestion, The Subconscious, The Mastermind, The Brain, Organized Planning, Persistence, Specialized Knowledge, and The Sixth Sense.

Secrets Of Transforming Thought Into Money

Throughout this philosophy you find the suggestion that thought backed by strong *desire* has a tendency to transmute itself into its physical equivalent. Before passing on, I wish to leave with you the suggestion that one may find in this story, and in the story of the organization of the United States Steel Corporation, a perfect description of the method by which thought makes this astounding transformation.

In your search for the secret of the method, do not look for a miracle, because you will not find it. You will find only the *eternal Laws of Nature*. These Laws are available to every person who has the *faith* and the *courage* to use them. They may be used to bring freedom to a nation, or to accumulate riches by an individual. There is no charge save the time necessary to understand and appropriate them.

> The person who desires riches in the same spirit that Samuel Adams desired freedom for the Colonies is sure to accumulate wealth.

Yes, **making a definite decision** *does* **make you a** *different* **person**. Tony Robbins correctly observes…

> Decide what you want, and believe that no challenge, no problem, no obstacle can keep you from it.
>
> When you decide that your life will ultimately be shaped not by conditions, but by your decisions, then, in that moment, your life will change forever.

Those who reach *decisions* promptly and definitely, know what they want, and generally get it. The leaders in every walk of life *decide* quickly, and firmly. That is the major reason why they are leaders. The world has the habit of making room for the man or woman whose words and actions show they know where they are going.

Bred In The Conventional School System

Indecision is a habit that usually begins in youth. The habit takes on permanency as the youth goes through grade school, high school, and even through college without *definiteness of purpose*. The major weakness of all educational systems is that they neither teach nor encourage the habit of *definite decision*.

The habit of *indecision* acquired because of the deficiencies of our school systems, goes with the student into the occupation he or she chooses…*if*…in fact, he or she *chooses* an occupation. Generally, the youth just out of school seeks any job that can be found. He takes the first place he finds, because he has fallen into the habit of *indecision*. Ninety-eight out of every hundred people working for wages today, are in the positions they hold because they lacked the *definiteness of decision to plan a definite position* and the knowledge of how to choose an employer or create their own business to order.

The Hidden Guide Demands It

Definiteness of decision **always requires courage, sometimes very great courage.** The 56 men who signed the Declaration of Independence staked their lives on the *decision* to affix their signatures to that document.

Decisions of great consequence demand great consequences. If you're going to step apart from the masses and purposefully accumulate wealth, you'll be asked more than once to put everything on the line. There is no other way.

The person who reaches a *definite decision* to procure a particular job or situation and make life pay the price he asks does not stake his life on that decision; but he does stake his *economic freedom.*

The effort can be rigorous, but the rewards are satisfying. John Milton asks it like this...

> *Which do you prefer, bondage with ease,*
> *or strenuous liberty?*

Most, of course, prefer bondage with ease. Financial independence, riches, desirable business and professional positions are not within reach of the person who neglects or refuses to *expect, plan,* and *demand* these things.

Even though you're surely discovering the **genuine elements of success**, no part of this philosophy can serve you, if you never make a *definite decision* to acquire riches.

This is a necessary first step. *Quickly,* breathe deep – muster the courage in this, your moment of truth. *Make that decision* now, that decision with the same spirit that Samuel Adams demonstrates, and you are sure to accumulate wealth.

Decide to acquire riches... How much? How? How will you benefit people? On what time schedule? What age(s) will you be then? What will you be doing?

When Do You Think You Should Start?

If you are serious about accumulating wealth in the reading of this book, then you'll *have* to make decisions and commitments in the same spirit of faith, and with the same willingness to face the hardships you'll encounter, that Hancock, Adams, Lee, and every one of the 56 demonstrated.

If you seek to do something great, there will always be hardships. After all, if anyone could do it, what would be great about it? Most people live lives of permanent "get-by" and worry with mountains of credit card debt. That's not where you proclaim you're going.

But, remember, time waits on no one. I would suggest *now* is the perfect time to begin. Start where you are, with the tools you have at hand, and better tools will be found as you go along.

Now is the *cause* for the consequences you desire. *Now* is the acceptable time.

> *Now* is the *cause* for the consequences you desire.
>   *Now* is the acceptable time.

If you don't start *now* you'll continue to pass through the years of your future journey on Earth in the same approximate condition you're in now.

The time will never be "just right." The right time is right now. Conditions are always imperfect. You must choose, and you must commit. That *decision* will be evident in your actions, as it was for the 56 signers of the American *Declaration of Independence*.

Elsewhere in this book, I refer to life as a checkerboard. It's like a battle, or a promotion, or a campaign. Life is uncertain — if we wish to live a life of contribution and fulfillment, the *time is now.*

Shakespeare says it superbly, in his character, Macbeth…

> There is a tide in the affairs of men
> Which, taken at the flood, leads on to Fortune.
> Omitted, all the voyage of their life
> Is bound in shallows and in miseries.
>
> On such a full sea are we now afloat,
> And we must take the current when it serves,
> Or lose our ventures.

Ready or not, *this* is the time…

Decision Moves The HoloCosm

Truly, there is a *magic power* in a *definite decision* of consequence. It changes all your life. It sets in motion a chain of compounding, directed consequences that ensures you against failure. It opens your spiritual connectivity with the HoloCosm, which then brings benefit back to you.

As the inspiring words of W.H. Murray, the first person known to have climbed to the summit of Mount Everest and returned, indicate everything else falls into place as you proceed:

Until one is committed, there is hesitancy… the chance to draw back, always ineffectiveness.

Concerning all acts of initiative there is one elementary truth, the ignorance of which kills countless ideas and splendid plans:

The moment one definitely commits oneself, then Providence moves, too.

All sorts of things occur to help one that would never otherwise have occurred.

A whole stream of events issues from the decision, raising in one's favor all manner of unforeseen incidents and meetings and material assistance, which no man could have dreamed would have come his way.

I have learned a deep respect for one of Goethe's couplets:

> *Whatever you can do, or dream you can, begin it.*
> *Boldness has genius, power, and magic in it.*

BONUS! 3 FREE Wealth-Building Gifts Worth $97 at HoloMagic.com

Most people will never experience this magic engagement with life, but for the responsible 2% who do – wealth becomes an accepted, expected, and *experienced* aspect of life.

PERSISTENCE
THE SUSTAINED EFFORT TO BUCK ALL ODDS

THE EIGHTH STEP TOWARD RICHES

"There is no effort without error or shortcoming."

– Theodore Roosevelt

chapter 8 ☞ Persistence is an essential factor in the procedure of transmuting *desire* into its monetary equivalent. The basis of persistence is the *power of will*.

Desire and willpower, when properly combined, make an irresistible pair. People who accumulate great Fortunes are generally known as cold-blooded, and sometimes ruthless. Often they are misunderstood. What they have is willpower, which they mix with persistence, and place back of their desires to insure the attainment of their objectives.

Knowing *Exactly* What You Want

Henry Ford has been generally misunderstood to be ruthless and cold-blooded. This misconception grew out of Ford's habit of following through in all of his plans with PERSISTENCE.

The majority of people are ready to throw their aims and purposes overboard, and give up at the first sign of opposition or misfortune. Often that opposition is no more than ridicule or well-meaning advice. Oftentimes, it's not even that – just an interior fear of what others might say.

Do you realize how *empty* the force is behind that?! It has no substance whatsoever, no money's at risk, and no bullets get fired… Rest assured – unless they change their ways – people in this arena will never meet with success. It's impossible!

Yes, most fail, over minors…

A few carry on *despite* all opposition, until they attain their goal. These few are the Fords, Carnegies, Rockefellers, and Edisons, Jobs, Robbins, Bezos, Gates, Waltons, Krocs, and Sanders…

There may be no heroic connotation to the word "persistence," but the quality is to the human character what carbon is to steel.

"Got'cha!"

> **PERSISTENCE**
>
> The building of a Fortune, generally, involves the interdependent, synergistic application of the entire thirteen principles of this philosophy. These principles must be understood, and they must be applied with *persistence* by all who accumulate money.

The building of a Fortune, generally, involves the interdependent, synergistic application of the entire thirteen principles of this philosophy. These principles must be understood, and they must be applied with *persistence* by all who accumulate money.

BONUS! 3 FREE Wealth-Building Gifts Worth $97 at HoloMagic.com

If you are following this book with the intention of applying the knowledge it conveys, your first test as to your *persistence* began, unannounced, when you discovered the six steps described in the first chapter.

Unless you are one of the two out of every 100 who already have a *definite goal* at which you are aiming and a *definite plan* for its attainment, you probably read the instructions, then passed on with your daily routine, never complying with those instructions.

The authors are checking up on you at this point, because lack of persistence is one of the major causes of failure. You said you were sincerely interested in getting rich... Even if you didn't purchase the book, you've at least read it to this point. If you haven't completed those six steps, *no matter how imperfectly you may do it* on your first pass, go back and do it now.

It's for *your* own good, not mine.

Good news! Also, as you work with it – on paper – it takes on a life of its own... It grows, morphs, and takes the substance and study you feed it to become even more than you dare imagine at the outset.

You don't have to get it right, at the start – that's nearly impossible. (And I don't use that world lightly.) The important thing is you *get started now...*

The Fuel That Powers Persistence

Moreover, experience with thousands of people has proven that lack of persistence is a weakness common to the majority of people. It is a weakness that may be overcome by effort. The ease with which lack of persistence may be conquered depends dominantly on two things:

1.   The *intensity of your desire*, which is the prime mover in this philosophy, and...

2.   Your *level of belief* that you'll actually achieve what you seek, which is the *faith* quantum quality.

BONUS! 3 FREE Wealth-Building Gifts Worth $97 at HoloMagic.com

The starting point of all achievement is *desire*. It is the fuel that powers persistence. Strong desire is the constant, expanding, take any setback in stride quantum fire that drives you to running. That's why it's chapter *one*. Keep this constantly in mind. A strong desire makes faith, auto-suggestion, the management of specialized knowledge, and all the other principles, very easy. *Persistence* always will be required, but it's not difficult to be persistent toward and with someone or something you truly love!

Weak desires bring weak results, just as a small amount of fire makes a small amount of heat. If you find yourself lacking in persistence, this weakness may be remedied by building a stronger fire under your desires.

For help building a fire under your desires, review the chapter on Auto-Suggestion, and apply the *Vakogëm* formula with passion to your desires *fulfilled*.

Then continue to read through to the end, then circle back to chapter one, and revise your "Formula For Riches" given in connection with the six steps.

"Mene, Mene, Tekel, Upharsin"

The eagerness with which you follow these instructions reveals clearly how much, or how little you really *desire* to accumulate money. You can be sure – ill or weal – the writing's on the wall.

If you find that you are indifferent, you may be sure that you have not yet acquired the *money consciousness* which you must possess before you can be sure of accumulating a Fortune.

Fortunes gravitate to those whose minds have been prepared to attract them just as surely as water gravitates to the ocean. There's a mutual attraction – a magnetism between riches and the heart of the wealth seeker. Or there isn't. Just like *real* life.

The great, great, great news is you can flip the switch and run *wealth current* through your being and your aura and make yourself a wealth electro-magnetic being.

This is exactly what's happening to you in the reading of this book.

> Fortunes gravitate to those whose minds have been prepared to attract them, just as surely as water gravitates to the ocean. There's a mutual attraction — a magnetism between riches and the heart of the wealth seeker. Or there isn't.

In this book may be found all the stimuli necessary to "attune" any normal being to the vibrations that will attract the object of your desires.

If you find you are weak in *persistence*, center your attention upon the instructions contained in the chapter on Power. Surround yourself with a *MasterMind* group, and through the cooperative efforts of the members of this group, you can develop persistence.

You will find additional instructions for the development of persistence in the chapters on Auto-Suggestion, Passion, and the Subconscious Mind. Follow the instructions outlined in these chapters with positive expectancy until your *habit* nature hands over to your subconscious mind a clear picture of the object of your *desire*. From that point on you will not be handicapped by lack of persistence.

If You Don't *Consciously* Install *Money Consciousness*...

Your subconscious mind works continuously, while you are awake, and while you are asleep.

Spasmodic, or occasional effort to apply the rules will be of no value to you. To get *results*, you must apply all of the rules until their application becomes a fixed *habit* with you. In no other way can you develop the necessary "money consciousness."

Poverty is attracted to one whose mind is favorable to it, as money is attracted to him whose mind has been deliberately prepared to attract it, and through the same laws. This is scary.

Here's the horrible thing, which you must power up against, unless you're willing to accept mediocrity, poverty, and desperation…

Poverty consciousness voluntarily *seizes the mind not occupied with money consciousness.*

A poverty consciousness develops without conscious application of habits favorable to it!

In modern terms, a poverty consciousness is the "default" position of the human consciousness at the present time in the present social order.

Discipline Required

The money consciousness, on the other hand, must be *consciously created* to order.

And that takes *thinking*, it takes work, it takes effort. Although because of the highly leveraged rewards, it's a *very light burden*, indeed!

Catch the full significance of the statements in the preceding paragraphs, and you will understand the importance of *persistence* in the accumulation of a Fortune.

Without *persistence*, you are defeated, even before you start. With intelligent *persistence,* short of an early death, you are destined to win.

Snap Out Of Your Mental Inertia

If you have ever experienced a nightmare, you will realize the value of persistence. You are lying in bed, half awake, with a feeling that you are about to smother. You are unable to turn over, or to move a muscle. You realize that you *must begin* to regain control over your muscles.

Through persistent effort of willpower, you finally manage to move the fingers of one hand. By continuing to move your fingers, you extend your control to the muscles of one arm, until you can lift it. Then you gain control of the other arm in the same manner. You finally gain control over the muscles of one leg, and then extend it to the other leg. *Then – with one supreme effort of will –* you regain complete control over your muscular system, and "snap" out of your nightmare. The trick has been turned step by step.

You may find it necessary to "snap" out of your mental inertia, through a similar procedure, moving slowly at first, then increasing your speed, until you gain complete control over your will. Be *persistent* no matter how slowly you may, at first, have to move. *With persistence will come success.*

If you select your "MasterMind" group with care, you will have in it, at least one person who will aid you in the development of *persistence.*

Some people who have accumulated great Fortunes did so because of *necessity.* They developed the habit of *persistence,* because they were so closely driven by circumstances they *had* to become persistent. Perhaps you may find yourself in that same situation. It's not so bad. If it guides you to do what you ought, it's very good.

There is no substitute for persistence! It cannot be supplanted by any other quality! Remember this, and it will hearten you, in the beginning, when the going may seem difficult and slow.

"Bravo!"

Those who have cultivated the *habit* of persistence seem to enjoy insurance against failure. No matter how many times they are defeated, they finally arrive up toward the top of the ladder.

Sometimes it appears that there is a hidden guide whose duty is to test postulants through all sorts of discouraging experiences. Those who pick themselves up after defeat and keep on trying arrive – and the world cries, "Bravo! I knew you could do it!" The hidden guide lets no one enjoy great achievement without passing the *persistence test*.

Those who can't take it, simply do not make the grade.

The Way The Triumphant Pass

That being the case, you could rightfully determine to steel yourself to it, and endure the slings and arrows of outrageous Fortune, because it's the way the triumphant have to pass.

Threat Into Opportunity

However, the science of NLP (Neuro-Linguistic Programming) has given us the concept of *reframing* – which really means nothing more than *changing the meaning*, usually done by changing internal associations with said event or condition.

So what could be disempowering – setbacks, delays, dishonesties, false affiliates, and adventures you encounter as you climb the ranks (you *will* encounter them, as they're part and parcel of the human nature, visible in all parts and professions) – you *reframe, recontext, reconceptualize* into an *empowering* event, simply by changing the *meaning* of the event.

So often you hear me say this philosophy is not new. You find in my humble opinion, the best, most actionable presentation of the philosophy that's ever been produced… And on this exact point you find Sun Tzu, in the oldest military treatise in the world, *The Art Of War*, talking about turning "misfortune into gain."

Instead of negative setbacks, they become positive steppingstones and *opportunities*. For example, instead of a partner who "ruined you" by embezzling $200,000, you've got a cheap lesson, quick in discerning character, so you can achieve all your goals successfully. Don't you find yourself more jazzed when you're tearing into *opportunities* than when you're beset by problems?!

Events and conditions just *are* – the meanings you *assign* to them are within your complete control. Remember the philosopher poet who says *you are master of your Fate?*... He's talking about this... You are master of your ship, because you can *choose* how to drive your organism. *Same winds, different direction.*

You can take the events that discourage and defeat common people, and engineer and condition them to progress and motivate you.

Isn't this what Edison did? Though *many* unenlightened laughed at his repeated failures and dissed his consuming interest in the light bulb as a folly, Edison saw *nothing of the sort.* What Edison saw with each experiment was progress.

Empowering difference.

The lottery of experiments began to talk... *There's more than one dimension* to any complex problem... Don't forget – Edison was entering entirely *new* ground! The message of the various elements and methods began to sound a message that Edison finally discerned. Without this effort and experimentation he never would have progressed to the breakthrough point.

The light bulb didn't come about with no *thinking.* It took massive thinking. A lot of alpha time.

> *Do you see the absolute and utter difference between Edison's attitude to repeated "defeat" and the ordinary person's?!*

I can't remember, do you?... What did the scoffers contribute to society? We do know that through Edison came a quantum leap.

In Other Words

The leading personal achievement scientists reach the same conclusion…

How do you design an interpretation system that **motivates people**? Answer: help people frame the world as a *series of opportunities* rather than as a series of threats. (Weick & Browning)

Of all the virtues we can learn, no trait is more useful, more essential for survival, and *more likely to improve the quality of life* than the **ability to transform adversity into an enjoyable challenge.** (Csikszentmihalyi)

Embrace Adventure

So if this is the most useful trait, essential to success, why don't you simply *embrace* adventure?

This frame makes the *necessary* quality of persistence *easy*. It's connecting with your goal, quest, and definite chief aim with intensity of purpose. There's no strife – there's *passion*.

There's no *discipline* required, in the conventional sense of the word – you're in *passion*. There are no failures, there's *engagement*, and calls on your prowess.

Problems aren't something to be avoided, but *opportunities* for you to turn to *advantage* and *abundance. Misfortune into gain.*

> Problems aren't something to be avoided, but *opportunities* for you to turn to *advantage* and *abundance.*

It's always been the way of the hero.

Don't expect smooth sailing all the time! It's the Law of Nature – like the Law of the Seas – it'll never happen.

Rather seek to become competent to navigate any sea, any airspace, and any situation you find yourself in with grace and success.

Isn't this the kind of pilot you would prefer to have if you were about to take off in turbulent weather? Or would you prefer a pilot unseasoned by adversity? Or, worse, one who loses it when things get turby?… Hmmm…

It's The Pathway To Success

Enter into the fray with gusto! Resolve to be bigger than every challenge, setback, delay, or disappointment. When those skirmishes, defeats, and dark days come, relish in the punishment, embracing it as a spur to *greater effort*. Don't just attempt a feigned effort at enjoying the adventures – *really enjoy* them!

Want a good reason?… It's the pathway to success.

Those who can "take it" are bountifully rewarded for their *persistence*. They receive, as their compensation, whatever goal they are pursuing. That is not all! They receive something infinitely more important than material compensation – the knowledge that *every failure brings with it the seed of an equivalent advantage.*

Phoenix Rising

Reverses and difficulties come to *everyone* engaged in a big effort. You cannot change the human experience into which you were born. However, if you exercise your consciousness and discipline, you can harness this natural phenomenon to your benefit.

It's the mythical story of the "phoenix" – the glory of triumph rising on wing from the ashes of defeat.

There are no exceptions to this rule, and all people who achieve outstanding success in any dimension, know from experience the soundness of persistence. They are the ones who have not accepted defeat as anything more than temporary. They are the ones whose *desires* are so *persistently applied* that defeat is finally changed into victory.

We, who are observers of life, see the overwhelmingly large number go down in defeat never to rise again. Then we see the few who take the jostles of defeat as an urge to greater effort. These, fortunately, never learn to accept life's reverse gear.

But what few *see*, what most never suspect of existing, is the silent, but irresistible *power,* which comes to the rescue of those who fight on in the face of discouragement. If we speak of this power at all, we call it *persistence*, and let it go at that.

One thing we know: if one does not possess *persistence*, one does not achieve noteworthy success in any calling.

Though It May Seem Like Vegas

As these lines are being written, I look up from my work, and see before me, less than a block away, the great mysterious "Broadway," the "Graveyard of Dead Hopes," and the "Front Porch of Opportunity." Interesting conjunction of opposites – like the Chinese ideogram for *opportunity*, which means *both* "danger" and "opportunity," depending on what you make of it. (P.S. If you would like to see a graphic image of what that Chinese ideogram looks like, visit **www.EastWestSuccess-MasterMind.com**)

From all over the world people come to Broadway, seeking fame, fortune, power, love, or whatever it is that human beings call success. Once in a great while someone steps out from the long procession of seekers, and the world hears that another person has mastered Broadway. But Broadway is not easily nor quickly conquered. She acknowledges talent, recognizes genius, and pays off in money, only after one has refused to *quit*.

Then we know this person has discovered the secret of how to conquer Broadway. The secret is always inseparably attached to one word: *persistence*!

Writing Into Riches

The secret is told in the struggle of Fannie Hurst, whose *persistence* conquered the Great White Way. She came to New York in 1915, to convert *writing into riches*. The conversion did not come quickly, *but it came*. For four years Miss Hurst learned about "The Sidewalks of New York" from first hand experience. She spent her days laboring, and her nights *hoping*. When hope grew dim, she did not say, "All right Broadway, you win!" She said, "Very well, Broadway, you may whip some, but not me. I'm going to force you to give up."

She exhibits a stellar example of the *reframing* technology we're speaking of…

One publisher (The *Saturday Evening Post*) sent her thirty-six rejection slips before she "broke the ice" and got a story across. The average writer, like the "average" in other walks of life, would have given up the job when the first rejection slip came. She pounded the pavements for four years to the tune of the publishers' "NO," because she was determined to win.

Then came the "payoff." The spell had been broken, the unseen guide had tested Fannie Hurst, and she could take it. From that time on publishers beat a path to her door. Money came so fast she hardly had time to count it. Then the moving picture industry discovered her, and money came not in small change, but in floods.

The moving picture rights to her latest novel, *Great Laughter*, brought $100,000.00, said to be *the highest price ever paid for a story before publication up to that time*. Her royalties from the sale of the book ran much more.

Briefly, you have a description of what *persistence* is capable of achieving. Fannie Hurst is no exception. **Wherever men and women accumulate great riches, you may be sure they first acquired** *persistence*. Broadway will give any beggar a cup of coffee and a sandwich, but it demands *persistence* of those who go after the big stakes.

The Singer With Passion

Kate Smith will say "Amen!" when she reads this. For years she sang, without money, and without price, before any microphone she could reach. Broadway said to her, "Come and get it, if you can take it." She did take it until one happy day Broadway got tired and said, "Aw, what's the use? You don't know when you're whipped, so name your price, and go to work in earnest." Miss Smith named her price! It was plenty. Away up in figures so high, that one week's salary is far more than most people make in a whole year.

The Rules Don't Change

Eighty years later, as a different person, with a different name and a different life, I cruise 16th Avenue in Nashville, Tennessee USA – home of country music. In my "Ford" pickup, I might add…

Different "music"… Different epoch… It's identically the same story… I see people driving four maypops without any spare who play so good they whip you to weep and elevate you to ecstasy in the same moments! There surely *is* a way to the top!… Broadway, Nashville, *your own field*…

The only *guaranteed* failure is *quitting!*

Truly, it pays to be *persistent!*

BONUS! 3 FREE Wealth-Building Gifts Worth $97 at HoloMagic.com

Being The *BEST* Not Required

And here is an encouraging statement, which carries with it a suggestion of great significance – thousands of singers who excel Kate Smith are walking up and down Broadway looking for a "break" – without success.

> The only *guaranteed* failure is *quitting!*

Countless others have come and gone, many of them sang well enough, but they failed to make the grade because they lacked the courage to keep on keeping on until Broadway became tired of turning them away.

While Elvis Presley and John Lennon and Paul McCartney made some of the sweetest music that's ever been made, nobody's ever said Bob Dylan and John Cash were "good" singers. Yet *each* of these singers made countless millions entertaining a hungry public.

What Makes The Magic

There's a magic that's more than the talent and training the person has – it's the magic of *desire* and *belief* so deep it drives you to persistent action.

It need not be hard to muster persistence… Like multi-millionaire marketer TJ Rohleder says, "When you are fixed on the goal, you don't even see the obstacles!" I know Rohleder intimately, we've earned multiple millions of dollars in joint projects, and I assure you this philosophy, in great degree, explains his outstanding success.

You discover how to capture and enlist that intensity of concentration in chapter ten on Passion.

To Cultivate Persistence

Persistence is a state of mind, therefore, it can be cultivated. Like all states of mind, persistence is based upon definite causes. Persistence,

BONUS! 3 FREE Wealth-Building Gifts Worth $97 at HoloMagic.com

principle number eight of The *NEW Think And Grow Rich* philosophy, can be massaged into massive proportions by incorporating…

1. *Definiteness of purpose.* Knowing what one wants is the first and, perhaps, the most important step toward the development of persistence. The *why* you want it can be even *more* important than the *what* it is… A strong motive gives one the seeming magic ability to surmount many difficulties.

2. *Desire.* It is comparatively easy to acquire and to maintain persistence in pursuing the object of intense desire. (See chapters one and ten.)

3. *Self-reliance.* Belief in one's ability to carry out a plan encourages one to follow the plan through with persistence. (Self-reliance can be developed through the principle described in the chapter on Auto-Suggestion).

4. *Definiteness of plans.* Organized plans, even though they may be weak and entirely impractical, encourage persistence. Planning is a recursive process, which improves with each experience, evaluation, or pass at your plans… provided you are *conscious*.

5. *Accurate Knowledge.* Knowing that one's plans are sound, based upon experience or observation, encourages persistence. "Guessing" instead of "knowing" destroys persistence.

6. *Co-operation.* Sympathy, understanding, and harmonious cooperation with others tend to develop persistence. Great success is not possible without developing and sharing it with others – without a select number of significant MasterMind groups.

7. *Willpower.* The habit of concentrating one's thoughts upon the building of plans for the attainment of a definite purpose leads to persistence. This "discipline" is made very light by the intensity of one's desire.

8. *Habit.* Persistence is the direct result of habit. The mind absorbs and becomes a part of the daily experiences upon which it feeds.

Fear, the worst of all enemies, can be effectively cured by forced repetition of acts of courage. Everyone who has seen active service in war knows this.

Affirmations can also cure fear − because with affirmations you are *feeding your mind the positive experience / drive you've consciously chosen.* Very powerful, and the reason why *auto-suggestion* is one of the thirteen pillars of this philosophy.

Before leaving the subject of *persistence*, take inventory of yourself, and determine in what particular, if any, you are lacking in this essential quality. Measure yourself courageously, point by point, and see how many of the eight factors of persistence you lack. The analysis may lead to discoveries that will give you a new grip on yourself.

Symptoms Of Lack Of Persistence

Here you will find the real enemies that stand between you and noteworthy achievement. Here you will find not only the "symptoms" indicating weakness of *persistence*, but also the *deeply seated subconscious causes* of this weakness.

Study the list carefully, and face yourself squarely, *if you really wish to know who you are and what you are capable of doing.*

BONUS! 3 FREE Wealth-Building Gifts Worth $97 at HoloMagic.com

These are the weaknesses that must be mastered by all who accumulate riches.

1. *Failure* to *recognize* and to *clearly define* exactly what one wants.

2. *Procrastination*, with or without cause (usually backed up with a formidable array of alibis and excuses).

3. *Lack of interest* in acquiring specialized knowledge.

> *People who are great at making*
> *excuses never get rich.*
> – Terence Storm

4. *Indecision*, the habit of "passing the buck" on all occasions, instead of facing issues squarely (also backed by alibis).

5. The habit of relying upon *alibis* instead of creating definite plans for the solution of problems.

6. *Self-satisfaction.* There is little remedy for this affliction, and no hope for those who suffer from it.

7. *Indifference*, usually reflected in one's readiness to compromise on all occasions, rather than meet opposition and fight it.

8. The habit of *blaming* others for one's mistakes, and accepting unfavorable circumstances as being unavoidable.

9. *Weakness of desire*, due to neglect in the choice of *motives* that impel action.

10. Willingness, even *eagerness to quit,* at the first sign of defeat (based upon one or more of the six basic fears).

11. *Lack of organized plans,* placed in writing where they may be analyzed.

12. The habit of *neglecting to move on ideas or to grasp opportunity* when it presents itself.

13. *Wishing* instead of *willing.*

14. The habit of *compromising with poverty,* instead of aiming at riches. General absence of ambition to be, to do, and to have.

15. *Searching for all the short-cuts to riches,* trying to *get* without *giving* a fair equivalent, usually reflected in the habit of gambling, endeavoring to drive "sharp" bargains.

16. *Fear of criticism,* failure to create plans and to put them into action, because of what other people will think, do, or say.

Thumbnail Of The Fear Of Criticism

Let us examine some of the symptoms of the fear of criticism. This enemy belongs at the head of the list, because it generally exists in one's subconscious mind, where its presence is not recognized.

The majority of people permit relatives, friends, and the public at large to so influence them that they cannot live their own lives, because they fear criticism.

A Bad Marriage

Huge numbers of people make a mistake in marriage, stand by the bargain, and go through life miserable and unhappy, because they fear criticism that may follow if they correct the mistake. (Anyone who has submitted to this form of fear knows the irreparable damage it does, by destroying ambition, self-reliance, and the desire to achieve.)

If you want to read a good — and controversial — essay that addresses the necessity to make a hard decision about your mate when you're determined to have success, read "Message To Friends Who Want To Become Millionaires," a special contribution by Ted Nicholas in Ted Ciuba's blockbuster marketing book, *Mail Order in the Internet Age*. Available at **www.MailOrderInTheInternetAge.com**

In The Name Of Duty

Millions of people neglect to acquire belated educations, after having left school, because they fear criticism. Countless numbers of men and women, both young and old, permit relatives to wreck their lives in the name of *duty*, because they fear criticism. Duty does not require any person to submit to the destruction of their personal ambitions and the right to live life their own way.

People refuse to take chances in business, because they fear the criticism which may follow if they fail. *The fear of criticism, in such cases is stronger than the desire for success.*

Too many people refuse to set high goals for themselves, or even neglect selecting a career, because they fear the criticism of relatives and "friends" who may say "Don't aim so high, people will think you are crazy."

Case Study: An Opportunity That Seeded A Million Millionaires

When Andrew Carnegie suggested I devote twenty years to the organization of a philosophy of individual achievement, my first impulse of thought was fear of what people might say.

The suggestion set out a goal for me, far out of proportion to any I had ever conceived. As quick as the crack of lightning, my mind cascaded alibis and excuses, all of them traceable to the inherent *fear of criticism*.

Something inside of me said,

- "You can't do it. The job is too big, and requires too much time."

- "What will your relatives think of you?"

- "How will you earn a living?"

- "No one has ever organized a philosophy of success, what right have you, who I remind you, are *poor*, to believe you can do it?"

- "Who are you, anyway, to aim so high?"

- "Remember your humble birth – what do you know about *philosophy*?"

- "People will think you are crazy!" (And they did.)

- "Why hasn't some other person done it already?"

These, and many other questions flashed into my mind, and demanded attention. It seemed as if the whole world had suddenly turned its attention to me with the purpose of ridiculing me into giving up all desire to carry out Mr. Carnegie's suggestion.

I had a fine opportunity, then and there, to kill off ambition before it gained control of me.

It happened again, in the dawning of the New Millennium, in another lifetime, another set of humble beginnings… *Another set of excuses!*

Funny thing about excuses – they all *seem* valid. Of course – they're a human defense mechanism. It takes desire and consciousness to root them out.

Ideas Need Immediate Action To Take

Later in life, after having analyzed thousands of people, I discovered that *most ideas are stillborn, and need the breath of life injected into them through definite plans of immediate action.* The time to nurse an idea is at the time of its birth. Every minute it lives gives it a better chance of surviving. The *fear of criticism* is at the bottom of the destruction of most ideas, which never reach the *planning* and *action* stage.

> Most ideas are stillborn, and need the breath of life injected into them through definite plans of immediate action.

You Make Your Own Breaks

Many people believe that material success is the result of favorable "breaks." There is an element of ground for the belief, because people digging into the turf always encounter more opportunities, by the simple fact they're stirring it up!

But those depending entirely upon luck, are nearly always disappointed, because they overlook another important factor, which must be present before one can be sure of success. It is the knowledge with which favorable "breaks" can be made to order.

During the Great American Depression, W. C. Fields, the comedian, lost all his money, and found himself without income, without a job, and his means of earning a living (vaudeville) no longer existing. Moreover, he was past sixty, when many men consider themselves "old." He was so eager to stage a comeback that he offered to work without pay, in a new field (movies). In addition to his other troubles, he fell and injured his neck. To many, that would have been the place to give up and *quit*. But Fields was *persistent*. He knew that if he carried on he would get the "breaks" sooner or later, and he did get them, *but not by chance*.

Marie Dressler found herself down and out, with her money gone, with no job, when she was about sixty. She, too, went after the "breaks," and got them. Her *persistence* brought an astounding triumph late in life, long beyond the age when most men and women are done with ambition to achieve.

Eddie Cantor lost his money in the 1929 stock crash, but he still had his *persistence* and his courage. With these, plus two prominent eyes, he exploited himself back into an income of $10,000 a week!

Persistence And Determination Are Omnipotent

Want some inspiration? Abraham Lincoln's life story reveals one of the greatest stories of persistence. He...

- Failed in business in '31
- Was defeated for the legislature in '32
- Again failed in business in '34
- Lost his sweetheart to death in '35
- Suffered a nervous breakdown in '36
- Was defeated in an election in '38
- Was defeated for Congress in '43
- Was defeated again for Congress in '46
- Was defeated again for Congress in '48
- Was defeated for the Senate in '55
- Was defeated for Vice President in '56
- Was defeated again for the Senate in '58
- Was elected President in '60

BONUS! 3 FREE Wealth-Building Gifts Worth $97 at HoloMagic.com

Truly, if one has *persistence*, one can get along very well without many other qualities.

It might seem that Abraham Lincoln served as the source for the inspired words of Calvin Coolidge…

> Nothing in the world can take the place of persistence. Talent will not; nothing is more common than unsuccessful individuals with talent. Genius will not; unrewarded genius is almost a proverb. Education will not; the world is full of educated derelicts. Persistence and determination are omnipotent.

The only "break" anyone can afford to rely upon is a self-made "break." These come through the application of *persistence*. The starting point is *definiteness of purpose*.

Few Have *Definite* Desires

Examine the first hundred people you meet, ask them what they want most in life, and ninety eight of them will not be able to tell you. If you press them for an answer, some will say *security*, many will say *money*, and a few will say *happiness*. Others will say *fame and power*, and still others will say *social recognition, ease in living, ability to sing, dance, or write*.

But none of them will be able to **define these terms**, or give the slightest indication of **a plan** by which they hope to attain these vaguely expressed wishes.

Riches do not respond to wishes. But they do respond to *definite* plans, fueled by *definite* desires, geared into action with relentless persistence.

How To Develop Persistence

There are four simple steps, which lead to the habit of *persistence*. These qualities make you invincible. They call for no great amount of intelligence, no particular amount of education, and little time or effort. The necessary steps are...

1. *A definite purpose backed by burning desire for its fulfillment,* a genuine determination to perform until you get what you're seeking.

2. *A definite plan, expressed in continuous action, applied with situational awareness.*

3. *A mind closed tightly against all negative and discouraging influences,* including negative suggestions of relatives, friends and acquaintances.

4. *A friendly alliance – a MasterMind – with one or more persons who will encourage you to follow through with both plan and purpose.*

These four steps are essential for success in all walks of life. The entire purpose of the thirteen principles of this philosophy is to enable one to take these four steps as a matter of *habit*.

- These are the steps by which one may control one's economic destiny
- They are the steps that lead to freedom and independence of thought
- They are the steps that lead to riches, in small or great quantities
- They lead the way to power, fame, and worldly recognition
- They are the steps which guarantee favorable "breaks"
- They are the steps that convert dreams into physical realities
- They lead, also, to the mastery of *fear, discouragement,* and *indifference*

There is a magnificent reward for all who learn to take these four steps. It is the privilege of writing one's own ticket, and of making life yield whatever price is asked.

International Romance Reveals Persistent Heart

I have no way of knowing the facts, but I venture to conjecture that Mrs. Wallis Simpson's great love for a man was not accidental, nor the result of favorable "breaks" alone. There was a burning desire, and careful searching at every step of the way. Her first duty was to love. What is the greatest thing on Earth? The Master called it *love* – not man-made rules, criticism, bitterness, slander, or political "marriages," but *love*.

She knew what she wanted, not *after* she met the Prince of Wales, but long *before* that. Twice when she had failed to find it, she had the courage to continue her search...

> To thine own self be true, and it must follow, as the night the
> day, thou canst not then be false to any man. (Shakespeare)

Her rise from obscurity was of the slow, progressive, *persistent* order, but it was *sure*! She triumphed over unbelievably long odds, and, no matter who you are, or what you may think of Wallis Simpson, or the king who gave up his crown for her love, she is an astounding example of applied *persistence*, an instructor on the rules of **self determination**, from whom the entire world might profitably take lessons.

When you think of Wallis Simpson, think of one who knew what she wanted, and shook the greatest empire on Earth to get it.

Follow Your Heart

And what of King Edward? What lesson may we learn from his part in one of the world's greatest dramas? Did he pay too high a price for the affections of the woman of his choice?

Surely, no one but he can give the correct answer. The rest of us can only conjecture. This much we know, the king came into the world without his own consent. He was born to great riches, without requesting them. He was persistently sought in marriage; politicians and statesmen throughout Europe tossed dowagers and princesses at his feet. Because he was the first born of his parents, he inherited a crown, which he did not seek, and perhaps did not desire. For more than forty years he was not a free agent, could not live his life in his own way, had little privacy, and finally assumed duties inflicted upon him when he ascended the throne.

Some will say, "With all these blessings, King Edward should have found peace of mind, contentment, and joy of living."

The truth is that back of all the privileges of a crown, the money, the fame, and the power inherited by King Edward, there was an emptiness that could be filled only by love.

His greatest *desire* was for love. Long before he met Wallis Simpson, he doubtless felt this great universal emotion tugging at the strings of his heart, beating upon the door of his soul, and crying out for expression.

And when he met a kindred spirit, crying out for this same holy privilege of expression, he recognized it, and without fear or apology, opened his heart and bade it enter. All the *National Enquirer* front pages in the world cannot destroy the beauty of this international drama, through which two people found love, and had the courage to face open criticism, renouncing *all else* to give it holy expression.

King Edward's *decision* to give up the crown of the world's most powerful empire for the privilege of going the remainder of the way through life with the woman of his choice was a decision that required courage. The decision also had a price, but who has the right to say the price was too great?

As a suggestion to any evil-minded person who chooses to find fault with the Duke of Windsor because his *desire* was for *love,* and for openly declaring his love for Wallis Simpson, and giving up his throne for her, let it be remembered that the *open declaration* was not essential. He could have followed the custom of clandestine liaison, which has prevailed in Europe for centuries, without giving up either his throne, or the woman of his choice, and there would have been *no complaint from either church or laity.* But this unusual man was built of sterner stuff. His love was clean. It was deep and sincere. It represented the one thing above *all else* he truly *desired,* therefore, he took what he wanted, and paid the price demanded.

Most of the world applauds the Duke of Windsor and Wallis Simpson, because of their *persistence* in searching until they found life's greatest reward. *All of us can profit* by following their example in our own search for that which we demand of life.

The Mystical Power Of Persistence

What mystical power gives to individuals of *persistence* the capacity to master difficulties? Does the quality of *persistence* set up in one's mind some form of spiritual, mental, chemical, or alchemical activity which gives one access to supernatural forces? Does Infinite Intelligence throw itself on the side of the person who still fights on, after the battle has been lost, with the whole world on the opposing side?

These and many other similar questions have arisen in my mind as I have observed men like Henry Ford, who started at scratch, and built an Industrial Empire of huge proportions, with little else in the way of a beginning, but *persistence.*

Or, Thomas Edison, who, with less than three months of schooling, became the world's leading inventor and converted *persistence* into the talking machine, the moving picture machine, and the incandescent light, to say nothing of half a hundred other useful inventions.

I had the happy privilege of analyzing both Edison and Ford, year by year, over a long period of years, and, therefore, the opportunity to study them at close range, so I speak from actual knowledge when I say that I found no quality save PERSISTENCE, in either of them, that even remotely suggested the major source of their stupendous achievements.

The Potency Of Persistence

As one makes an impartial study of the prophets, philosophers, "miracle" men, and religious leaders of the past, one is drawn to the inevitable conclusion that *definiteness of purpose,* faith, concentration of effort, and *persistence* were the major sources of their achievements.

Consider, for example, the strange and fascinating story of Mohammed; analyze his life, compare him with men of achievement in this modern age of industry and finance, and observe how they have one outstanding trait in common: *persistence!*

If you are keenly interested in studying the strange power, which gives potency to *persistence,* read a biography of Mohammed, especially the one by Essad Bey. This brief review of that book, by Thomas Sugrue, in the *Herald Tribune,* will provide a preview of the rare treat in store for those who take the time to read the entire story of one of the most astounding examples of the power of PERSISTENCE known to civilization.

The Last Great Prophet

Mohammed was a prophet, but he never performed a miracle. He was not a mystic; he had no formal schooling; he did not begin his mission until he was forty. When he announced that he was the Messenger of God, bringing word of the true religion, as you might expect, he was ridiculed and labeled a lunatic. Children tripped him and women threw filth upon him. He was banished from his native city, Mecca, and his followers were stripped of their worldly goods and sent into the desert after him.

When he had been preaching ten years he had nothing to show for it but banishment, poverty and ridicule. Yet before another ten years had passed, he was dictator of all Arabia, ruler of Mecca, and the head of a New World religion, which was to sweep to the Danube and the Pyrenees before exhausting the impetus he gave it. That impetus was three-fold: the power of words, the efficacy of prayer and man's kinship with God.

His career never made sense. Mohammed was born to impoverished members of a leading family of Mecca. Because Mecca, the crossroads of the world, home of the magic stone called the Caaba, great city of trade and the center of trade routes, was unsanitary its children were sent to be raised in the desert by Bedouins. Mohammed was thus nurtured, drawing strength and health from the milk of nomad, vicarious mothers. He tended sheep and soon hired out to a rich widow as leader of her caravans. He traveled to all parts of the Eastern World, talked with many men of diverse beliefs and observed the decline of Christianity into warring sects. When he was twenty-eight, Khadija, the widow, looked upon him with favor, and married him. Her father would have objected to such a marriage, so she got him drunk and held him up while he gave the paternal blessing. For the next twelve years Mohammed lived as a rich and respected and very shrewd trader.

Then he took to wandering in the desert, and one day he returned with the first verse of the Koran and told Khadija that the archangel Gabriel had appeared to him and said that he was to be the Messenger of God.

The Koran, the revealed word of God, was the closest thing to a miracle in Mohammed's life. He had not been a poet; he had no gift of words. Yet the verses of the Koran, as he received them and recited them to the faithful, were better than any verses, which the professional poets of the tribes could produce. This, to the Arabs, was a miracle. To them the gift of words was the greatest gift; the poet was all-powerful. In addition the Koran said that all men were equal before God, that the world should be a democratic state – Islam. It was this political heresy, plus Mohammed's desire to destroy all the 360 idols in the courtyard of the Caaba, which brought about his banishment. The idols brought the desert tribes to Mecca, and that meant trade. So the businessmen of Mecca, the capitalists, of which he had been one, set upon Mohammed. Then he retreated to the desert and demanded sovereignty over the world.

The rise of Islam began. Out of the desert came a flame, which would not be extinguished – a democratic army fighting as a unit and prepared to die without wincing. Mohammed had invited the Jews and Christians to join him, for he was not building a new religion. He was calling all who believed in one God to join in a single faith. If the Jews and Christians had accepted his invitation Islam would have conquered the world. They didn't. They would not even accept Mohammed's innovation of humane warfare. When the armies of the prophet entered Jerusalem not a single person was killed because of his faith. When the crusaders entered the city, centuries later, not a Moslem man, woman, or child was spared.

You're not igniting a religion – but if you apply a style of drive and persistence like Mohamed exhibited, you will, as surely, manifest the riches you desire.

POWER OF THE MASTER MIND
THE DRIVING FORCE

THE NINTH STEP TOWARD RICHES

"Nobody gets rich by themself."
–TJ Rohleder

chapter 9 Power is essential for success in the accumulation of money.

Plans are inert and useless without sufficient *power* to translate them into *action*. In other words, thinking BIG not connected with actually carrying out your plans is meaningless... The stuff of buffoons.

This chapter describes the method by which you may attain and apply real *power*.

Power may be defined as "organized and intelligently directed *knowledge*." Power, as the term is here used, refers to *organized* effort, sufficient to enable an individual to transmute *desire* into its monetary equivalent.

Power is required for the accumulation of money. Power is necessary for the retention and growth of money after it has been accumulated!

Organized effort is produced through the coordination of effort of two or more people, who work toward a *definite* end, in a spirit of harmony.

Simply put, isn't it logical – since every person has their own unique bent and strengths… since every person has certain weaknesses – that a harmonious affiliation between partners with *complementary skills, interests,* and *abilities,* with a common goal in a spirit of absolute trust and *direction* should progress the team further than fragmented individuals could?

This is the magic *synergy* we sing of… The result is greater than the sum of the input parts… The individual benefit is greater than it could be were the individual to attempt to go it alone.

It's *That* Important…

Let us ascertain how power may be acquired. If **power is "organized knowledge,"** let us examine the sources of knowledge:

1. ***Accumulated Experience*.** Anything in the world you want is available on the Internet. Sure, the accumulated experience of humanity (or that portion which has been organized and recorded) may be found in any well-equipped public or university library… But the Internet continues with *on the minute* precision, while libraries lag months or years behind. Although any library of respect today, itself has Internet availability.

2. ***Experiment and Research*.** In the field of science, and in practically every other walk of life, participants are gathering, classifying, and organizing new facts daily. This is the source to which one must turn when knowledge is not available through "accumulated experience." Here, too, the Internet is the hottest tool for discovery and collaboration ever encountered! Further, you begin to step into Higher Powers here… Frequently you *need* a new idea, to test a new alternative… *But what is that idea or alternative?* Creative imagination must often be used.

3.   *Infinite Intelligence.* This source of knowledge may be contacted through the procedure described in other chapters, purposefully, with the aid of creative imagination.

Knowledge may be acquired from any of the foregoing sources.

Knowledge Is *Not* Power

And while knowledge, by itself, is *not* power (contrary to the saying you may have heard)… **Knowledge may be converted into *power* by organizing it into definite plans** *and by expressing those plans in terms of action.*

You Need Others

Examination of the three major sources of knowledge will readily disclose the difficulty an individual would have, if they depended upon their efforts alone, in assembling knowledge and expressing it through definite plans in terms of *action.*

> Knowledge may be converted into *power* by organizing it into definite *plans* and by expressing those plans in terms of *action.*

How Big Are Your Objectives? While there's nothing wrong with humble plans… You *are* reading *The NEW Think And Grow Rich*…

If your plans are comprehensive, and if they contemplate large proportions, you must induce others to cooperate with you before you can inject into them the necessary element of *power.*

Gaining Power Through The "MasterMind"

The "MasterMind" may be defined as…

BONUS! 3 FREE Wealth-Building Gifts Worth $97 at HoloMagic.com

The coordination of knowledge, effort, and resources, in a spirit of harmony between two or more people for the attainment of a definite purpose.

No individual may have great power without availing himself of the "MasterMind"

In a preceding chapter, instructions were given for the creation of *plans* for the purpose of translating *desire* into its monetary equivalent. It will require the good will, cooperation, and partnership of others.

The felicitous news is, if you carry out these instructions with *persistence* and intelligence, and use discrimination in the selection of your "MasterMind" group, your objective will be halfway reached, even before you begin to recognize it.

> *"As the seed is planted,
> the plant does grow."*

So you may better understand the "intangible" potentialities of power available to you through a properly chosen "MasterMind" group, we will here explain two characteristics of the MasterMind principle, one of which is economic in nature, and the other spiritual.

MasterMind Yields Economic Benefits

The economic feature is obvious. Economic advantages may be created by any person who surrounds himself or herself with the advice, counsel, and personal cooperation of a group of capable individuals willing to lend him or her wholehearted aid, in a spirit of *perfect harmony*.

BONUS! 3 FREE Wealth-Building Gifts Worth $97 at HoloMagic.com

This form of *cooperative alliance* has been the basis of nearly every great Fortune. Your understanding of this great truth may definitely determine your financial status.

Mysterious Spiritual Power

The spiritual phase of the MasterMind principle is much more abstract, and more challenging to comprehend, because it is of the spiritual forces, with which the human race, as a whole, is not well acquainted. You may catch a significant suggestion from this statement...

No two minds ever come together without, thereby, creating a third, invisible, intangible force which may be likened to a third mind.

Jesus said it a different way, and it's certainly been promoted to religious ends, but this great man speaks of the *identical spiritual principle* – associated with the issue at hand...

"Wherever two or more are gathered in my name, there am I in the midst of you."

When people gather together, something bigger than little fragmented selves blooms.

One obvious example to make it clear is when three complementary partners unite and form a corporation to do business. That corporation is a third-party entity, separate and distinct from each of the individuals who are furthering its Fortunes. In this metaphor, *it* is the MasterMind.

It's called synergy, in which the whole is greater than the sum of the parts. The spiritual laughs at logic, and affirms 1 + 1 = 11!

There Is Only One Spirit

Keep in mind the fact that there are only two known elements in the whole Universe, energy and matter. It is a well- known fact that matter

BONUS! 3 FREE Wealth-Building Gifts Worth $97 at HoloMagic.com

may be broken down into units of molecules, atoms, and electrons. There are units of matter, which may be isolated, separated, and analyzed.

But when you go so far, you see that these subatomic particles of matter are *waves and units of energy…*

The human mind field is a form of energy, a part of it being spiritual in nature. When the minds of two people are coordinated in a *spirit of harmony*, the spiritual units of energy of each mind form an affinity, which animates the "spiritual" phase of the MasterMind.

Powerful Enough To Change Your Life

The MasterMind principle or rather the economic feature of it, was first called to my attention by Andrew Carnegie 100 years ago. Discovery of this principle was responsible for the choice of my life's work.

It happened again, as Ted Ciuba, when as a budding author in a new lifetime, the words of Napoleon Hill first planted the MasterMind concept in my fertile mind, mystery though it was… Was it ironic? Was it coincidental?

As a budding 20 year old in Los Angeles I found my first copy of Napoleon Hill's famous *Think And Grow Rich* in an old, dimly-lit used bookstore at the top of a long climb in 1970… Didn't know until over thirty years passed… And destiny served up my turn… Napoleon Hill passed to that great Infinite Intelligence that same year… Discovery of this principle was responsible for the riches I currently enjoy and the liberty and gift I have to update this important work.

Mr. Carnegie's MasterMind group consisted of a staff of approximately fifty people with whom he surrounded himself, for the *definite purpose* of manufacturing and marketing steel. He attributed his entire Fortune to the *power* he accumulated through this "MasterMind."

Reality Chiclets – Analyze the record of any person who has accumulated a great Fortune, and many of those who have accumulated modest

Fortunes, and you will find that they have either consciously, or unconsciously employed the "MasterMind" principle.

Great Power Can Be Accumulated Through *No* Other Principle!

Energy is Nature's *universal set of building blocks*, out of which she constructs every material thing in the Universe, including the human animal and every form of animal and vegetable life and beyond and below. Through a process, which only Nature completely understands, *she* translates energy into matter.

Fortunately, just like electricity in your home or the engine in your auto, you don't have to understand *how* it works to use it.

Nature's building blocks are available to *you* in the energy involved in *thinking!*

Battery Metaphor Illustrates MasterMind Principle

Let me explain how this happens from a 1918 example; something that was current when I was doing the research that became *Think And Grow Rich.* You'll easily see its implications.

The human brain may be compared to an electric battery.

It's a well-known fact that an individual battery provides energy in proportion to the number and capacity of the cells it contains. This accounts for the fact that some brains are more efficient than others.

Today, we've got bigger batteries that do the job fine for big rigs, fire and emergency equipment, etc. Problem solved in this instance, more capacity. But follow the *metaphor.*

In 1918 (when Ford sales constituted one half of the auto industry's output!), things were a bit more crude. We had developed the need for and built early versions of delivery trucks, construction, and emergency equipment, but we didn't quite have the technology to build a single-cased high-capacity battery.

And engines didn't start so easily as they do today. Lots of time 6-volts wasn't enough cranking power to give a stubborn engine the chance to fire up.

Easily enough overcome… It's a well-known fact that a group of electric batteries *wired together in a certain way* provides more energy than a single battery. So, by simply teaming batteries to the accomplishment of a single end, it is possible to double and quadruple battery power and output.

The brain functions in a similar fashion…

> *A group of brains coordinated (or connected) in a spirit of harmony provide more thought-energy than a single brain, just as a group of electric batteries provides more energy than a single battery*
>
> *That enhanced power is available to each individual member of the team, and can be applied to your definite chief aim.*

Spiritual Synergy

Through this metaphor it becomes immediately obvious that the MasterMind principle holds the secret of the *power* wielded by men who surround themselves with other men of brains. That's because there's another important principle that comes into play here, and that's *synergy*.

Human brains coordinated together create *more* energy than the simple sum of their parts. If 1 + 1 does not equal 2, but 11, then, by the same holoprocess, 6 + 6 + 6 + 6 doesn't equal 24, but 6,666. There's a HUGE difference there!

The power that's generated is available at every single outlet – available to each individual member of the team.

You are in the realm of the spiritual phase of the MasterMind principle.

When a group of individual brains are coordinated and function in harmony, the increased energy created through that alliance, becomes available to every individual brain in the group.

You Become Like Those You Associate With

It is a well-known fact that Henry Ford began his business career under the handicap of poverty, illiteracy, and ignorance. It is an equally well-known fact that, within the inconceivably short period of ten years, Mr. Ford mastered these three handicaps, and that within twenty-five years he made himself one of the richest men in America.

Connect with this fact, the additional knowledge that Mr. Ford's most rapid strides became noticeable from the time he became a personal friend of Thomas A. Edison, and you will begin to understand what the influence of one mind upon another can accomplish.

Go a step farther, and consider the fact that Mr. Ford's *most outstanding achievements* began from the time that he formed the acquaintances of Harvey Firestone, John Burroughs, and Luther Burbank (each a man of great brain capacity), and you will have further evidence that *power* may be produced through a friendly alliance of minds.

There is little, if any, doubt, that Henry Ford was one of the best-informed men in the business and industrial world. The question of his wealth needs no discussion. That's like debating Bill Gate's wealth. *What's the difference if you err two or three hundred million dollars?!!* Analyze Mr. Ford's intimate personal friends, some of whom have already been mentioned, and you will be prepared to understand the following statement…

BONUS! 3 FREE Wealth-Building Gifts Worth $97 at HoloMagic.com

"Humans take on the nature and the habits and the power of thought of those with whom they associate in a spirit of sympathy and harmony."

More simply, my mother always warned, "You become like those you associate with."

> *A group of brains coordinated (or connected) in a spirit of harmony provide more thought energy than a single brain, just as a group of electric batteries provides more energy than a single battery*
>
> *That enhanced power is available to each individual member of the team, and can be applied to your definite chief aim.*

Henry Ford whipped poverty, illiteracy, and ignorance by allying himself with great minds, whose vibrations of thought he came to know and entone with.

Through his association with Edison, Burbank, Burroughs, and Firestone, Ford added to his own brain power the sum and substance of the intelligence, experience, resources, contacts, knowledge, and spiritual forces of these four men. Moreover, he made use of the MasterMind principle through the methods of procedure described in this book.

This principle is available to you!

The Genius Of Harmony

We have already mentioned Mahatma Gandhi. Perhaps the majority of those who have heard of Gandhi look upon him as merely an eccentric little Indian man, who went around without formal wearing apparel, making trouble for the British government.

Sure, Gandhi was a bit eccentric, but, during his epoch, *he was the most powerful human living.* (Estimated by the number of his followers and their faith in their leader.)

Moreover, he is probably the most powerful man who has *ever* lived. He exercised *passive* power, but it was very real. It conquered the well-ordered, well-trained, fully funded British Empire – without ever firing a shot.

Let us study the method by which he attained his stupendous *power.* It may be explained in a few words…

> Gandhi came by *power* through inducing over two hundred million people to coordinate, with mind and body, in a spirit of *harmony*, for a *definite purpose.*

In brief, Gandhi accomplished a *miracle*, for it is a miracle when two hundred million people can be induced – not forced – to cooperate in a spirit of *harmony*, for a limitless time. If you doubt this is a miracle, try to induce *any two people* to cooperate in a spirit of harmony for any length of time.

Every individual who manages a business knows what a difficult matter it is to get employees to work together in a spirit even remotely resembling *harmony*.

Spiritual Principles Most Important In *Think And Grow Rich* Philosophy

The list of the chief sources from which *power* may be attained culminates, as you have seen earlier in this chapter, with *Infinite Intelligence. Duh!!!*

When two or more people coordinate in a spirit of *harmony*, and work toward a definite objective, they place themselves in position, through that alliance, to absorb power directly from the great universal storehouse of Infinite Intelligence.

When two or more people coordinate in a spirit of *harmony*, and work toward a definite objective, they place themselves in position, through that alliance, to absorb power directly from the great universal storehouse of Infinite Intelligence.

This is the greatest of all sources of power. It is the source to which the genius turns. It is the source to which every great leader turns (whether they be conscious of the fact or not).

The other two major sources from which the knowledge necessary for the accumulation of *power* may be obtained are no more reliable than the five animal senses. The senses are not always reliable. *Infinite Intelligence does not err.*

Read, Think & Meditate

In subsequent chapters, the methods by which Infinite Intelligence may be most readily contacted are adequately described.

This is not a course on religion. No fundamental principle described in this book should be interpreted as being intended to promote any religious agenda or to interfere either directly, or indirectly, with any person's religious habits. This book has been confined, exclusively, to instructing the reader how to transmute the *definite purpose of desire for money* into its monetary equivalent.

Read, *think*, and meditate as you read. Soon, the entire subject will unfold, and you will see it in perspective. You are now seeing the detail of the individual chapters.

Money, Like A Good Spouse, Doesn't Come By Accident, But Must Be Pursued

Money is as shy and elusive as the "old time" maiden. It must be wooed and won by methods not unlike those used by a determined lover in pursuit of the girl of his choice. And, coincidental as it is, the *power* used in the "wooing" of money is not greatly different from that used in wooing a maiden. That power, when successfully used in the pursuit of money must be mixed with *faith*. It must be mixed with *desire*. It must be applied through a plan, and that plan must be launched into *action* and followed with *persistence*.

When money comes in quantities known as "the big money," it flows to the one who accumulates it, as easily as water flows down hill.

There exists a great unseen stream of *power*, which may be compared to a river; except that one side flows in one direction, carrying all who get into that side of the stream, onward and upward to *wealth* – and the other side flows in the opposite direction, carrying all who are unfortunate enough to get into it (and not able to extricate themselves from it), downward to misery and *poverty*.

Every man who has accumulated a great Fortune has recognized the existence of this stream of life. It consists of one's *thinking process*. The positive emotions of thought form the side of the stream, which carries one to Fortune. The negative emotions form the side that carries one down to poverty.

This carries a thought of stupendous importance to the person who is following this book with the object of accumulating a Fortune.

Water, left to its own devices, always seeks the lowest level. In the same way, it's the nature of your thoughts… Either you work your way into the upward stream (which then becomes easy to maintain), or, don't worry you flow downstream to poverty and the wailing miseries of mediocrity.

Ordinary people don't dream, but mail-order multi-millionaire, TJ Rohleder, spots it right on when he says…

"People think and grow *poor*, too! Whatever thoughts you hold, you experience! It's the *same* law, working both ways!"

If you are in the side of the stream of *power,* which leads to poverty, this may serve as an outboard motor by which you may navigate the wake to the other side of the stream. It can serve you *only* through application and use.

Merely reading and passing judgment on it, either one way or another, will in no way benefit you.

Some people undergo the experience of alternating between the positive and negative sides of the stream, being at times on the positive side, and at times on the negative side.

Poverty and riches often change places. The Great American Market Crash of 1929 taught the world this truth, although the world did not long remember the lesson. Every business reversal – though it's part of the natural cycle of nature in business – humbles a new group of business people. Those who weather the rough waves, like the ship tried at sea, go on to great things.

Most people, through their own misunderstanding, lack of education, or plain laziness, don't get it. It's for this reason several governments require business opportunity advertisers to clearly state, after *true* testimonials, "these results are atypical."

Poverty may, and generally does, *voluntarily,* take the place of riches.

When riches take the place of poverty, the change is usually brought about through intense desire grasped with faith that drives well-conceived plans, carefully and persistently executed in consort with a MasterMind team.

Poverty needs no plan. It needs no one to aid it. It is ruthless. It is, as mentioned earlier, the *default* human mechanism. *Look around for the evidence!*

Riches are shy and timid. They have to be "attracted."

ANYBODY CAN
WISH FOR RICHES

AND MOST DO...

But, only a few know that a BURNING DESIRE

passionate enough to drive you create DEFINITE PLANS and

implement them with PERSISTENCE...

IS THE ONLY DEPENDABLE MEANS
OF ACCUMULATING WEALTH.

PASSION
PASSION MAKES DISCIPLINE *EASY!*

THE TENTH STEP TOWARD RICHES

"He who possesses the source of enthusiasm achieves great things."

– I Ching

chapter 10 ⊂══► Sex desire is the most powerful of human desires. When driven by this desire, men develop drive, interest, keenness of imagination, courage, willpower, persistence, and creative ability unknown to them at other times.

So strong and impelling is the desire for sexual affiliation that men freely run the risk of life and reputation to indulge it.

When harnessed, and redirected along other lines this motivating force maintains all of its attributes of drive, interest, keenness of imagination, courage, persistence, and creative ability, which may be used as powerful creative forces in literature, art, or in any other profession or calling, including, of course, the accumulation of riches.

Enrich Body, Mind And Spirit

Transmutation is, in simple language, the changing or transferring of one element, or form of energy, into another. *Sex transmutation* is simple and easily explained. It means the switching of the mind from thoughts of physical expression, to thoughts of some other nature.

The desire for sexual expression is inborn and natural. The desire cannot and should not be submerged or eliminated.

But the innate sexual drive should be given an outlet through forms of expression that enrich the body, mind and spirit of you and of all humanity.

If not given this form of outlet, through transmutation, it will seek outlets through purely physical channels.

A river may be dammed, and its water controlled for a time, but eventually, it will force an outlet. The same is true of the drive for sex. It may be submerged and controlled for a time, but its very nature causes it to be ever seeking means of expression.

On the other hand, just as water is harnessed to achieve great ends – like at Hoover Dam in Nevada USA which provides electricity to an entire region by harnessing the power in accord with its *nature,* so you, too, can accomplish great things when you harness this powerful force of Nature to achieve worthy goals.

A High Sex Drives Success!

Scientific research has disclosed these significant facts:

1. The men of greatest achievement are men with high sex drives; men who have learned the art of sex transmutation.

2. The men who have accumulated great Fortunes and achieved

outstanding recognition in literature, art, industry, architec-
ture, and the professions, were motivated by the influence of
a woman.

The research from which these astounding discoveries were made
went back through the pages of biography and history for more than
two thousand years. Wherever there was evidence available in connection
with the lives of men and women of great achievement, it indicated most
convincingly that they possessed highly developed sex natures.

Why It's So Important For Success-Driven People To Know About And Harness This Phenomenon

Vibrations of an exceedingly high rate are the only vibrations picked
up and carried, by the Cosmos, from one brain to another. Thought is
energy traveling at an exceedingly high rate of vibration. Thought which
has been modified or "stepped up" by any of the major emotions vibrates
at a much higher rate than ordinary thought, and it is this type of thought
which passes from one brain to another, through the broadcasting machinery of the human brain.

*The emotions generated around sex stand at the head of the list of human emo-
tions, as far as intensity and driving force are concerned.*

That fact alone should drive you to investigate how you can harness
this powerful force to your personal wealth quest.

The brain which has been stimulated by the emotions surrounding
sex vibrates at a much more rapid rate than it does when that emotion is
quiescent or absent.

The result of sex transmutation is the increase of the rate of vibration
of thoughts to such a pitch that the creative imagination becomes highly
receptive to ideas, which it picks up from the Cosmos.

BONUS! 3 FREE Wealth-Building Gifts Worth $97 at HoloMagic.com

When the brain is vibrating at a rapid rate, it not only attracts thoughts and ideas released by other brains through the medium of the Cosmos, but it gives to one's own thoughts that "feeling" which is essential before those thoughts will be picked up and acted upon by your own subconscious mind.

So, you will see that the broadcasting principle is the factor through which you mix feeling, or emotion with your thoughts and pass them on to your subconscious mind, and to the entire Universe.

An Irresistible Force

The emotions surrounding sex form an "irresistible force," against which there can be no such opposition as an "immovable body."

> When *driven* by the emotions surrounding sex…Men become gifted with a **super power** for action.

That is the secret of this entire concept.

When **driven** by these emotions, individuals become gifted with a super power for action.

Understand this truth, and you will catch the significance of the statement that the transmutation of your sexual desires can lift you to the status of a genius.

Actuate this secret, and you harness the greatest power known to humanity to achieve your ends!

The emotions generated around sex contain the secret of creative ability. Of course, it's around "good sex" where the power comes, which is more than just the streetwalker variety – it includes love and romance, too.

Commitment To Do Or To Die

Oftentimes the spirit, which immediately vaults people to prominence, is the spirit of "Do or Die!"

It means, short of an early death, *nothing* will deter you. Even if you can't be certain of the exact date of arrival, you can be certain of the fact.

There's a magic – opened by the quality we call "Faith" – in *knowing* only an early encounter with death can stop you.

Willpower Required

The transmutation of sex energy calls for the exercise of willpower, to be sure, but the reward is worth the effort.

Further, there are techniques to let the *imagination* take over in this regard, rendering the willpower easy to muster. In fact, you can direct your nervous system – when your desire is sufficient – to make the proper choices your choices of preference. To make it a passion you are driven by.

Let's take an example from the weight loss world. You can easily see how it applies in business and to your grand pursuits.

The heavily overweight person *wants* to lose weight. They know how much better they would feel, how much better their health would be. Not the least of which is how much better he or she would look.

They decide countless times to lose weight. And make the determination to resist the temptation to overeat and to avoid evil things like sweets and desserts.

The resolve lasts maybe one meal… Maybe two temptations.

The issue lies in thinking the wrong thoughts…

A slim person doesn't have those temptations… A slim person wouldn't overeat. It doesn't feel good. Being "disciplined" is not an issue, because a trim person doesn't feel the compulsion to pig out, and, in fact, would feel *bad* overeating.

BONUS! 3 FREE Wealth-Building Gifts Worth $97 at HoloMagic.com

The person battling excessive weight may feel bad about *having* over-eaten, but the reason why they overeat is because they feel good *doing* it.

Think the thoughts those in the situation you want to create think. Find out what their thoughts are, and model them.

A person who sees themselves as a fat person, battling to lose weight, has set themselves up for failure. They grit their teeth, clench their fists, and make the solemn resolve to make the right choice.

That's relying on willpower.

Einstein holographically observed, "Whenever the will and the imagination are in conflict, the imagination will win."

Rather, if they could discover and model the attitudes and thoughts of a trim, positive person, the result they desire would grow to fruition over time. A slim, trim, healthy person isn't battling any food demons.

It is the focus of this book, and this chapter, in particular, to reveal how to *think* and *grow rich*. How to think the thoughts the wealthy person thinks... What those thoughts are... In what manner and with what character the wealthy person thinks those thoughts. When you grasp and apply the holomagic secret of this text and this philosophy, when you're coming from the right space, your financial independence grows to fruition over time.

As an aside, even though an in-depth investigation of Neuro-Linguistic Programming (NLP) is beyond the scope of this book, every serious wealth seeker will seek out and strategize using NLP in the empowerment and vivification of their desires, aims and goals.

Dog Your Quest

The mystery of sex transmutation talks of a *passion* for your quest!

If you could dog your wealth quest, your enterprise, your

project with the same intent-fulness, *passion*, and persistence of a male dog chasing a female in heat, how much "discipline" would you need?

Your progress would be greater. Setbacks would not have any duration nor significance.

There lies the magic in sex transmutation.

It's about *loving* what you do. It's being *passionate* in what you do!

When love and passion drive you – work is not work. It is easy. It is doing what you'd most prefer to do most in all the world! With passion, you don't have to *force* yourself to work on your project, career, or finances… It's not like a "job." You find it impossible to do otherwise – by nature.

Fortunate, indeed, is the person who has discovered how to give the emotions generated around sex an outlet through some form of creative effort, for he has, by that discovery, lifted himself to the status of a genius.

When you pursue your single definite chief aim single-mindedly, distractions don't come up. That powerful focus is made *easy* by intense desire.

Harness This Male Instinct To Fight

Destroy the sex glands, whether in man or beast, and you remove the major source of action. For proof of this, observe what happens to any animal after it has been castrated. A bull becomes as docile as a cow after it has been altered sexually. Sex alteration takes out of the male, whether man or beast, all the *fight* that was in him. Sex alteration of the female has the same effect.

The Ten Mind Stimuli

The human mind responds to stimuli, through which it may be "keyed up" to high rates of vibration. On this higher level, with this enthusiasm,

BONUS! 3 FREE Wealth-Building Gifts Worth $97 at HoloMagic.com

you find you *naturally* attack everything you do with the energy that creates success from your own efforts, as well as pluck the strings of the entire HoloCosm, so that everything responds to you in magnetic harmonics.

"What you think about, you bring about." Enthusiasm generates a tremendous power. Therefore, it's important to consider… The stimuli to which the mind responds most freely are...

1. The desire for sex expression

2. Love

3. A burning desire for fame, power, or financial gain, *money*

4. Music

5. Friendship between either those of the same sex, or those of the opposite sex

6. A MasterMind alliance based upon the harmony of two or more people who ally themselves for spiritual or temporal advancement

7. Mutual suffering, such as that experienced by people who are persecuted

8. Meditation / auto-suggestion

9. Fear

10. Narcotics and alcohol

The desire for sexual expression comes at the head of the list of stimuli, which most effectively "step-up" the vibrations of the mind and start the "wheels" of physical action. Eight of these stimuli are natural and constructive. Two are destructive. The list is here presented for the purpose of enabling you to make a comparative study of the major sources of mind stimulation. From this study, it will be readily seen that the emotion of sex is, by great odds, the most intense and powerful of all mind stimuli.

> Your sexual drive should be given an outlet through forms of expression which enrich the body, mind and spirit of humanity. If not given this form of outlet, through transmutation, it will seek outlets through purely physical channels.

That being the case, it merits our closest attention and study to harness this power. On a personal scale, it holds the same promise as a nuclear plant, which makes cities and industries purr, yet, mismanaged sows a wasteland, like Chernobyl.

This comparison is necessary as a foundation for proof of the statement that transmutation of sex energy may lift one to the status of a genius.

Let us find out what constitutes a genius.

Not Available Through Ordinary Thought

Some wisecracker has said that a genius is a man who "wears long hair, eats queer food, lives alone, and serves as a target for the joke makers."

A better definition of a genius is, "a person who has discovered how to increase the vibrations of thought to the point where he can freely communicate with sources of knowledge not available through the ordinary rate of vibration of thought."

The statement is so easily said, yet so few… Only the exceptional capture and put to use its essence.

BONUS! 3 FREE Wealth-Building Gifts Worth $97 at HoloMagic.com

The person who thinks will ask some questions concerning this definition of genius.

The first question is… "If I'm reading this book and philosophy to get *rich*, then why should I care about being a "genius"?

The reason is simple. To *do* the exceptional – i.e. get rich in service to humanity – you must *be* exceptional. The truth is, though most people associate being a "genius" with academics and science, one who excels in any field is a "genius."

Assuming you buy into the advantages being a "genius" gives you, the next overwhelming question is, "*How* may one communicate with sources of knowledge which are not available through the *ordinary* rate of vibration of thought?"

This question is coupled with, "Are there known sources of knowledge which are available only to genii, and if so, *what are these sources*, and exactly how may they be reached?"

We shall offer proof of the soundness of some of the more important statements made in this book – or at least we shall offer evidence through which you may secure your own proof through experimentation, and in doing so, we shall answer all these questions.

The Human Mind Responds To Stimulation

The human mind responds to stimulation. **Among the greatest and most powerful of these stimuli is the urge for sex**. When harnessed and transmuted, this driving force is capable of lifting men into that higher sphere of thought which enables them to master the sources of worry and petty annoyance which attack their pathway on the lower plane. That's when the creative imagination is given free reign.

Unfortunately, only the genii have made this discovery. Others experience the urge of sex without discovering one of its major potentialities

— a fact which accounts for the great number of "others" as compared to the limited number of genii.

For the purpose of refreshing the memory, in connection with the facts available from the biographies of certain men, we here present the names of a few men of outstanding achievement each of whom was known to have been driven by strong sexual desires.... The genius which was theirs, undoubtedly found its source of power in transmuted sex energy:

George Washington	Thomas Jefferson
Napoleon Bonaparte	Elbert Hubbard
Elbert H. Gary	William Shakespeare
Oscar Wilde	Woodrow Wilson
Abraham Lincoln	Ralph Waldo Emer-
Andrew Jackson	Robert Burns
Enrico Caruso	Paul McCartney
Donald Trump	Richard Branson
Glenn Turner	Anthony Robbins
Corey Rudl	

Lincoln was a notable example of a great leader who achieved greatness through the discovery and use of his faculty of creative imagination. He discovered and began to use this faculty as the result of the stimulation of love which he experienced after he met Anne Rutledge, a statement of the highest significance in connection with the study of the source of genius.

"Uh Oh!"

The pages of history are filled with the records of great leaders whose achievements may be traced directly to the influence of women who aroused the creative faculties of their minds through the stimulation of sex desire. Napoleon Bonaparte was one of these. When inspired by his first wife, Josephine, he was irresistible and invincible. When his "better judgment" or reasoning faculty prompted him to put Josephine aside, he began to decline. His defeat and St. Helena were not far distant.

If good taste would permit, we might easily mention scores of well-known men across the international scene who climbed to great heights of achievement under the stimulating influence of their wives, only to drop back to destruction *after* money and power went to their heads, and they put aside the old wife for a new one. Napoleon was not the only man to discover that sex influence, from the right source, is more powerful than any substitute of expediency, which may be created by mere reason or animal passion.

Your own knowledge of biography and current events will enable you to add to this list.

Sex Energy *Is* Creative Energy

Find if you can, a single man in all the history of civilization who achieved outstanding success in any calling who was not driven by a well-developed sex nature.

If you do not wish to rely upon biographies of men not now living, take inventory of those whom you know to be men of great achievement, and see if you can find one among them who is not highly sexed.

It can get real simple here…

> **Sex energy is the creative energy of all genii. There never has been, and never will be a great leader, builder, or artist lacking in this driving force of sex.**

"Many Are Called, Few Choose"

Surely, no one will misunderstand these statements to mean that *all* who are highly sexed are genii! Man attains to the status of a genius *only* when, and *if,* he stimulates his mind so that it draws upon the forces available through the creative faculty of the imagination.

Chief among the stimuli with which this "stepping up" of the vibrations may be produced is sex energy.

Any person who can harness that tremendous sexual energy to productive ends can accomplish great things!

The mere possession of this energy is not sufficient to produce a genius. In my profession we say it is a "necessary, but not sufficient" cause of genius. The energy must be transmuted from desire for physical contact into some other form of desire and action before it will lift one to the status of a genius.

Far from becoming genii because of great sex desires, the majority of men lower themselves, through misunderstanding and misuse of this great force, to the status of the lower animals.

Want a simple jumpstart on harnessing this secret? Here it is… Instead of moving on sex directly, copulating and falling asleep, which, after all, any animal can do, *do something* to show and merit love. Express the drive in other channels. Note how you feel after this "test" of achievement.

Expand this awareness to your bigger motives.

Why Men Seldom Succeed Before Forty

I discovered, from the analysis of over 25,000 people, that men who succeed in an outstanding way, seldom do so before the age of forty, and more often they do not strike their real pace until they are well beyond the age of fifty. This fact was so astounding that it prompted me to go into the study of its cause most carefully, carrying the investigation over a period of more than twelve years.

This study disclosed the fact that **the major reason why the majority of men who succeed do not begin to do so before the** age of forty to fifty is their tendency to *dissipate* their energies through over indulgence in physical expression of the emotion of sex. They are too scattered to concentrate their creative energies on the development of a single project.

Noteworthy Achievement

The majority of men never learn that the urge of sex has other possibilities which far transcend in importance that of mere physical expression. The majority of those who make this discovery do so after having wasted many years at a period when the sex energy is at its height, prior to the age of forty-five to fifty. This usually is followed by noteworthy achievement.

If you want evidence that most men do not begin to do their best work before the age of forty, study the records of the most successful men known to the American people, and you will find it.

Henry Ford had not "hit his pace" of achievement until he had passed the age of forty. Andrew Carnegie was well past forty before he began to reap the reward of his efforts. James J. Hill was still running a telegraph key at the age of forty. His stupendous achievements took place after that age.

Biographies of American industrialists and financiers are filled with evidence that the period from forty to sixty is the most productive age of man.

Colonel Sanders didn't even start the now worldwide Kentucky Fried Chicken store until he got his first Social Security check upon retirement at age 62. He was insulted by the terrible joke, and he went to work in earnest.

Ray Kroc, founder of the McDonald's chain, at age 52 tried to persuade the McDonald brothers to build more restaurants – obviously the public *liked* what they were doing! They couldn't be bothered, as they were too busy flipping hamburgers. He built his empire after that age.

Between the ages of thirty and forty, man begins to learn (if he ever learns) the art of sex transmutation. This discovery is generally accidental, and more often than otherwise, the man who makes it is totally unconscious of his discovery.

He may observe that his powers of achievement have increased around the age of thirty-five to forty, but in most cases, he is not familiar with the cause of this change. Nature begins to harmonize the emotions of love and sex in the individual between the ages of thirty and forty, so that he may draw upon these great forces, and apply them jointly as stimuli to action.

> The desire for sexual expression is by far the strongest and most impelling of all the human emotions, and for this very reason this desire, when harnessed and transmuted into action, other than that of physical expression, may raise one to the status of a genius.

The lives of many men up to, and sometimes well past the age of forty, reflect a continued dissipation of energies, which could have been more profitably turned into better channels. Their finer and more powerful emotions are sown wildly to the four winds. Out of this habit of the male grew the term, "sowing his wild oats."

Omega Energy

Obviously, when we're dealing with sexual energy, we're dealing with the *Creative Energy*. It treats of the male-female energy.

It's come of fashion in recent days to call this combining of male-female energies "omega energy."

There's another aspect in the calming that comes with age... And that's an ability to harness the universal rhythms of Nature. That's what sex energy is, you know, the male-female tension that, when it connects, creates an offspring which itself becomes independent.

We see this duality throughout Nature, in the day and the night, in the morning and evening, in cold and hot, in high and low, in alpha and beta, the rise and fall of tides, in give and receive, in the rhythm of all wave forms and vibration, the peak and the trough, in the positive and negative electrical charges that output work.

The Eastern philosophy calls it *Yin-Yang* energy, which best translates as *Life Force.*

You, female, need the male; you, male, need the female. Without both parties, nothing is born.

Omega Energy speaks of the balance of both energies to be optimally effective. And surely, when all of Nature operates on the principle of duality, no sane person could argue against it.

There is a right way to characterize your actions in the world, and it has to do with incorporating both aspects of behavior – the yang and the yin, the male and the female, the testosterone and the estrogen.

Balance the Yin and Yang energies to apply your life force, your passion, your energies, sensitivities, and motives to accomplish wealth

In any coming together (mating) of duality, a third, an offspring or effect, is created.

This shouldn't be a surprising idea, living as we do in a creative Universe. Indeed, the entire *Think And Grow Rich* philosophy is premised on the *growth* metaphor of planting seeds (male/action) in the soil (female/medium) that grow into wealth (offspring/result).

Again, it's all about being *conscious* in the preparation of, selection of, and nurturing of the seeds of wealth you intend to sprout. The law never varies; it works. You do your part right, and you receive the riches you went after.

Take A Page From The Sports Book

It might be good to note here how the coaches play high stakes pro football by conserving the sexual juice of the players in the days leading up to the game. The aim, of course, is to control and direct its release for accomplishment on the big day. That speaks of another way to employ the principle of balance.

This is the mystery of sex transmutation.

Control, direct, unleash the energy to accomplish.

That female inspiration for the male drive is *exactly* what we're speaking of…. (Of course, it's *male* inspiration for the female.)

Harness it to accomplish great things.

The Strongest Force

The desire for sexual expression is by far the strongest and most impelling of all the human emotions, and for this very reason this desire, when harnessed and transmuted into action, other than that of physical expression, may raise one to the status of a genius.

This, by the way, is not to be interpreted as suggesting you become celibate. Far from it. There's a sordid history that reveals the perversions that develop when you seek to block the sexual urge. We are suggesting you *harness* that energy you normally use to chase a mating partner to productive, higher ends.

We celebrate this drive!

It would be safe to assume we are suggesting you engage in physical sex in moderation – if you do, the benefit is you'll get more out of it, too. Then use this drive to inspire you to creative breakthrough! (Think about it, *creativity IS* Nature's purpose behind this drive, isn't it?)

BONUS! 3 FREE Wealth-Building Gifts Worth $97 at HoloMagic.com

The "Other Woman"

One of America's most able businessmen frankly admitted that his attractive secretary was responsible for most of the plans he created. He admitted that her presence lifted him to heights of creative imagination such as he could experience under no other stimulus.

A number I've spoken to on this theme think "forbidden fruit" is too racy an idea to admit to… In my preferred language, it's *la fruta prohibida* – much more emotion, I promise you. But, don't forget, our first responsibility is not political correctness, but *results*. **The sex drive is *powerful*.** Wherever it comes from. The Gods made it that way, not you.

Which is precisely why I'm instructing you to **harness that power to achieve great things**.

Another of the most successful men in America owes most of his success to the influence of a very charming young woman, who has served as his source of inspiration for more than twelve years. Everyone knows the man to whom this reference is made, but not everyone knows the *real source* of his achievements.

Sex Is The Best Stimulant

History is not lacking in examples of people who attained to the status of genii as the result of the use of artificial mind stimulants in the form of alcohol and narcotics. Edgar Allen Poe wrote the "Raven" while under the influence of liquor, "dreaming dreams that mortal never dared to dream before."

James Whitcomb Riley did his best writing while under the influence of alcohol. Perhaps it was then he saw "the ordered intermingling of the real and the dream, the mill above the river, and the mist above the stream." Robert Burns wrote best when intoxicated, "For Auld Lang Syne, my dear, we'll take a cup of kindness yet, for Auld Lang Syne."

The entire history of rock and roll, from Elvis Presley to Elvis Costello is intertwined with drug use. From the harmonic Beatles to the raunchy Rolling Stones, and the artists on the scene today...

But let it be remembered that many such folks have destroyed themselves in the end. Nature has prepared her own potions with which we may safely stimulate our minds so they vibrate on a plain that enables them to tune into fine and rare thoughts that come from the creative Universe. No satisfactory substitute for Nature's stimulants has ever been found. Sex is the best stimulant for the human animal. Embrace it.

The Destiny Of Civilizations

It is a fact well known to psychologists that there is a very close relationship between sex desires and spiritual urges – a fact which accounts for the peculiar behavior of people who participate in the orgies known as religious "revivals," common among the primitive/fundamentalist types.

The world is ruled, and the destiny of civilizations is established by *human emotions*. People are influenced in their actions, not by reason so much as by *feelings*.

The creative faculty of the mind is set into action entirely by *emotions*, and not by cold reason. The most powerful of all human emotions are generated around sex.

There are other mind stimulants, some of which have been listed, but no one of them, nor all of them combined, can equal the driving power of sex.

For this reason you easily wrap your mind around the importance of studying how to harness sexual energy! **Can you imagine putting the influence of the strongest force of humanity behind your plans?!!**

A mind stimulant is any influence, which will either temporarily, or permanently, increase the vibrations of thought. The ten major stimulants, described, are those most commonly resorted to.

BONUS! 3 FREE Wealth-Building Gifts Worth $97 at HoloMagic.com

Through the medium of one or more of the mind stimulants one may commune with Infinite Intelligence, or enter, at will, the storehouse of the subconscious mind, either one's own, or that of another person, a procedure which is all there is of genius.

Simply put, it's entering into a higher consciousness, and love is the most effective facilitator.

Sales Charisma

A teacher who has trained and directed the efforts of more than 30,000 sales people made the astounding discovery that highly sexed people are the most efficient salespersons. The explanation is that the factor of personality known as "personal magnetism," or "charisma," is nothing more or less than sexual energy. Highly sexed people always have a plentiful supply of magnetism. Just call it a good personality.

Through cultivation and understanding, this vital force may be drawn upon and used to great advantage in the relationships between people.

This energy may be communicated to others through the following media:

1. The handshake. The touch of the hand indicates, instantly, the presence of magnetism, or the lack of it.

2. The tone of voice. Charisma, or sexual energy, is the factor with which the voice may be colored, or made musical and charming.

3. Posture and carriage of the body. Highly sexed people move briskly, and with grace and ease.

4. The vibrations of thought. Highly sexed people mix the emotion of sex with their thoughts, or may do so at will, and in that way, may influence those around them.

5.   Body adornment. People who are highly sexed are usually
      very careful about their personal appearance. They usually
      select clothing of a style becoming to their personality, phy-
      sique, complexion, etc.

When employing sales personnel, the more capable sales manager
looks for the quality of charisma as the first requirement of a salesperson.
People who lack sexual energy will never become enthusiastic nor inspire others with enthusiasm, and enthusiasm is one of the most important requisites in salesmanship, no matter what one is selling.

The public speaker, orator, preacher, lawyer, or salesperson, who is
lacking in sexual energy is a "flop," as far as being able to influence others
is concerned. Call it *boring*.

Couple with this the fact that most people can be influenced only
through an appeal to their emotions, and you will understand the importance of sexual energy as a part of the salespersons' native ability. Master
salespersons attain the status of mastery in selling, because they, either
consciously, or unconsciously, transmute the energy of sex into *sales enthusiasm!* In this statement may be found a very practical suggestion as to
the actual meaning of sex transmutation.

The salesperson who knows how to take their mind off the subject of
sex, and direct it in sales effort with as much enthusiasm and determination as they would apply to its original purpose, has acquired the art of
sex transmutation, whether they know it or not. The majority of salespersons who transmute their sexual energy do so without being in the least
aware of what they are doing, or how they are doing it.

Discipline Has Its Rewards

Transmutation of sex energy calls for more willpower than the average
person cares to use for this purpose. However, those who find it difficult

to summon willpower sufficient for transmutation may gradually acquire this ability. Though this requires willpower, the reward for the practice is more than worth the effort.

After all, all we're saying is *conserve your sexual energy, the most powerful driver of all creation, and direct it to noteworthy pursuits.* Don't sow your wild oats. Be inspired by a worthy love and worthy causes – move on your definite chief aim in the same spirit.

It's always easier to follow your animal passions of the moment, as former Malaysian Prime Minister Datuk Seri Dr. Mahathir Mohamad observes…

> "Most people give in to their baser instincts, thinking more of short-term pleasures and gains than the kind of sustained self-restraint required in order to practice what is good and reject what is bad."

Discipline is almost a bad word… However, that's among what Confucius calls the "masses." Among the *elite*, those with vision, the productive, the actualizing, *discipline* is a very good term. Following its dictates – concentrating your time, energy, and effort towards *goal achieving* ends, rather than merely tension relieving ends, gives you full sail under power to achieve all the good things in your life you are motivated to achieve.

Those who embrace this philosophy apply to the "willing discipline" theory, believing *to be inspired* makes all necessary effort light. Review again the weight-loss example cited earlier in this chapter to make engaging the magic of discipline to your ends easy for you.

Speaking of discipline, it goes without saying that every person who desires the true riches of life understands **you must maintain your health to make sustained noteworthy achievements.** You need to implement a lifestyle that includes good nutrition, aerobic exercise, adequate rest, recreation, and a social and spiritual component. Cultivate good habits and avoid excess in all things. There are all kinds of literature and programs on a healthy, holistic lifestyle.

The majority of humans live lives that Shakespeare identifies as… "a tale told by an idiot, full of sound and fury, signifying nothing."

You, however, live a life of energy harnessed to a practical application. You are an actualizing being. Fruitful.

Sexual "Open Season" Is *Not* What We're Talking About

Intemperance in sex habits is just as detrimental as intemperance in habits of drinking and eating. No person can avail himself of the forces of their creative imagination while dissipating them. Man is the only creature on Earth who violates Nature's purpose in this connection. Every other animal indulges its sex nature in moderation, and with purpose, which harmonizes with the Laws of Nature. Every other animal responds to the call of sex only "in season." Man's inclination is to declare "open season."

The Rich Get Richer, The Poor Get Poorer

From these brief references to the subject, it may be readily seen that ignorance on the subject of sex transmutation doles stupendous penalties upon the ignorant on the one hand, and withholds equally stupendous benefits from them, on the other.

You can see why it's so important to learn about this subject and to harness your sex drives to achieve your goals.

If you don't proactively harness them, they will (through your neglect or ignorance) leave you to the waste heap. Riches require insight, imagination, discipline, planning, and effort; poverty needs no plan, nor effort, nor discipline.

Elevate The Sex Urges To Achieve Great Things

Sex, alone, is a mighty urge to action, but its forces are like a cyclone – often uncontrollable. When you mix the emotion of love with the emotion of sex, the result is calmness of purpose, poise, accuracy of judgment, and balance. What person, who has attained to the age of forty, is so unfortunate as to be unable to analyze these statements, and to corroborate them by their own experience?

When driven by his desire to please a woman, based solely upon the emotion of sex, a man may be, and usually is, capable of great achievement, but his actions may be disorganized, distorted, and totally destructive. When driven by his desire to please a woman, based upon the motive of sex alone, a man may steal, cheat, and even commit murder. But when the emotion of *love* is mixed with the emotion of sex, that same man will guide his actions with more sanity, balance, and reason.

Criminologists have discovered that the most hardened criminals can be reformed through the influence of a woman's love. There is no record of a criminal having been reformed solely through the sex influence. These facts are well known, but their cause is not.

Reformation comes, if at all, through the heart, or the emotional side of man, not through his head, or reasoning side. Reformation means, "a change of heart." It does not mean a "change of head." A man may, because of reason, make certain changes in his personal conduct to avoid the consequences of undesirable effects, but **genuine reformation comes only through a change of heart, through a *desire* to change**.

Love, romance, and sex all stimulate emotions capable of driving men to heights of super achievement. Love is the emotion, which serves as a safety valve and insures balance, poise, and constructive effort. When combined, these three drivers may lift one to an altitude of a genius.

There are genii, however, who know little of the emotion of love. Most of them may be found engaged in some form of action which is destructive, or at least, not based upon justice and fairness toward others. If good taste would permit, we could name dozens of genii in the field of industry, finance, and politics, who ride ruthlessly over the rights of their fellow beings. They seem totally lacking in conscience. You can easily supply your own list of such individuals.

The emotions are states of mind. Nature has provided man with a "chemistry of the mind" which operates in a manner similar to the principles of chemistry of matter. It is a well known fact that, through the aid of chemistry of matter, a chemist may create a deadly poison by mixing certain elements – none of which are, in themselves harmful – in the right proportions. The emotions may, likewise, be combined so as to create a deadly poison. The emotions of sex and jealousy, when mixed, may turn a person into an insane beast.

The presence of any one or more of the destructive emotions in the human mind, through the chemistry of the mind, triggers the release of a poison, which may destroy one's sense of justice and fairness. In extreme cases, the presence of any combination of these emotions in the mind may destroy one's reason.

There's a bit of discipline required, but for the motivated, it's *willing* discipline. The road to genius consists of the development, control, and use of sex, love, and romance. Briefly, the process may be stated as follows:

Live with a higher purpose! Encourage the presence of these emotions as the dominating thoughts in your mind, and discourage the presence of all the destructive emotions. Your mind is a creature of habit. It thrives upon the dominating thoughts fed it. With *consciousness*, one may discourage the presence of any emotion, and encourage the presence of any other.

Control of the mind, through the power of will, is not difficult. Control comes from desire, persistence, and habit. The secret of control lies in understanding the process of transmutation. When any negative emotion presents itself in one's mind, it can be transmuted into a positive, or constructive emotion, by the simple procedure of changing one's thoughts.

The Mind As A Software Program

That's why it's so important to construct in advance energizing, empowering, affirmative thoughts and emotions, so you can drop them into place anytime you need, on command.

The human organism is like a computer. It's *not* the computer that determines the output and benefit it delivers. It's not even the *software* program.

The excellent operational efficiency of the computer and the software not withstanding… It's what you put *into* the computer that determines what you get as output. "Garbage in, garbage out."

Positive, empowering thoughts, thoughts of your definite chief aim, mixed with faith, images of achievement, positive self-talk, reminders of the *value* of what you pursue, these are the emotionalized input you use to *consciously think* and *grow rich.*

When you think these thoughts, not only do you communicate positive messages that animate you to perform the actions you need to achieve your goals (self-fulfilling prophecy), these thoughts also connect with universal intelligence so that synchronicity and serendipity can work for you.

In short, you work the Universe the same way you work yourself, and in working yourself, you work the Universe.

Universal Forces

Man's greatest motivating force is his desire to please women! The hunter, who excelled during prehistoric days, before the dawn of civilization, did so, because of his desire to appear great in the eyes of woman. Man's nature has not changed in this respect. The "hunter" of today brings home no skins of wild animals, but he indicates his desire for her favor by supplying fine clothes, motorcars, trips, and wealth. Man has the same desire to please women that he had before the dawn of civilization. The only thing that's changed is his method of pleasing her.

Men who accumulate large Fortunes, and attain to great heights of power and fame, do so, mainly, to satisfy their desire to please women. It is this inherent desire of man to please women, which gives women the power to make or break a man.

The same holds true of women of achievement. Of course, by nature, women are more holistically oriented – yet love drives a woman, too. Women find great satisfaction and drivers in love – love of their mate, children, and family.

Some men know that they are being influenced by the woman of their choice, their wives, sweethearts, mothers, sisters, or daughters, but they tactfully refrain from rebelling against the influence because they are intelligent enough to know *no man is happy or complete without the modifying influence of the right woman.*

It serves a lesson to men and women both, of whatever sexual orientation… The person who does not recognize this important truth, deprives them self of the power which has done more to help individuals achieve success than all other forces combined.

THE SUBCONSCIOUS MIND
THE CONNECTING LINK

THE ELEVENTH STEP TOWARD RICHES

chapter 11 ⇌ *The subconscious mind is multidimensional.* One of its characteristic aspects consists of a field of consciousness in which every impulse of thought that reaches the objective mind through any of the five senses is classified and recorded, and from which thoughts may be recalled or withdrawn as letters may be taken from a filing cabinet.

It receives and files sense impressions or thoughts, regardless of their nature.

It also is the sending station between your heart and soul and the HoloCosm, Infinite Intelligence. Here's your point of power...

You may *voluntarily* plant in your subconscious mind any plan, thought, technique, or purpose which you desire to translate into its physical or monetary equivalent.

The subconscious acts first on the dominating desires, which have been mixed with emotional feeling put forth in faith.

The Subconscious Mind Works Day And Night

Through a method or procedure unknown to conventional humanity, the subconscious mind tunes into and draws upon the forces of Infinite Intelligence for the power with which it voluntarily transmutes one's desires into their physical equivalent, making use, always, of the most practical media by which this end may be accomplished.

You cannot entirely control your subconscious mind, but you can voluntarily hand over to it any plan, desire, or purpose you wish transformed into concrete form. Read, again, instructions for using the subconscious mind, in the chapter on Auto-Suggestion. Make your images holographic, present tense, real, excited, colorful, loud, moving, and extreme.

Enter into the fantasy… This is the language the subconscious vibes with…

Another feature of the subconscious mind is that it is the individualization of the creative intelligence in the human animal. (Actually, all creatures, but our discussion here is limited to the human animal.)

The subconscious of every individual is connected by *being* Infinite Intelligence. It's a spiritual realm, in which you interact with the subconscious of every other individual, force and item in creation. Your subconscious affects all things through the law of vibration and attraction (otherwise known as electricity and magnetism). As well, it is affected by the spiritual dimension of all things and organisms… according to its wavelength. Just like *x-rays* and magnets only interact with other items on their vibrational wavelength.

These are scientific facts in the New Millennium still not realized by staid institutions and the masses, consciously deployed by achievers in this new age.

There is plenty of evidence to support the contention that the subconscious mind is the connecting link between the finite mind of man and Infinite Intelligence. It is the intermediary through which one may draw upon the forces of Infinite Intelligence at will. It alone contains the secret process by which mental impulses are modified and projected into their spiritual equivalent. It alone is the medium through which prayer may be transmitted to the source capable of answering prayer. As well, it is the medium through which answers, ideas, plans, and motivations arrive and play before you from Infinite Intelligence.

The Human Body Metaphor

Here's a workable metaphor… We are, each of us, complex cells in a larger being. Just as, in the human being, a burn on the leg or a cut on the arm draws an immediate response from the whole organism – meaning you may stop, hold the wound, jump up and down, faint, and a host of other possibilities. As well, the body consciousness dispatches a whole army of white blood cells autonomically hustling in a predictable response to fight infection.

In the same way, a call in one sector of Infinite Intelligence marshals and sends from the greater resources of the holobody, all things needful to satisfy whatever demand arises.

Deepak Chopra speaks of this reality…

> This lump of flesh and bones is not your body… This limited personality you experience is not your self. Your body is actually infinite and one with the Universe. Your spirit encompasses all spirits and has no limit in time or space.

The NEW Think And Grow Rich presents the science of harnessing that phenomenon to practical ends, transmuting desire into money.

BONUS! 3 FREE Wealth-Building Gifts Worth $97 at HoloMagic.com

Staggering To Imagine!

The possibilities of creative effort connected with the subconscious mind are stupendous and imponderable. They inspire one with awe.

I never approach the discussion of the subconscious mind without a feeling of littleness and inferiority due, perhaps, to the fact that humanity's entire stock of knowledge on this subject is so pitifully limited.

The very fact that *the subconscious mind is the connecting link, the medium and channel of communication between the thinking mind of man and Infinite Intelligence,* is of itself, a thought that almost blows one's circuits!

The Raw Material

After you have accepted, as a reality, the existence of the subconscious mind, and understand its possibilities as a medium for transmuting your *desires* into their physical or monetary equivalent, you comprehend the full significance of the instructions given in the chapters on *Desire, Faith,* and *Auto-Suggestion.*

It is the way of the initiate…

You also understand why you have been repeatedly admonished to *make your desires clear, and to reduce them to writing.* You also understand the necessity of *persistence* in carrying out instructions.

The subconscious mind is just a tool to manifest your currently dominant thought or image. It works all the time. It cannot *not* work. Through its magic interaction with the HoloCosm it reflects in your experience the issues of your mind and heart.

Therefore it becomes of stunning importance in the process of transmuting desire into money that you give your subconscious and the HoloCosm specific instructions and holoimages of the fulfillment you would have…

BONUS! 3 FREE Wealth-Building Gifts Worth $97 at HoloMagic.com

It's almost as if your subconscious is a computer. The computer is just a tool… It does what it's told to do. It processes whatever data or input it gets…Without discrimination. Whatever you feed it, it manifests.

The discrimination comes from a higher level, above that of the tool of the computer or the subconscious.

It works as surely with images of squalor and "barely getting by" as it does with abundance.

Everything Goes Subconscious

The thirteen principles are the stimuli with which you acquire the ability to reach and to influence your subconscious mind. Do not become discouraged, if you cannot do this upon the first attempt. Remember that the subconscious mind may be voluntarily directed only through habit, under the directions given in the chapter on *Faith*. You have not yet had time to master faith. Be patient. Be persistent.

It requires consciousness to start to be effective, and it requires conscientious practice and effort to gain the skill on demand.

A good many statements in the chapters on Faith and Auto-Suggestion are repeated here, for the benefit of your subconscious mind. Remember, your subconscious mind functions voluntarily, whether you make any effort to influence it or not. This naturally suggests to you that thoughts of fear and poverty, and all negative thoughts, serve as stimuli to your subconscious mind, unless you master these impulses and give it more desirable food upon which it may feed.

This is a recognition that places tremendous responsibility on your shoulders. Knowing how the process works gives you absolute freedom to pick and make your life to order! It really is that serious.

BONUS! 3 FREE Wealth-Building Gifts Worth $97 at HoloMagic.com

The subconscious mind does not remain idle! If you fail to plant consistently positive and intentful *desires* in your subconscious mind, it feeds upon the thoughts that reach it as the result of your neglect. That could mean the media, politicians with an agenda, and negative victim friends are feeding your mind.

Which do you believe is more conducive to your financial wellbeing?

Manage Your Mind

We have already explained that thought impulses, both negative and positive, are reaching the subconscious mind continuously, from the sources mentioned in the chapter on Passion.

For the present, it is sufficient if you remember that you are living daily in the midst of all manner of thought impulses, which are reaching your subconscious mind without your knowledge. Some of these impulses are negative, some are positive.

You are now engaged in trying to restrict and manage the flow of negative impulses, and to voluntarily influence your subconscious mind through positive images and impulses associated with your *desire*.

When you achieve this, you possess the key that unlocks the door to your subconscious mind and all manner of manifestation. Moreover, you control that door so completely, that no undesirable thought may influence your subconscious mind. You have risen to Master of your Soul, creator of your destiny.

The Prime Mover

Everything the individual creates *begins* in the form of a thought impulse. No person can create anything that is not first conceived in *thought*.

All Things Work Together

Through the aid of the imagination, *desire* – thought impulse – may be assembled into plans. The imagination, when under control, may be used for the creation of plans or purposes that lead to success in one's chosen occupation.

All thought impulses intended for transmutation into their physical equivalent, voluntarily planted in the subconscious mind, must pass through the imagination and be mixed with faith. The mixing of faith with a plan or purpose intended for submission to the subconscious mind may be done *only* through the imagination.

From these statements, you will readily observe that voluntary use of the subconscious mind calls for coordination and application of all the principles.

Thoughts Are Things

Ella Wheeler Wilcox gave evidence of her understanding of the power of the subconscious mind when she wrote:

> *You never can tell what a thought will do*
> *In bringing you hate or love*
> *For thoughts are things, and their airy wings*
> *Are swifter than carrier doves.*
> *They follow the law of the Universe –*
> *Each thing creates its kind,*
> *And they speed o'er the track to bring you back*
> *Whatever went out from your mind.*

Wilcox understood the truth that thoughts which go out from one's mind also imbed themselves deeply in one's subconscious mind, where they serve as a magnet, pattern, or blueprint by which the subconscious mind in an interactive dance with the HoloCosm translates them into their physical equivalent.

Thoughts are truly things, for the reason that every material thing begins in the form of thought-energy.

Impact Created By *Emotion*

The subconscious mind is more susceptible to influence by impulses of thought mixed with "feeling" or emotion, than by those originating solely in the reasoning portion of the mind. In fact, there is much evidence to support the theory that *only* emotionalized thoughts have any *action influence* upon the subconscious mind.

It is a well-known fact that emotion, or feeling, rules the majority of people. If it is true that the subconscious mind responds more quickly to, and is influenced more readily by thought impulses well mixed with emotion, it is essential to become familiar with the more important of the emotions.

Therefore, the vital importance of communicating to your subconscious in holoimages of the *Vakogëm* kind.

Inject The Positives

There are seven major positive emotions and seven major negative emotions. The negatives voluntarily inject themselves into the thought impulses, which insure passage into the subconscious mind. The positives must be injected, through the principle of auto-suggestion, into the thought impulses which an individual wishes to pass on to his or her subconscious mind.

These emotions, or feeling impulses, may be likened to yeast in a loaf of bread, because they constitute the *action* element which transforms thought impulses from the passive to the active state. Thus may one understand why thought impulses, which have been well mixed with emotion, are acted upon more readily than thought impulses originating in "cold reason."

You are preparing yourself to influence and control the "inner audience" of your subconscious mind, in order to hand over to it the *desire* for money, which you wish transmuted into its monetary equivalent. It is essential, therefore, that you understand the method of approach to this "inner audience." You must speak its language, or it will not heed your call. It understands best the language of emotion or feeling.

Let us, therefore, describe here the seven major positive emotions and the seven major negative emotions, so that you may draw upon the positives and avoid the negatives when giving images, affirmations, and instructions to your subconscious mind.

It's like the lyrics of the Harold Arlen song Johnny Mercer sings so well, "You've got to accentuate the positive, eliminate the negative, latch on to the affirmative, and don't mess with Mr. In Between."

The Seven Major Positive Emotions

These are the positive emotions you foster in your life and affairs...

1. *Desire*
2. *Faith*
3. *Love*
4. *Sex*
5. *Enthusiasm*
6. *Romance*
7. *Hope*

There are other positive emotions, but these are the seven most powerful, and the ones most commonly used in creative effort.

BONUS! 3 FREE Wealth-Building Gifts Worth $97 at HoloMagic.com

Master these seven emotions (they can be mastered only by *use*) and the other positive emotions will be at your command when you need them.

Remember, in this connection, that you are studying a book which is intended to help you develop a "money consciousness" by filling your mind with positive emotions. It wouldn't make sense, fitting yourself to become money conscious, to go filling your mind with negative emotions. That is *not* the plan.

The Seven Major Negative Emotions

That being said, here's a rundown of the seven major negative emotions you must avoid like the plague. That others indulge them is of no consequence to you. You are on a totally different agenda, consciously using the emotions and the subconscious to sow and reap positive results in your life, transmuting desire into money.

Others have the delusional luxury of blaming Fate, circumstance, and others for their bad positions, for all the good it does them…

But you know we all create our own circumstances.

These primary emotions are…

1. *Fear*
2. *Jealousy*
3. *Hatred*
4. *Revenge*
5. *Greed*
6. *Superstition*
7. Anger

There are others, but this is not a negative things class. These are sufficient for the day and the destruction that they wreak.

The Pivot

Positive and negative emotions cannot occupy the mind at the same time. One or the other must dominate. This is your point of liberation!

This gives you the opportunity to *ensure* **that positive emotions constitute the dominating influence of your mind**.

Your Habits Are Your Life

Here the law of *habit* will come to your aid. Form the habit of applying and using the positive emotions!

Consciously and with forethought begin to practice the specific positive emotions that lead to your fulfillment. Reframe every happening into a life-affirming, empowering event. Eventually, the positive emotions dominate your mind so completely that the negatives cannot enter it. Celebrate that day, because your riches are already on their way!

Operator Alert!

There is something you should know...

- Only by following these instructions literally, consciously, and continuously can you gain control over your subconscious mind.

- The presence of a single lurking negative is sufficient to destroy all chances of constructive aid from your subconscious mind.

Let's consider a common manifestation of this self-sabotage...

Why Most Prayer Doesn't Work

If you are an observing person, you must have noticed that most people resort to prayer *only* after everything else has *failed!* Or else they pray by a ritual of meaningless words. And, because it is a fact that most people who pray, do so *only after everything else has failed*, they go to prayer with their minds filled with *fear* and *doubt,* which are the emotions the subconscious mind picks up on, and passes on to Infinite Intelligence. Likewise, that is the emotion which Infinite Intelligence receives and *acts upon.*

If you pray for something, but have fear as you pray that you may not receive it, or that your prayer will not be acted upon by Infinite Intelligence, your prayer will have been in vain.

Even worse – remember, what you think about you bring about – you will find yourself in the same situation as the ancient God-fearing character, Job, who wailed, "What I feared has come upon me!"

Those "fears" were *emotionalized thoughts* – the *wrong* emotion. They work the same for everybody, God-fearing or not. The subconscious delivers according to your emotionalized thoughts, good or bad. What you are emotionally attached to – be it ill or weal – is that which Infinite Intelligence mirrors back to you.

It's a metaphysical Universe – the laws of mind are exact, under every circumstance.

Prayer does, sometimes, result in the realization of that for which one prays. If you have ever had the experience of receiving that for which you prayed, go back in your memory, and recall your actual *state of mind* while you were praying, and you will know, for sure, that the theory here described is more than a theory.

Scientific Prayer

Already various schools, educational organizations, and developed churches teach the "science of prayer," though, indeed, this concept still is little accepted by mainstream, institutional, foot-in-the-past religion.

Indeed, this is the promise of the New Millennium. Witness for a starter, Ernest Holmes' classic, *Science Of Mind*. The level of consciousness of humanity is rising rapidly. One day soon no one will approach Universal Mind in a state of fear, for the very good reason that there will be no such emotion as fear.

Ignorance, superstition, and false teaching will have disappeared, and humanity will have risen to its true status as a child of Infinite Intelligence. A few have already attained this blessing. But you can't see them – because they look like ordinary people.

If you have further interest in this elevated relationship with Infinite Intelligence, just put your antennae up, and broadcast your interest. Advocates of the science will see you and respond.

If you believe this prophecy is far-fetched, take a look at the human race in retrospect. Less than 200 years ago, we believed lightning to be evidence of the wrath of God, and feared it. Now, thanks to the power of *faith*, we have harnessed lightning and made it turn the wheels of industry and stimulate the flow of electrons through the Internet.

Not much more than 100 years ago, we believed the space between the planets to be nothing but a great void, a stretch of dead nothingness. Now, thanks to this same power of *faith*, we know that far from being either dead or a void, the space between the planets is very much alive, that it is one of the highest forms of vibration known, excepting, perhaps, the vibration of *thought*.

Moreover, we know that this living, pulsating, vibratory energy that permeates every atom of matter and fills every niche of space connects every human brain with every other human brain and with Infinite Intelligence.

A Club So Exclusive You Can't Buy Your Way In

There are no tollgates between the finite human mind and Infinite Intelligence. The communication costs nothing except patience, faith, persistence, understanding, and a *sincere desire* to communicate.

Moreover, the approach can be made only by the individual them self. Paid prayers are worthless. Infinite Intelligence does no business by proxy. You either go direct, or you do not go.

You may buy prayer books and repeat them until the day of your doom, without avail. Thoughts that you wish to communicate to Infinite Intelligence must undergo transformation, such as can be given only through your own subconscious mind.

The Radio Metaphor

The method by which you communicate with Infinite Intelligence is very similar to that through which the vibration of sound is communicated by radio. If you understand the working principle of radio, you know that sound cannot be communicated through the Cosmos until it has been "stepped up," or changed into a rate of vibration which the human ear cannot detect.

The radio broadcasting station steps up the vibration millions of times. Only in this way can the vibration of sound be communicated through the Cosmos.

After this transformation has taken place, the cosmic waves pick up and carry the energy (which originally was in the form of vibrations of sound within the human range) to radio receiving sets, and these receiving sets step down that energy, back to its original rate of vibration, so it is recognized as sound.

In the same manner, the subconscious mind is the intermediary which steps up your prayers into terms which Infinite Intelligence can recognize, presents the message, and brings back the answer, stepping it down in the form of a definite plan, idea, meeting, or circumstance for procuring the object of your prayer.

Your Reward Is The Riches You Seek

Understand this principle, and you will know why mere words read from a prayer book cannot, and will never serve as an agency of communication between the mind of man and Infinite Intelligence.

Before your prayer will reach Infinite Intelligence, it must be transformed from its original *thought* vibration into *spiritual* vibration.

Faith is the only known agency that gives your thoughts a spiritual nature. *Faith* and *fear* make poor bedfellows. Where one is found, the other cannot exist.

Your discipline is to design and direct your thoughts – your reward is the riches you seek. Your subconscious happens in between.

THE BRAIN
BROADCASTING AND RECEIVING
STATION FOR THOUGHT

THE TWELFTH STEP TOWARD RICHES

chapter 12 ☞ The brain interpenetrates all the other twelve principles of this holographic wealth philosophy.

In the dawning years of the twentieth century the author, working in conjunction with the late Dr. Alexander Graham Bell and Dr. Elmer R. Gates, observed that every human brain is both a broadcasting and receiving station for the vibration of thought.

Through the medium of the Cosmos, in a fashion similar to that which the radio broadcasting and receiving phenomenon advantages… Every human brain is *capable* of both transmitting and of receiving vibrations of thought, which are being released by other brains or the HoloCosm itself (although all things happen *within* the HoloCosm, of course).

Note the emphasis on the word *capable*. Because every human brain is *capable* doesn't mean every human exercises this option. For most people it's just an accidental breakthrough from the other realms, from time to time. Obviously – in the very fact you find yourself this deeply involved in this book this moment – you have already far distanced yourself from the maddening crowd.

There are techniques that give you the power to *consciously with fore-sight and design, use and benefit from* these overwhelming insights, and they are described completely in this present treatise, *The NEW Think And Grow Rich*.

How It Works

The creative imagination is the aspect of the brain-mind continuum that is the "receiving set" of the brain. It receives thoughts. It is the agency of communication between the four sources from which one may receive thought stimuli and your conscious or reasoning mind.

By way of quick summary, those four sources are....

1.   Consciously from other people

2.   Your own subconscious

3.   Subconsciously from other people

4.   Infinite Intelligence

When stimulated, or "stepped up" to a high rate of vibration, the mind becomes more receptive to the vibration of thought which reaches it through the Cosmos from outside sources. This "stepping up" process takes place through the positive emotions, or the negative emotions. Through the emotions, the vibrations of thought may be increased.

Your transmissions are also stronger, clearer, and more effective, with less interference, when you mind is stimulated. Vibrations of an exceed-ingly high rate are the only vibrations picked up and carried, by the Cosmos, from one's brain to another source. Thought is energy traveling at an exceedingly high rate of vibration. Thought that has been modified or "stepped up" by any of the major emotions vibrates at a much higher rate than ordinary thought, and it is this type of thought that transmits its electro-magnetic waves throughout the HoloCosm.

Have You Ever Been So Intensely Sexually Involved You "Forgot" *Yourself?*

The emotion of sex stands at the head of the list of human emotions, as far as intensity and driving force are concerned. The brain which has been stimulated by the emotion of sex, vibrates at a much more rapid rate than it does when that emotion is quiescent or absent.

The result of passion is the increase of the rate of vibration of thoughts to such a pitch that the creative imagination becomes highly receptive to ideas transmitted both from others' brains as well as, *Infinite Intelligence* itself, which it picks up from the Cosmos.

Further, when the brain is vibrating at a rapid rate, it not only attracts thoughts and ideas released by other brains through the medium of the Cosmos, but it gives to one's own thoughts that "feeling" which is essential before those thoughts are picked up and acted upon by your own subconscious mind, by the subconscious minds of others, and the HoloCosm.

Amp Up Your Broadcasting Station For Spectacular Results

An important point of control and power is the factor through which you mix feeling, or emotion, with your thoughts and pass them on to your subconscious mind.

The subconscious mind then becomes the "sending station" of the brain, through which vibrations of thought are broadcast.

The creative imagination is the "receiving set," through which the vibrations of thought are picked up from the Cosmos.

BONUS! 3 FREE Wealth-Building Gifts Worth $97 at HoloMagic.com

Both of these domains are interlaced with the activity of your brain. *Direct your mind.*

Along with the important factors of the subconscious mind and the faculty of the creative imagination, which constitute the sending and receiving sets of your mental broadcasting machinery, consider now the principle of auto-suggestion, which is the medium by which you may put into operation your "broadcasting" station.

Through the instructions described in the chapter on Auto-Suggestion, you were definitely informed of the method by which *desire* may be transmuted into its monetary equivalent. To thumbnail it… *Dive passionately into* the images of fulfillment *of your definite chief aim* a la *Vakogëm.*

The technical operation of your mental "broadcasting" station is a comparatively simple procedure. You have three principles to bear in mind and to apply when you wish to use your broadcasting station: the *Subconscious Mind, Creative Imagination, and Auto-Suggestion.*

The catalytic factor is the *intensity* of emotion you direct into your intended outcomes, plus the *faith* you have that you *will* achieve your definite chief aim. Therefore, we use words like *passion* to reveal the route. Words like *determination, obsession, willpower,* and *steel* to express your will. The stimuli through which you put these three principles into action have been fully described – the procedure begins with *desire.* Amplify your desire.

The Greatest Forces Are "Intangible"

Through the dark ages which have passed, humankind has depended too much upon the physical senses, and has limited the pursuit of knowledge to physical things, which we could see, touch, weigh, and measure.

But there's light coming from the East. Not to trivialize what we're speaking of… Quoting the words of a popular hit song some years back,

BONUS! 3 FREE Wealth-Building Gifts Worth $97 at HoloMagic.com

this is the "Age of Aquarius," the most marvelous of all ages – an age in which flowers an appreciation, understanding, and use of the intangible forces of the world about us. More and more grasp it daily, as we pass through this age: the "other self" is more powerful than the physical self we see when we look into a mirror.

The consciousness of the human race will reach a critical mass, and this level will generally be more available to all. But for the exceptional, it's available now. *You are a leading light.*

There's a long continuum between the physical self, the soul that carries the impress of your experiences and desires, the connection point, called your Higher Self, and Infinite Intelligence. And that, as many of the prophets, wise men, and poets have told us, can be harnessed to benefit ourselves – with the one proviso we ourselves enrichen in the same degree we enrich others.

"Forgive Them"

Sometimes people speak lightly of the intangibles, the things that they cannot perceive through the five senses. *Talk about a reframe from error into light!* When we hear them, it should *remind us* that all of us are controlled by forces which are unseen and intangible.

We Are Not "Above" The Laws Of Nature – We Are *Nature Manifest!*

The whole of humankind has not the power to cope with, nor to control the colossal intangible force wrapped in the rolling waves of the oceans.

Humanity doesn't have the capacity to understand the intangible force of gravity, which keeps this little Earth suspended in mid-air, and keeps humans from falling off of it, much less the power to control that force.

BONUS! 3 FREE Wealth-Building Gifts Worth $97 at HoloMagic.com

We are entirely subservient to the intangible force that comes with a thunderstorm and its evil sister, the tornado.

And we are just as helpless in the presence of the intangible force of electricity. Even after over 200 years, we still do not even know what electricity is, where it comes from, or what its purpose is!

Nor is this by any means the extent of humanity's ignorance in connection with things unseen and intangible.

For all the good thousands upon thousands of researchers, chemists, botanists, alchemists, and other scientists working on it have done, we still do not understand the intangible force and intelligence wrapped up in the soil of the Earth – the force which provides humanity with every morsel of food we eat, every article of clothing we wear, every dollar we carry in our pockets.

Nor, of course, with all the bruited accolades the "name" hospitals and research facilities genuinely deserve, have they pulled the trick of initiating and sustaining cellular, animal, or human life.

"Life" is the province of the Gods...

Last, but not least, humanity, with all its boasted culture and education, understands little or nothing of the intangible force, the greatest of all the intangibles, of *thought*. **Humanity knows little concerning the physical brain, and its vast network of intricate machinery through which the power of thought is translated into its material equivalent.**

The Incredible Complexity Of The Human Brain

But humanity is now entering an age that shall yield enlightenment on the subject. Already science has turned their attention to the study of this stupendous thing called a brain, and, while they are still in the kindergarten stage of their studies, they have uncovered enough knowledge to know that the central switchboard of the human brain, the number of lines which connect the brain cells one with another, equals the figure one, followed by *millions* of zeros!!

"The figure is so stupendous," said Dr. C. Judson Herrick, of the University of Chicago, "that astronomical figures dealing with hundreds of millions of light years, become insignificant by comparison. It has been determined that there are [billions of] nerve cells in the human cerebral cortex, and we know that these are arranged in definite patterns. These arrangements are not haphazard. They are orderly.

The brain contains more than 100 billion nerve cells, *each* of which connects with as many as 10,000 other neurons in an infinitely complex network of nerve processes.

This complex network exceeds the sole purpose of carrying on the physical functions incidental to growth and maintenance of the physical body.

The Media Of Communication

In this cosmic soup, *everything* is in intercommunication with everything else…

> This same system, which gives billions of brain cells the media for communication one with another, which interconnects billons of stars in a single galaxy… with billions of dancing galaxies to choose from, provides, also, the means of communication with other intangible forces.

Thought, thoughts of others, the subconscious, and Infinite Intelligence are *meant* to be in the domain of our human experience. It just doesn't happen in the 10% realm. Even when it does, it's a unique, non-repeatable breakthrough experience.

BONUS! 3 FREE Wealth-Building Gifts Worth $97 at HoloMagic.com

You've been given the keys throughout this book to consciously access that vast 90% brain reservoir few people dare tread…To get inspiration, motivation, ideas, plans, resources, associations – you'll be in good company with the world's leading thinkers, inventors, motivators, governors, businessmen, mystics, poets, and artists.

To See The End In The Beginning
Rhine Into Quantum

After the first version of this book had been written, just before the manuscript went to the publisher, there appeared in the *New York Times*, an editorial showing that at least one great university, and one intelligent investigator in the field of mental phenomena, are carrying on an organized research through which conclusions have been reached that parallel many of those described in this and the following chapter.

At the time, I celebrated the appearance of this reputable reference to what to many seemed "out there" conversation. There's been a *lot* of progress over the ensuing decades… Rhine was right, of course. Following in the tradition, famed researchers have led the way into the HoloGraphic Universe and Quantum reality, and given substantiation and explanations that never existed before. It's all the same, Rhine into Quantum – **normal reality is so stupendous it's *paranormal!***

Don't be fooled by appearances of discrete, fragmented separateness…

What you aim to do through the means of this philosophy is of the paranormal level, also. The proper term for it is *psychokinesis* – the movement of *matter* by *mind*. Of course, if, as scientists tell us, all is just a form of vibration, the mystics agree thousands years, hence… We each are participating in the cosmic soup in accord with definite rules…

BONUS! 3 FREE Wealth-Building Gifts Worth $97 at HoloMagic.com

You do have the ability to manifest the reality of wealth through the same mysterious channels Nature uses…. *Realize, you* are *Nature!* If you choose it. *Vibration.*

For some it comes quickly, intuitively, in early sync… For others it comes neither quick nor intuitively… And for others, not quick, but intuitively after all. For all who follow this philosophy, it *does* come.

The following is a reprint of that brief editorial analyzing the work carried on by Dr. Rhine and his associates at Duke University….

"What is 'Telepathy'?

A month ago we cited on this page some of the remarkable results achieved by Professor Rhine and his associates in Duke University from more than a hundred thousand tests to determine the existence of 'telepathy' and 'clairvoyance.' These results were summarized in the first two articles in *Harpers Magazine.* In the second, which has now appeared, the author, E. H. Wright, attempts to summarize what has been learned, or what it seems reasonable to infer, regarding the exact nature of these 'extrasensory' modes of perception.

The actual existence of telepathy and clairvoyance now seems to some scientists enormously probable as the result of Rhine's experiments. Various percipients were asked to name as many cards in a special pack as they could without looking at them and without other sensory access to them. About a score of men and women were discovered who could regularly name so many of the cards correctly that 'there was not one chance in many a million of their having done their feats by luck or accident.'

But how did they do them? These powers, assuming that they exist, do not seem to be sensory. There is no known organ for them. The experiments worked just as well at distances of several hundred miles as they did in the same room. These facts also dispose, in Mr. Wright's opinion, of the attempt to explain telepathy or clairvoyance through any physical theory of radiation. All known forms of radiant energy decline inversely as the square of the distance traversed. Telepathy and clairvoyance do not. But they do vary through physical causes as our other mental powers do. Contrary to widespread opinion, they do not improve when the percipient is asleep or half-asleep, but on the contrary, when he is most wide-awake and alert. Rhine discovered that a narcotic will invariably lower a percipient's score, while a stimulant will always send it higher. The most reliable performer apparently cannot make a good score unless he tries to do his best.

One conclusion that Wright draws with some confidence is that telepathy and clairvoyance are really one and the same gift. That is, the faculty that 'sees' a card face down on a table seems to be exactly the same one that 'reads' a thought residing only in another mind. There are several grounds for believing this. So far, for example, the two gifts have been found in every person who enjoys either of them. In every one so far, the two have been of equal vigor, almost exactly. Screens, walls, distances, have no effect at all on either.

Wright advances from this conclusion to express what he puts forward is no more than the mere 'hunch' that other extra-sensory experiences, prophetic dreams, premonitions of disaster [intuitions, psychokinesis] and the like, may also prove to be part of the same faculty. The reader is not asked to accept any of these conclusions unless he finds it necessary, but the evidence that Rhine has piled up must remain impressive.

How To Stimulate Your Mind To Quantum Levels

My associates and I have discovered what we believe to be an ideal condition under which the mind can be stimulated so that thought can be transmitted to the Cosmos – *to have an effect* –that the thoughts of others and impressions from the Cosmos can be received.

It's an easy entry into the HoloGraphic Universe. An advanced technique comes in chapter thirteen.

The conditions to which I refer, consist of a close working alliance between myself and two members of my staff. Through experimentation and practice, we have discovered how to stimulate our minds so that we can, by a process of blending our three minds into one, find the solution to a great variety of personal, business, and governmental problems which are submitted by my clients.

The procedure is simple. We sit down at a conference table, focus with a brief invocation, clearly state the nature of the problem we have under consideration, drop into a four minute music-guided meditation, return to consciousness, then begin discussing it.

It is not improper here to introduce again the idea that your sexually switched on thoughts and motivations both bring to and allow you to take from the MasterMind the greatest contributions. In other words, *not* that you entertain nor act out any sexual attraction with your working partners… but that you, yourself, are charged with vitality and life force. Review again chapter ten on Passion, if you have any questions about what we recommend.

Each contributes whatever thoughts may occur. You get a kool feeling and enter a new level quite effortlessly with this method of mind stimulation – it places each participant in communication with unknown sources of knowledge definitely outside your own experience.

BONUS! 3 FREE Wealth-Building Gifts Worth $97 at HoloMagic.com

If you understand the principle described in the chapter on the MasterMind, you, of course, recognize the round-table procedure here described as being a practical application of the MasterMind.

This method of mind stimulation, through harmonious discussion of definite subjects between three people, illustrates the simplest and most practical use of the MasterMind.

Participation in an *effective* MasterMind always steps up your vibes and puts you into the realm where you can both broadcast into and receive from the great HoloCosm.

> *By adopting and following a similar plan you may come into*
> *possession of the famous Carnegie secret briefly alluded to*
> *in the introduction.*

If it means nothing to you at this time, mark this page and read it again after you have reread this holobook a few times... You'll be amazed at the difference in meaning! It won't be because the *words* have changed, but because *you* have. That noticeable change is a demonstration of your increasing power...

You're about to leap to another level...

THE SIXTH SENSE
INFINITE INTELLIGENCE CONTACTS YOU
– INSPIRATION AND SYNCHRONICITY

chapter 13 ⌾ The "thirteenth" principle is known as the *sixth sense*. The sixth sense is the "receiving set" from Infinite Intelligence through which ideas, plans, and thoughts flash into the mind. The "flashes" are sometimes called "hunches," "inspirations," or "intuition."

The sixth sense operates in that portion of the subconscious mind, which has been referred to as the creative imagination.

The broadcasting station of the brain touches the subconscious, which contacts or stimulates the HoloCosm.

The *sixth sense* is when communication comes the other way, from Infinite Intelligence to the individual. This communication comes without any effort from, or demands by, the individual.

Make no mistake, all the principles in this book, but especially the last two we've discussed, the *subconscious* and the *brain*, lead you to where you can actually work the HoloCosm on your own behalf.

That is, you can intentionally contact Infinite Intelligence, usually through some form of meditation, and receive replies, usually in the sixth sense state of meditation itself, in a hunch, inspiration, idea, or plan that strikes you, or in a synchronicity that occurs in your life.

This principle still seems "*way* out there" for some people. That's a shame. Holding outdated training or preconceived notions that prohibit one from looking closely at and learning how to cooperate with *huge* forces is a serious mistake.

You are, after all, presumably reading this book to get rich, and the great achievers of all time have been those who discovered how to use and be used by the great Infinite Intelligence, the *HoloCosm*.

This principle is the apex of *The NEW Think And Grow Rich* philosophy. It can be assimilated, understood, employed, and benefited from *only* by first mastering the other twelve principles.

While the HoloCosm can't be *forced* to yield its answers, guidance, introductions, and opportunities, it doesn't have to be by chance, either. We have the ability to proactively stimulate the HoloCosm, creating conditions favorable for a reply. It is the nature of the HoloCosm to respond in kind. If you aspire to the genius state, you'll want to learn to operate this amazing force to your wellbeing, also.

The Miracles Of The Sixth Sense

The sixth sense defies easy description. It cannot be described to a person who has not mastered the other principles of this philosophy, because such a person has no knowledge, and no experience with which the sixth sense may be compared. Understanding of the sixth sense comes only by meditation, through mind development from within.

The sixth sense is the medium of contact Infinite Intelligence uses to communicate with the finite mind of man. For this reason, it is a mixture of both the mental and the spiritual. It is the point at which the Universal Mind contacts the individuated human mind.

After you have mastered the principles described in this book, you will be prepared to accept as truth a statement which may, otherwise, be incredible to you, namely...

> Through the aid of the sixth sense, you are warned of impending dangers in time to avoid them, and notified of opportunities in time to embrace them. You are given inspired ideas, plans, and determinations you can use to become wealthy.

> Through the aid of synchronicity, a function of the sixth sense, without your volitional effort, you are guided to meet the people who can further your success, encounter the books and seminars that pole vault your progress, and receive messages and directions from the Cosmic in the smallest things – like a billboard alongside the highway, or a few choice words on a TV program you catch as you pass through the mini-mart.

There comes to your aid, and to do your bidding, with the development of the sixth sense, a "guardian angel" who opens to you at all times the door to the Temple of Wisdom.

Whether or not these are statements of truth, you will never know, except by following the instructions described in the pages of this book, or some similar method of procedure.

The authors are neither believers in, nor advocates of "miracles," for the reason they have enough knowledge of Nature to understand that Nature never deviates from her established laws. Some of her laws are so incomprehensible they produce what appear to be "miracles."

To Move The HoloCosm

The reality of a "sixth sense" has been well established. This sixth sense speaks to you through creative imagination. The faculty of creative

BONUS! 3 FREE Wealth-Building Gifts Worth $97 at HoloMagic.com

imagination is one the majority of people never use during an entire lifetime, and if used at all, it usually happens by mere accident.

A relatively small number of people use, *with deliberation and purposeful planning*, the faculty of creative imagination. Those who use this faculty voluntarily, and with understanding of its functions, are *genii*.

This is your call, right now, to join this group, and to harness the powerful drivers of the sixth sense to your own road to riches. This chapter contains all you need to know.

The faculty of creative imagination is the direct link between Infinite Intelligence and the finite human mind. All so-called revelations, referred to in the realm of religion, and all discoveries of basic or new principles in the field of invention, take place through the faculty of creative imagination. Inspired literature and art enters under this same cover.

When ideas or concepts flash into one's mind, through what is popularly called a "hunch," they come from one or more of the following sources:

1.   Infinite Intelligence

2.   One's subconscious mind, wherein is stored every sense impression and thought impulse which has ever reached the brain through any of the five senses

3.   From the mind of some other person who has just released the thought, or picture of the idea or concept, through conscious thought, or

4.   From another person's subconscious storehouse

There are no other *known* sources from which "inspired" ideas or "hunches" may be received.

Above The Horizon

The creative imagination functions best when the mind is vibrating (due to some form of mind stimulation) at an exceedingly high rate. That is, when the mind is functioning at a rate of vibration higher than that of ordinary, normal thought.

When brain action has been stimulated, through one or more of the ten mind stimulants, perhaps with a period of meditation, it has the effect of lifting the individual far above the horizon of ordinary thought, and permits him or her to envision distance, scope, and quality of *thoughts* not available on the lower plane, such as that occupied while one is engaged in the solution of the problems of business and professional routine.

When lifted to this higher level of thought, through any form of mind stimulation, an individual occupies, relatively, the same position as one who has ascended in an airplane to a height from which he may see over and beyond the horizon line which limits his vision, while on the ground.

Moreover, while on this higher level of thought, the individual is not hampered or bound by any of the stimuli which circumscribe and limit his vision while wrestling with the problems of gaining the three basic necessities of food, clothing, and shelter. He is in a world of thought in which the *ordinary*, work-a-day thoughts have been as effectively removed as are the hills and valleys and other limitations of physical vision, when he rises in an airplane.

While on this exalted plane of *thought*, the creative faculty of the mind is given freedom for action. The way has been cleared for the sixth sense to function. It becomes receptive to ideas which could not reach the individual under any other circumstances.

The Difference That Makes The Difference

The "sixth sense" is the faculty that marks the difference between a genius and an ordinary.

The creative faculty becomes more alert and receptive to vibrations originating outside the individual's subconscious mind the more this faculty is used. There's also the factor of how much the individual relies upon and makes demands upon it for thought impulses. This faculty can be cultivated and developed only through use.

That which is known as one's "conscience" operates entirely through the faculty of the sixth sense.

The great artists, writers, musicians, and poets become great because they acquire the habit of relying upon the "still small voice" which speaks from within, through the faculty of creative imagination. It is a fact well known to people who have "keen" imaginations that their best ideas come through so-called "hunches."

Great Speeches From Great Connections

There is a great orator who does not attain to greatness until he closes his eyes and begins to rely entirely upon the faculty of creative imagination. When asked why he closed his eyes just before the climaxes of his oratory, he replied, "I do it because then I speak ideas which come to me from within."

Do not fail to notice the give and take. Proactively, the orator closes his eyes – to facilitate contact. Then *receives* the inspiration of the HoloCosm.

A Few Minutes' Meditation

One of America's most successful and best-known financiers followed the habit of closing his eyes for two or three minutes before making a decision.

When asked why he did this, he replied, "With my eyes closed, I am able to draw upon a source of superior intelligence."

These are forms of meditation, the conscious art of connecting with the Higher Power, to open the flow of Creative Intelligence.

Go Into Your Room

The late Dr. Elmer R. Gates, of Chevy Chase, Maryland, created more than 200 useful patents through the process of cultivating and using the creative faculty. His method is both significant and interesting to one interested in attaining to the status of genius, in which category Dr. Gates, unquestionably belonged. Dr. Gates was one of the really great, though less publicized scientists of the world.

In his laboratory, he had what he called his "personal communication room." It was practically sound proof, and so arranged that all light could be shut out. It was equipped with a small table, on which he kept a pad of writing paper. In front of the table, on the wall, was an electric pushbutton, which controlled the lights.

Dr Gates was *proactive* about stimulating communication from Infinite Intelligence. When Dr. Gates desired to draw upon the forces available to him through his creative imagination, he would go into this room, seat himself at the table, shut off the lights, and enter the alpha state. He would then *concentrate* upon the *known* factors of the invention on which he was working, remaining in that position until ideas began to "flash" into his mind in connection with the *unknown* factors of the invention.

Again you see a form of meditation in motion. Some people add candles, incense, music, water and crystals to facilitate contact, especially when they're in their own space.

On one occasion, ideas came through so fast that he was forced to write for almost three hours. When the thoughts stopped flowing, and he examined his notes, he found they contained a minute description of principles that had no parallel among the known data of the scientific world. Moreover, the answer to his problem was intelligently presented in those notes. In this manner Dr. Gates completed over 200 patents, which had been begun, but not completed, by "half-baked" brains. Evidence of the truth of this statement is in the United States Patent Office.

Dr. Gates earned his living by "sitting for ideas" for individuals and corporations. Some of the largest corporations in America paid him substantial fees, by the hour, for "sitting for ideas."

Inspired Ideas Are More Reliable

The reasoning faculty is often faulty, because it is largely guided by one's accumulated experience. Not all knowledge that one accumulates through "experience" is accurate. It's certainly limited! Ideas received through the creative faculty are much more reliable, for the reason that they come from sources more reliable than any which are available to the reasoning faculty of the mind.

The major difference between the genius and the ordinary "crank" inventor, may be found in the fact that the genius works through his faculty of creative imagination, while the "crank" knows nothing of this faculty. The scientific inventor (such as Mr. Edison and Dr. Gates) makes use of both the synthesizing and the creative faculties of imagination.

How To Work The HoloCosm

For example, the scientific inventor, or "genius," begins an invention by organizing and combining the known ideas, or principles accumulated through experience, through the synthesizing faculty (the reasoning faculty).

If he finds this accumulated knowledge to be insufficient for the completion of his invention, he then draws upon the sources of knowledge available to him through his creative faculty.

The method by which he does this varies with the individual, but this is the sum and substance of his procedure:

He stimulates his mind so that it vibrates on a higher-than-average plane, using one or more of the ten mind stimulants or some other stimulant of his choice.

He enters the alpha meditative state and concentrates upon the known factors (the finished part) of the invention, and creates in mind a perfect picture of the unknown factors (the unfinished part) of the invention.

He holds this picture in mind until it has been taken over by the subconscious mind, then relaxes and **clears his mind** of *all* thought.

And **waits** for the answer to "**flash**" into his mind.

Meditation – pure and simple. Meditation to stimulate Infinite Intelligence. Meditation in which you receive from the HoloCosm, in the form of an idea, angle, answer, action, plan, or synchronicity.

Results Not Always Instantaneous

Sometimes the results are both definite and immediate. At other times, the results are negative, depending upon the state of development of the "sixth sense," or creative faculty. Sometimes results are delayed… Or displayed so that only the hardy dare the attempt, like…

Mr. Edison tried out more than 10,000 different combinations of ideas through the synthesizing faculty of his imagination before he "tuned in" through the creative faculty and got the answer, which perfected the incandescent light. His synthesizing experience, of course, was fuel to guide the creative intelligence. His experience was similar when he produced the talking machine.

There is plenty of reliable evidence that the faculty of creative imagination exists. This evidence is available through accurate analysis of men and women who have become leaders in their respective callings, without having had extensive educations.

Lincoln was a notable example of a great leader who achieved greatness through the discovery and use of his faculty of creative imagination. He discovered and began to use this faculty as the result of the stimulation of love which he experienced after he met Anne Rutledge, a statement of the highest significance in connection with the study of the source of genius.

The HoloCosm: All Is One

Creative imagination comes as close to being a miracle, as anything most people have ever experienced, and it appears so only because it is a mighty force, mysterious in its operation.

This much the authors do know – that there is a power, or a first cause, or an intelligence, which permeates every atom of matter, and embraces every unit of energy perceptible to man – that this Infinite Intelligence converts acorns into oak trees, causes water to flow down hill in response to the law of gravity, follows night with day, and winter with summer, each maintaining its proper place and relationship to the other.

The power is all that there is, and all that exists, exists within it – like in some huge cosmic stew. *All* pieces are the stew – all pieces are affected by and affect, interdependently, all other pieces, making the stew, stew. This is the HoloCosm.

This Intelligence may, through the principles of this philosophy, be induced to aid in transmuting *desires* into concrete, or material form.

The authors have this knowledge, because they have discovered it in the lives of the most successful men and women.

The authors have this knowledge because they have been taken with the fascination of it, secured advanced training in it, experimented with it, and *experienced it.*

> This intelligence may, through the principles of this philosophy, be induced to aid in transmuting *desires* into concrete or material form.

Step by step, through the preceding chapters, you have been led to this, the last principle. If you have mastered each of the preceding principles, you are now prepared to accept, without being skeptical, the stupendous claims made here. If you have not mastered the other principles, you must do so before you may determine, definitely, whether or not the claims made in this chapter are fact or fiction.

Invisible Counselors

While I was passing through the age of "hero worship," I found myself trying to imitate those whom I most admired. Moreover, I discovered that the element of *faith,* with which I endeavored to imitate my idols, gave me great capacity to do so quite successfully.

I have never entirely divested myself of this habit of hero-worship, although I have passed the age commonly given over to such. My experience has taught me that the best way to become truly great is to emulate the great, by feeling and action, as nearly as possible.

This is called *modeling.*

Remember, though you can't force the HoloCosm to respond, any more than you can force the growth of a tree, you can contact the Holo-Cosm in such a way as to stimulate the response you desire. Both metaphysical processes, growth and thought, eventuate in material form.

Here I'll give you another method for contacting, harnessing, and directing Infinite Intelligence to do your bidding, and hint at the possibilities that can be yours.

BONUS! 3 FREE Wealth-Building Gifts Worth $97 at HoloMagic.com

Long before I had ever written a line for publication, or endeavored to deliver a speech in public, I followed the habit of reshaping my own character, by trying to imitate the nine men whose lives and life works had been most impressive to me. These nine men were, Emerson, Paine, Edison, Darwin, Lincoln, Burbank, Napoleon, Ford, and Carnegie. Every night, over a long period of years, I held an imaginary Council meeting with this group whom I called my "Invisible Counselors."

The procedure is this. Just before going to sleep at night, I shut my eyes and saw, in my imagination, this group of individuals seated with me around my Council Table. Here I had not only an opportunity to sit among those whom I considered to be great, but I actually dominated the group, by serving as the Chair.

I had a very *definite purpose* in indulging my imagination through these nightly meetings. My purpose was to rebuild my own character so it would represent a composite of the characters of my imaginary counselors. I was projecting an outcome. Realizing, as I did, early in life, that I had to overcome the handicap of birth in an environment of ignorance and superstition, I deliberately assigned myself the task of voluntary rebirth through the method here described.

A Mystical MasterMind

Being an earnest student of psychology, I knew, of course, that all individuals become what they are, because of their *dominating thoughts and desires.*

I knew that every deeply seated desire has the effect of causing one to seek outward expression through which that desire may be transmuted into reality. I knew that self-suggestion is a powerful factor in building character, that it is, in fact, the sole principle through which character is built.

With this knowledge of the principles of mind operation, I was fairly well armed with the equipment needed in rebuilding my character. In these imaginary Council meetings I called on my Cabinet members for the knowledge and qualities I wished each to contribute, addressing myself to each member in audible words, as follows…

> "Mr. Emerson, I desire to acquire from you the marvelous understanding of Nature which distinguished your life. I ask that you make an impression upon my subconscious mind of whatever qualities you possessed which enabled you to understand and adapt yourself to the Laws of Nature. I ask that you assist me in reaching and drawing upon whatever sources of knowledge are available to this end.

> "Mr. Burbank, I request that you pass on to me the knowledge which enabled you to so harmonize the Laws of Nature that you caused the cactus to shed its thorns, and become an edible food. Give me access to the knowledge which enabled you to make two blades of grass grow where one grew before, and helped you to blend the coloring of the flowers with more splendor and harmony, for you, alone, have successfully gilded the lily.

> "Napoleon, I desire to acquire from you, by emulation, the marvelous ability you possessed to inspire men, and to arouse them to greater and more determined spirit of action. Also to acquire the spirit of enduring *faith*, which enabled you to turn defeat into victory, and to surmount staggering obstacles. Emperor of Fate, King of Chance, Man of Destiny, I salute you!

> "Mr. Paine, I desire to acquire from you the freedom of thought and the courage and clarity with which to express convictions, which so distinguished you!

BONUS! 3 FREE Wealth-Building Gifts Worth $97 at HoloMagic.com

"Mr. Darwin, I wish to acquire from you the marvelous patience, and ability to study cause and effect, without bias or prejudice, so exemplified by you in the field of natural science.

"Mr. Lincoln, I desire to build into my own character the keen sense of justice, the untiring spirit of patience, the sense of humor, the human understanding, and the tolerance, which were your distinguishing characteristics.

"Mr. Carnegie, I am already indebted to you for my choice of a life work, which has brought me great happiness and peace of mind. I wish to acquire a thorough understanding of the principles of organized effort, which you used so effectively in the building of a great industrial enterprise.

"Mr. Ford, you have been among the most helpful of the men who have supplied much of the material essential to my work. I wish to acquire your spirit of persistence, the determination, poise, and self confidence which have enabled you to master poverty, organize, unify, and simplify human effort, so I may help others to follow in your footsteps.

"Mr. Edison, I have seated you nearest to me, at my right, because of the personal cooperation you have given me during my research into the causes of success and failure. I wish to acquire from you the marvelous spirit of *faith*, with which you have uncovered so many of Nature's secrets, the spirit of unremitting toil with which you have so often wrestled victory from defeat."

My method of addressing the members of the imaginary Cabinet would vary, according to the traits of character in which I was, for the moment,

most interested in acquiring. I studied the records of their lives with pains-
taking care. After some months of this nightly procedure, I was astounded
by the discovery that these imaginary figures became, apparently real.

The Plot Thickens

Each of these nine men developed individual characteristics, which
surprised me. For example, Lincoln developed the habit of always being
late, then walking around in solemn parade. When he came, he walked
very slowly, with his hands clasped behind him, and once in a while, he
would stop as he passed, and rest his hand, momentarily, upon my shoulder. He always wore an expression of seriousness upon his face. Rarely
did I see him smile. The cares of a sundered nation made him grave.

That was not true of the others. Burbank and Paine often indulged
in witty repartee, which seemed at times to shock the other members of
the cabinet. One night Paine suggested that I prepare a lecture on "The
Age of Reason," and deliver it from the pulpit of a church that I formerly
attended. Many around the table laughed heartily at the suggestion. Not
Napoleon! He drew his mouth down at the corners and groaned so
loudly that all turned and looked at him with amazement. To him the
church was a pawn of the State, not to be reformed, but to be used, as a
convenient inciter to mass activity by the people.

On one occasion Burbank was late. When he came, he was excited
with enthusiasm, and explained that he had been late, because of an experiment he was making, through which he hoped to be able to grow
apples on any sort of tree. Paine chided him by reminding him that it was
an apple that started all the trouble between man and woman. Darwin
chuckled heartily as he suggested that Paine should watch out for little
serpents, when he went into the forest to gather apples, as they had the

habit of growing into big snakes. Emerson observed, "No serpents, no apples," and Napoleon remarked, "No apples, no state!"

Lincoln developed the habit of always being the last one to leave the table after each meeting. On one occasion, he leaned across the end of the table with his arms folded, and remained in that position for many minutes. I made no attempt to disturb him. Finally, he lifted his head slowly, got up and walked to the door, then turned around, came back, and laid his hand on my shoulder and said, "My boy, you will need much courage if you remain steadfast in carrying out your purpose in life. But remember, when difficulties overtake you, the common people have common sense. Adversity will develop it."

This proved too true on more than one occasion in more than one lifetime.

Your Desires Serve As Magnets

One evening Edison arrived ahead of all the others. He walked over and seated himself at my left, where Emerson was accustomed to sit, and said, "You are destined to witness the discovery of the secret of life. When the time comes, you will observe that life consists of great swarms of energy, or entities, each as intelligent as human beings think themselves to be. These units of life group together like hives of bees, and remain together until they disintegrate, through lack of harmony. These units have differences of opinion, the same as human beings, and often fight among themselves.

"These meetings which you are conducting will be very helpful to you. They will bring to your rescue some of the same units of life that served the members of your Cabinet, during their lives. These units are eternal. *They never die!* Your own thoughts and *desires* serve as the magnet, which attracts units of life from the great ocean of life out there. Only the friendly units are attracted – the ones which harmonize with the nature of your *desires.*"

The other members of the Cabinet began to enter the room. Edison got up, and slowly walked around to his own seat. Edison was still living when this happened. It impressed me so greatly that I went to see him, and told him about the experience. He smiled broadly, and said, "Your dream was more a reality than you may imagine it to have been." He added no further explanation to his statement.

These meetings became so realistic that I became fearful of their consequences, and discontinued them for several months. The experiences were so uncanny, I was afraid if I continued them I would lose sight of the fact that the meetings were purely experiences of my imagination.

Was It A Dream Or A Visitation?

Have eyes and see! Here's another instance of the sixth sense in action, come in the middle of the night. Open yourself to the phenomenon.

Some six months after I had discontinued the practice I was awakened one night, or thought I was, when I saw Lincoln standing at my bedside. He said,

> The world will soon need your services. It is about to undergo a period of chaos, which will cause men and women to lose faith, and become panic stricken.
>
> Go ahead with your work and complete your philosophy. That is your mission in life. If you neglect it, for any cause whatsoever, you will be reduced to a primal state, and be compelled to retrace the cycles through which you have passed during thousands of years.

I was unable to tell, the following morning, whether I had dreamed this, or had actually been awake, and I have never since found out which it was, but I do know that the dream, if it were a dream, was so vivid in my mind the next day that I resumed my meetings the following night.

This was not the first time I received the "wake-up call" under the perilous threat of destruction. Nor, as lifetimes progress, do I expect it will be the last, either.

At our next meeting, the members of my Cabinet all filed into the room together, and stood at their accustomed places at the Council Table, while Lincoln raised a glass and said, "Gentlemen, let us drink a toast to a friend who has returned to the fold."

After that, I began to add new members to my Cabinet, until now it consists of more than fifty, among them Akhenaton, Ulysses, Christ, St. Paul, Galileo, Copernicus, Aristotle, Plato, Socrates, Homer, Cagliostro, Shakespeare, Voltaire, Bruno, Spinoza, Drummond, Kant, Schopenhauer, Newton, Confucius, Elbert Hubbard, Brann, Ingersol, Wilson, William James, Parahamansa Yogananda, Bill Gates, Tolly Burkan, Donald Trump, Martha Stewart, Oprah Winfrey, Richard Branson, Dan Kennedy, Ron LeGrand, Brett McFall, Tom Hua, T. Harv Eker, Armand Morin, and Tony Robbins.

Speaking On Verboten Subjects

Napoleon Hill said, "This is the first time that I have had the courage to mention this. Before this I have remained quiet on the subject, because I knew I would be misunderstood if I described my unusual experience."

Ted Ciuba says, "Thank the Gods the world has progressed to the point where we are pretty much free to express our metaphysical opinions, and not be blackballed." (Ya, ya, I know it's not perfect yet... Nor will it ever be.) Nevertheless, we have made great spiritual progress over the last 100 years. History will look back on us and confirm this.

BONUS! 3 FREE Wealth-Building Gifts Worth $97 at HoloMagic.com

Imaginary, But Very Real

For the timid reader, or those whose religious beliefs would interfere with the greater message at hand, lest I be misunderstood, I wish here to state most emphatically, that I still regard my Cabinet meetings as being in a sense purely imaginary.

But I feel entitled to suggest that, in this HoloGraphic Universe, while the members of my Cabinet may be purely fictional, and the meetings existent only in my own imagination, they have led me into glorious paths of adventure, rekindled an appreciation of true greatness, encouraged creative endeavor, emboldened the expression of honest thought, and stimulated *millions* of dollars, for years running on years!

In short, imaginary, but very *real!*

Somewhere in the cell structure of the brain may be located an organ which receives vibrations of thought ordinarily called "hunches." So far, science has not discovered where this organ of the sixth sense is located, but this is not important. Being spiritual in nature, looking in the brain for a receiver organ may be looking in the wrong place, anyway.

The fact remains that human beings do receive accurate knowledge, impressions, and guidance through sources other than the physical senses.

Such knowledge, generally, is received when the mind is under the influence of extraordinary stimulation.

Any emergency, which arouses the emotions and causes the heart to beat more rapidly than normal, may, and generally does, bring the sixth sense into action. Anyone who has experienced a near accident while driving knows that on such occasions, the sixth sense often comes to one's rescue, and aids, by split seconds, in avoiding the accident.

These facts are mentioned preliminary to a statement of fact which I shall now make, namely, that during my meetings with the "Invisible

Counselors," I find my mind most receptive to ideas, thoughts, and knowledge which reach me through the sixth sense. I can truthfully say I owe entirely to my "Invisible Counselors" full credit for such ideas, facts, or knowledge as I receive through "inspiration."

MasterMind Partners

My original purpose in conducting Council meetings with imaginary beings was solely that of impressing my own subconscious mind, through the principle of auto-suggestion, with certain characteristics which I desired to acquire.

In more recent years my experimentation has taken on an entirely different trend. I now go to my imaginary counselors with every difficult problem that confronts me and my clients. The results are often astonishing, although I do not depend entirely on this form of counsel.

Spiritual Forces

You, of course, have recognized that this chapter covers a subject that a majority of people are not familiar. The sixth sense is a subject of great interest and benefit to the person whose aim is to accumulate vast wealth.

Henry Ford undoubtedly understands and makes practical use of the sixth sense. His vast business and financial operations make it necessary for him to understand and use this principle. The late Thomas A. Edison understood and used the sixth sense in connection with the development of inventions, especially those involving basic patents, in connection with which he had no human experience and no accumulated knowledge to guide him, as was the case while he was working on the talking machine and the moving picture machine.

Nearly all great leaders, such as Napoleon, Bismarck, Joan of Arc, Christ, Buddha, Confucius, and Mohammed, understood, and probably made use of the sixth sense almost continuously. The major portion of their greatness consisted of their knowledge of this principle.

The sixth sense is not something that one can take off and put on at will. Ability to stimulate and use this great power comes slowly, through application of the other principles outlined in this book. Seldom does any individual come into workable knowledge of the sixth sense before the age of forty. More often the knowledge is not available until one is well past fifty, and this, for the reason that the spiritual forces, with which the sixth sense is so closely related, do not mature and become usable except through meditation, self-examination, and serious thought.

No Apologies

No matter who you are, or what may have been your purpose in reading this book, you can profit by it without understanding the principle described in this chapter. This is especially true if your major purpose is that of accumulation of money or other material things.

The chapter on the Sixth Sense was included because the book is designed for the purpose of presenting a complete philosophy by which individuals may unerringly guide themselves in attaining *whatever they ask of life.*

The starting point of all achievement is *desire.* **The finishing point is that brand of** *knowledge* **which leads to understanding... understanding of self, understanding of others, understanding of the Laws of Nature, and understanding** *happiness,* **which then leads on to enlightened action which, while it profits the impulse source, enriches the world at the same time.**

Hence, the ancient, empowering admonition inscribed on the Oracle at Delphi, "Man, know thyself."

This sort of understanding comes in its fullness only through familiarity with, and engagement with the HoloCosm. Therefore, this principle had to be included as a part of this philosophy, for the benefit of those who demand more than money – for those who demand *actualization* along with their money.

Layers Of Growth And Ability

Having read the chapter, you must have observed that while reading it, you were lifted to a high level of mental stimulation. Splendid! Come back to this chapter again a month from now, read it once more, and observe that your mind will soar to a still higher level of stimulation.

Repeat this experience from time to time, giving no concern as to how much or how little you learn at the time, and eventually you will find yourself in possession of a power that will enable you to throw off discouragement, master fear, overcome procrastination, and draw freely upon your imagination.

Meet with your own Invisible Counselors to achieve your own ends.

Then you will have felt the touch of that unknown "something" which has been the moving spirit of every truly great thinker, leader, artist, musician, writer, statesman, and businessperson. Then you will be in a position to transmute your *desires* into their physical or financial counterpart easily.

Nothing Works If You Don't Work It

You now have all the insight and tools you need to become self-determining.

BONUS! 3 FREE Wealth-Building Gifts Worth $97 at HoloMagic.com

You may pass on this incredible idea of transmuting your *desires* into *riches,* like a narrow brush with death that you didn't even know you had.

Like when an airplane you're on doesn't have that mid air collision it could have had, while you, as a passenger in life, didn't even know what *nearly* happened. Thank the Gods, however, for the pilot's sixth sense.

If you do not begin to follow instructions and create your life to order, you will never even know how close you brushed to a whole new, magnificent, different destiny.

Reread this book 22 times, if that's what it takes for you to assume this same holomagic power millions of others have found and testify to, the power to *think* and *grow rich,* the power of transmuting desire into money!

The Reward Is Worthy Of Your Effort

In parting, I would remind you, "Life is a checkerboard, and the player opposite you is *time.* If you hesitate before moving, or neglect to move promptly, your men will be wiped off the board by *time.* You are playing against a partner who does not tolerate *indecision!*"

Previously, you may have had a logical excuse for not having forced life to come through with whatever you asked, but that alibi is now obsolete, because you are in possession of the Master Key that unlocks the door to life's bountiful riches.

The Master Key is intangible, but it is powerful! It is the privilege of creating, in your own mind, a *burning desire* for a definite form of riches. There is no penalty for the use of the Key, but there is a price you must pay if you do not use it. The price is *failure.* There is a reward of stupendous proportions if you put the Key to use. It is the satisfaction that comes to all who conquer self and allow life to ante up whatever is asked.

The reward is worthy of your effort.

BONUS! 3 FREE Wealth-Building Gifts Worth $97 at HoloMagic.com

Now... Having just taken in the principles and done the exercises in this book... Having processed the info and taken actual steps, having just done the things that distinguish you from the masses of mediocrity, having just re-steered your entire destiny and financial future...

What do you think is worthy of this moment?....

Celebrate!

THE BEGINNING OF THE BEST

OF YOUR LIFE!

⤞ appendix A ⤝

WHY WRITE A "NEW" THINK AND GROW RICH?

This is one of those blue elephants in the room we can't ignore so let's discuss it outright.

You're not the first to think this, so go right ahead...

"Who are you, Ted Ciuba, to possibly believe you could ADD something to Napoleon Hill's Think And Grow Rich, the greatest success classic of all time?!"

I admit, at first exposure the very idea sounds like some fruit from California announcing he's re-written the Bible!

It did to me. Rest assured, I had further moments of doubt myself – until an uncertain event occurred.

Think And Grow Rich Is Not A Sacred Work

Yes, like the works of Homer and Shakespeare, select works of Napoleon Hill are in *public domain*. But that doesn't mean they're whores. Attested to in the way it's been accepted and sworn to by so many for so long, there's a *magic* in each of these works, including specifically...

Think And Grow Rich is not *literature*. Even though it's placed as a classic. Neither is it a *sacred* work, though it treats of things *spiritual*.

To the contrary, looking at it *correctly* – Wouldn't it be *amazing* if a "how to" manual *didn't* need updating after 100 years of service?

What other body of knowledge and practice has not progressed? Can the *science of personal achievement* be any different?

Invisible Counselors

Nor would Napoleon Hill let it go that easy. He knew he'd found in me a kindred spirit, a vessel capable of rendering the updates *Think And Grow Rich* needed, and indeed, a colleague capable of being persuaded.

Sometimes, I'm careful in saying – because I don't want to invite any challenges and contests – someone willing to "roll with the punches" and never lose sight of their goal, never be discouraged by events... Be inspired and motivated by all – like Edwin Barnes accepting the lowliest job in the Edison organization *simply to progress ONE beloved step more!!*

Maybe like someone getting knocked off his ash on a rented motorbike recognizing there's global significance on his head.

When the first inspirations to update *Think And Grow Rich* came, I shied away in defense. I tried to compartmentalize it out of my awareness, and get on with my other projects.

But the *idea*, conceived with a powerful impulse of life force, sprung root at the instant of its birth, and continued to grow – and developed a life and form of its own.

I began to consider the idea closely, diving into yet another study of the book. Studying deeper, applying the principles to make more money in my own affairs. Making notes, searching out with both a writer's and an editor's eye how to incorporate some of the new insights and progress of the ensuing decades of the book's life.

But I kept thinking of that California nut.

A Fate That Involves Both You And Me

Before I continue, I must advise you... It's funny how Fate is, sometimes. This is a fate that involves both you and me.

Then came a defining moment...An end to thought and consideration, and a fast move to accomplish it.

Not Your Ordinary Vacation

It was a nice evening along the beachfront in the Dominican Republic.

Though you won't see it when you fly in on a tour, find welcome staff at the cabin door, get swept through customs and immigration, are shuttled over to the resort with other people exactly like you, and play on the resort beach and eat at the four onsite resort restaurants the entire six days you are there...

You can't imagine the poverty there!

They've got shanty families of 12-15 people living in cramped houses. The entire house is no larger than the average American's living room! Ten houses fitting inside the lot line, of an average American starter home.

I wasn't either one of those types...

Speaking Spanish, being an insider, I'd rented a 100cc motorcycle from one of the local boys in Boca Chica. Doing that, you can get the motorcycle for a full 8 hours, for the same rate those tourist types at Hilton's *La Hamaca* pay for a single hour.

I wasn't one of them, either...

Then there's me, cruising the barrios – Monday, 17 November 2003, more or less 7:30 pm. Dusk leaning into night.

Fast Forward

At the moment the horrible thought struck me, *"I could have been born here!"* I felt headlights screaming at me like Chinese fireworks. I clutched under the blare of Gabriel's horn in the approaching car. It was a dry Caribbean night – I remember confusing images of rain – hard to see, slippery, cold...

In those fast-forward seconds my fate was not my own… I lived, but not because of my own prowess… Infinite Intelligence had a higher purpose for me…

Waking up, I discovered myself on my back, looking up through the tall grass swaying in a gentle Caribbean evening breeze… Disconnected… with a connection… I could see it, hear it, feel it… As a consciousness… It was very pleasant time. I was *totally* in the moment.

I didn't feel any connection to my body, but I was *seeing* out my body's eyes…

First, I consciously blinked a few times… I moved a finger, a couple next, then my hands… *Things are looking good!* Then my toes, my feet… Couldn't move my legs. I paused and thought it over… I was able to shift my head, lift my head, and get up on my elbows. I lay back down, rested, and gave thanks *I was alive!*

In that moment I heard my voice again… I can't begin to describe my shock upon hearing that brutish, unadjusted thing… The strange sound broke the rhythm of the gentle Caribbean silence, and, different, I was back.

Those accelerated moments were the final impetus of the work you see before you…

"Work That Only *You* Can Do"

Maybe Napoleon arranged the whole thing just to get me into action, for it was his warnings I heard, his urging to do the work that needs to be done…

Work that only **YOU** *can do…*

There's nobody else, so if you lay back on this one, it simply will not get done, and you will have to go into your next generation with the awful responsibility you cowarded out on a Cosmic directive destined to help *millions.*

"Nobody's immortal."

So quick the visit, the mission, and the resolve. A few seconds changed a lifetime and a legacy. Something I can't forget and barely can remember.

Carpe Diem
Seize The Day!

It was a call to contribute *while* I still have the day to do it! Not to *waste* the day. One of those "2 x 4" *ah-ha* moments…

I shortly went to acquiring a copy of the public domain version of *Think And Grow Rich,* to use as my source text… And even "miraculously" the domain name "**ThinkAndGrowRich.com**" – only synchronicity could have pulled that off. Something happening at a higher level.

I stilled myself, entered the mystical conference room… I read, studied, researched, applied, tested, prepared, and wrote for two years.

And my business affairs prospered. These years coincided with the rise to prominence of the global *World Internet Summit.* See it at **www. TheWorldInternetSummit.com**

And I had the opportunity in *fast forward* to meet with thousands of businesspersons of every race, nationality, level of success, desire, mindset… I traveled extensively, including stops in Panamá, Colombia, the Dominican Republic, Mexico, Canada, United Kingdom, Australia, New Zealand, Japan, China, Hong Kong, Malaysia, and Singapore. I worked with thousands, and helped them make money. Meanwhile analyzing them, their obstacles, their successes, their obstacles overcome… The commonalities… Their failures. The slight regional differences in doing business or measuring success…

Always with a mind to testing and rendering the secret to you. *You* are the one I am writing to.

I set off on a renewed success, training, development, and "wealth" cultural enrichment program that lasted years...

And now you see the result, in this book before you.

Hill And Ciuba MasterMind

What I've done has not taken anything away from Napoleon Hill, but, in a true MasterMind or Joint Venture, has *synergized* our energies, each bringing and receiving very real benefit from the participation of the other.

What I've done is what Napoleon Hill wants. Every decision we made, we made together. In our Thirteenth level MasterMind.

What Napoleon Hill and I have done *together* is much greater than what either of us could have ever done individually. The essence of a robust MasterMind partnership. When there is that special chemistry, 1 + 1 does not equal 2, it equals 11!

A Timeless Classic

Think And Grow Rich is a timeless classic. As such I didn't feel any compulsion to change just a few of the characters, stories, or examples of the original.

It, therefore, feels very comfortable for those who know the original *Think And Grow Rich*. The characters, stories, qualities are like the cast and setting of a Shakespearian play – dressed in a day, conveying universal truths.

I did add in a number of more up-to-date examples, but that has not been my focus. My effort is to update the expression of the *principles* of the original *Think And Grow Rich* philosophy. Add more explanation... Clarify... Remove some of the confusions in the former version... Smooth some of the sharper edges. Add more power and impact to other items. To reflect life in the modern era we live in.

Creaking With The "Isms" Of An Antique Era

There were shortcomings, of course, in a book as old as this classic. Certain themes that rub us sore today kept popping up, like sexism, racism, Americanism... Now I don't want to insinuate that Napoleon Hill had any shortcomings of character in this regard. He was, in fact, a better, more tolerant, more liberal, specimen than most of his time. But *he was of his time.*

It's been 100 years since Napoleon began organizing the philosophy that became *Think And Grow Rich.* There's been *huge progress* in those years. This redo is sensitive to this progress. Reborn of a new age, refined by a new person...

It's also **more accessible to young people**, of any race, creed, and country, the people who can best benefit from a close reading of this philosophy.

A Few Other Differences

I've introduced a few other items, like...

Adjusting the confusing incongruity between the chapter number and the principle. Now things are clear: chapter one treats of principle one, chapter two explores principle two, etc.

I also addressed the inherent employeeism in the original work, opting for the truth as J. Paul Getty says it in *How To Be Rich*, "To be rich you must have your own business." Or like Robert Kiyosaki's *rich* dad, ¿no?... Thus you won't suffer the long essay on submitting a good resume.

I also blend in the Quantum view of reality. The first edition of this book was written in a time when you couldn't talk about the concepts of Quantum reality without relying solely on the language of mysticism and spirituality (which seemed like religious blasphemy).

Today we can. Everything the mystical tradition has taught for millennia, physicists on the cutting edge of reality are now exploring. *Embrace the spiritual* is a constant theme of *The NEW Think And Grow Rich*, as it was the original... It's just more explicit – we live in a spiritual Universe that responds to our thoughts.

Indeed, all the world, including our focus in this present work – *RICHES* – is a realm of "what you think is what you get."

What do you think *Infinite Intelligence* is?

You are co-creator of your own experience.

Method Of Rewriting

We are "co-authors," Napoleon Hill and Ted Ciuba.

This was a heavy trip! Not just writing with a co-author of Napoleon Hill's stature... But writing with one who entered the Grave Beyond some decades ago...

It makes a respectful person think...

> "So how did you, Ted Ciuba, go about writing the *"New"* *Think And Grow Rich?"*

You deserve to know.

First, it wasn't anything like channeling. It wasn't reincarnation – I'm not him.

The best perspective is to see the principles of chapter thirteen in motion. We blend through a sympathetic connection, and now you have the same person writing over an extended period of time. This also stretches the mind. It's a joint "I," someone who lived a longer life than normally possible...

You've surely heard it said that most humans use less than 10% of their mind capacity. This book, in testimony to the methodology it *teaches*, was accomplished in that vast other 90% ordinary people know nothing of...

As businessmen, as authors, as success students ourselves, together we penned *The New Think And Grow Rich*. (Of course, this time we used a computer and word processor.)

It is, also, a living testament to the MasterMind shared in this very work… Ted Ciuba and Napoleon Hill – two men driven to discover, apply, and reveal the secrets of wealth to the world.

Members of the same brotherhood, teamed for a common cause… Neither one of which could accomplish as much without the other… When you climb to the point you understand the thirteenth principle – you'll understand this MasterMind.

From invisible counselors to visible co-workers.

Napoleon has said writing *Think And Grow Rich* was his life's work. It was my destiny to update it.

Celebrate The Magic

Celebrate the magic inside, dear reader, as you read, study, and apply the secret, and demonstrate very real benefits in your own life and affairs.

May you prosper forever!

Ted Ciuba

World's TOP *Think And Grow Rich* Expert

Co-Author of *The* NEW *Think and Grow Rich*

America's Foremost Internet Marketing Consultant

Original Founder of **www.TheWorldInternetSummit.com**

⇒ *appendix B* ⇐

ABOUT THE PERSONALITIES OF
THE NEW THINK AND GROW RICH

Many of the personalities Napoleon Hill refers to are unfamiliar to modern readers. And certainly are unfamiliar to readers from different cultures, because it's so American populated.

Nevertheless, it works fine, because, like a good movie, everything you need to understand the meaning, as far as the science of personal achievement goes, is crafted into the account itself.

In the same way, many of the currently modern well-known references will not be so well known in future times...

So... As a **free gift to readers** of this book who might like some brief historical insight into the personalities cited in *The NEW Think And Grow Rich,* surf to...

www.HoloMagic.com/ntr/personalities.ntr.html

⇒ *appendix* 𝒞 ⇐

ABOUT THE AUTHORS

Napoleon Hill	Ted Ciuba
b. 26 October 1883	b. 29 October 1951
d. 8 November 1970	d. ?

Napoleon Hill (b. 26 October 1883, d. 8 November 1970) and **Ted Ciuba** (b. 29 October 1951, d. ?), co-authors. For those into that sort of thing, they were both Scorpio, born just a few days apart, both the firstborn son. My astrology friends say they both fit the part. Some say they even look remarkably similar.

Their lifetimes overlapped, but they never "physically" met one another. Hill passed away at 87 years of age, a mere six months after the young Ciuba finished his high school studies, some four months prior to encountering his first copy of *Think And Grow Rich* in a mysterious manner.

They say an author reveals themselves in their work, and while, as authors, both men admit there is some truth to that, as far as psychology and philosophy go, as wordgicians, they also affirm much is hidden, too.

So here's a few bits you might not find in the reading of the text...

Both were born into a rough upbringing in a rural environment... Hill was born in backwoods Virginia... The Butcher Hollow kind of environment... Ciuba was born in and ran the canyons of North Texas.

There were some rough and rambunctious years growing up... Neighbors... police... schools... fathers of young girls... And many people predicted they wouldn't make it past the county jail.

As it turned out... Those dilemmas were just the frustrations of being a panther caged in a zoo...

The thread that starts early... Both boys felt the calling to letters early on – recognizing that would be their route to the top. Both boys received a typewriter from their encouraging mother figures... Napoleon at age twelve, from his step-mother, trying to tame his wild ways; Ted at age eight, from his mother, a used Royal blue typewriter from a pawn shop as a Christmas gift, encouraging her boy's odd inclinations.

Once he reached age, Hill quickly escaped his environment, and made way to Chicago. He encountered both rapid success and spectacular crashes, several times running. Ciuba passed a procession of adventurous years as a roustabout in the Texas oilfields, an accountant in a Denver office, a salesperson of commissioned goods, and an English instructor at California State University; finally, as an Internet Marketer things propelled him into the big time, with *World Internet Summit* his crowning achievement in that field.

Both Hill and Ciuba tended toward letters... Both were more than a little familiar with the works of Socrates, Plato, Virgil, Chaucer, Shakespeare, and Milton, among others. Perhaps this classical influence nurtured their lifelong interest in metaphysics and the spiritual life.

As a young reporter wet behind the ears, on his first assignment in a new job, Hill walked into the palatial wealth of Andrew Carnegie... Right then and there, Hill discovered and adopted his life's purpose.

As a budding twenty-year old in Los Angeles in 1971, Ciuba found his first copy of Napoleon Hill's famous *Think And Grow Rich* in an old, dimly lit, mysterious used bookstore at the top of a long climb in Los Angeles... Seedtime was long... Though they had him in preparation all the while, he didn't determine his destiny on *The NEW Think And Grow Rich* project till a near-death experience in the Dominican Republic struck the wake up gong...

True to their turning, both, in their "settled" adult life turned out as persons of words and influence... Both turned out to be a journalist, author, teacher, and speaker. Both wrote and published a number of books. To make their living in a commercially viable field, both finally found themselves, with their word expertise, in the copywriting and info products profession, and, as such, became salesmen, businessmen, marketers, and promoters. Neither ever lost his passion for investigation, writing, teaching, and speaking.

One final similarity... separated by 69 years distance, both published their own version of the book in their 54th year: Napoleon Hill's *Think and Grow Rich* in 1937 and Ted Ciuba's *The NEW Think And Grow Rich* in 2006.

Finally, it is the fervent desire and aim of both men, individually, and in MasterMind, that you embrace the wisdom encoded in the very title of this book to *"Think and Grow Rich!"*

"Discover The "Secret" In A Magical Mastermind Study Of The 1937 *Original Publication* Of Napoleon Hill's Success Classic, *Think And Grow Rich!*"

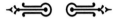

ACHIEVER'S MASTERMIND

You actively participate in working study sessions... DE-SIGNED WITH THE SOLE PURPOSE OF MAKING YOU WEALTHY!

Includes:

1. Sixteen Achiever's Master-Mind Sessions In Audio

2. Achiever's MasterMind Study Chapters

3. *Achiever's MasterMind* Study Guides

Bonuses include word-for-word transcriptions!

- How to do direct imprinting into your nervous system, so that you're driven to success!

- How to harness the awesome unseen power that has created Fortunes with one secret 6-step technique. (Takes less than 5 minutes to implement.)

- The 8-part, no-fail secret the winners in the wealth game use to... Create your own "breaks"

- And much, much more!

Digital Version – Save $$$! – Audio and print files downloadable instantly!

Physical Version - so you can feed CD's into your CD player and carry the convenient notebooks with you!

www.AchieversMasterMind.com

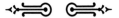

Co-author of *The NEW Think And Grow Rich*, Ted Ciuba, journeyed East to forge this collaboration. The entire event was captured, and is available to you now as the...

East-West Success MasterMind
Study of *Think and Grow Rich*

Share the excitement that got people tuning in from Singapore, Malaysia, China, Hong Kong, Vietnam, Korea, Philippines, Thailand, India, Australia, UK, USA, Africa, and Latin America!

The purpose of the MasterMind is quite simple...

In a MasterMind study of the success philosophy outlined in the original *Think And Grow Rich*...

> *"One of the most important days of my life was the day I began to read* Think and Grow Rich.*" -* W. Clement Stone

> *"I was invited to participate in the MasterMind study of* Think And Grow Rich *by my friend Ted Ciuba. That 8-week program transformed my own Consciousness of Wealth..." - Dan Klatt*

- To merge the BEST of both East and West to enable any willing human being, anywhere on this planet *or any other planet or moon*, to THINK WITH INTENT...

- To control and direct your thinking to receive the *natural result* of RICHES in your life!

www.EastWestSuccessMasterMind.com

WHO ELSE WOULD LIKE TO HAVE *THE NEW THINK AND GROW RICH* CO-AUTHOR TED CIUBA MOTIVATE AND TRAIN YOUR GROUP?

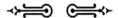

Schedule permitting, Ted Ciuba welcomes speaking and training invitations from businesses, organizations, associations, and promoters.

Through a brief but thorough pre-event questionnaire, Ted Ciuba makes each presentation unique to each group.

You can request fees and opportunities by contacting our organization by email at **info@ehaste.com** or from the website at **www.HoloMagic.com**

You'll get information on how to make it *free* to you, too!

Additional Copies Of *The NEW Think And Grow Rich* At a Discount

This book reveals the key to unlocking your wealth, the secret formula to riches, the combination to the vault of abundance in modern terms and in modern ways.

Individuals have bought this book, looking to forge their destiny of riches. They've in turn, bought this book for their friends and family members, hoping to impart the mystical magic of its power. Suggested to their employers, to distribute the book and train on it.

Entrepreneurs and coaches buy this book for their team members. Insurance and real estate companies buy this book for all the personnel in their organizations. Multi-level companies and all sales forces make this book required reading - to achieve outstanding success at any age.

Companies have even bought this book and *given* it to their *customers*! Talk about an enlightened company!

To get a discount on multiple copies of *The NEW Think And Grow Rich*, and to purchase an *original* version of *Think And Grow Rich* visit.

www.HoloMagic.com/ntr/multiple.html

Printed in the United States
70631LV00003B/355-396